COMEDY FILMS
1894–1954

By John Montgomery

1. *Buster Keaton and Roscoe (Fatty) Arbuckle outside the Metro Studios (1920)*

COMEDY
FILMS
1894—1954

John Montgomery

Preface by
Norman Wisdom

London
GEORGE ALLEN & UNWIN LTD
RUSKIN HOUSE MUSEUM STREET

*Printed in Great Britain
by Hazell Watson & Viney Ltd,
Aylesbury, Bucks*

To
Margot Grahame

by Norman Wisdom

I FELT HONOURED when, in 1954, I was asked to write the foreword to this book, for I was then very much a new boy in film comedy.

The first comedian I remember seeing on the screen was Eddie Cantor, the wonderful clown with the big eyes and the expressive face. What a comic, I thought! I laughed so much, watching him in a film called *Whoopee*, that I nearly fell off my seat.

I used to creep off on Saturday afternoons to the old Grand cinema in the Edgware Road, where for ninepence I could watch my favourites. There was a wonderful atmosphere in the old Grand, with its hard tip-up seats, its worn red carpet, and the thick grey haze of smoke which hung over our heads like a fog. How I loved going to the pictures. Nowadays I'm lucky if I can find the time to go; but when we were young, we all enjoyed the westerns, the blood-and-thunder action dramas, and the serials. But for me the comedies came first, and I little thought that one day I would be up there on the big screen, trying to make people laugh.

Since I started filming I have been called many things. It's like being back in the army. People call me *pint-sized*, *rubber-boned*, *a shy nervous little man, a clown with a whipped-dog expression*, and *Chaplin's successor*. I do not mind being called anything, but not Chaplin's successor. To me Chaplin is unique, and always will be. And in any case, I want to be myself.

In this book the late W. C. Fields is quoted as having once said that film comedy is often too refined. Well, isn't that true? I think audiences still enjoy knockabout, still want to laugh at visual gags and broad slapstick humour. People tell me that they enjoyed my first film *Trouble in Store* because it was good honest knockabout, with a touch of sentiment, and situations which could, after all, happen to any of us—or nearly any of us. We all struggle, and work, and lose our jobs, and hope to get new jobs, and try to succeed. But it seems to me that a little laughter goes a long way, and that as that great comedienne Gracie Fields says, we must look up and laugh—and keep laughing.

This book is almost a complete history of most of the men and women who have kept the world laughing since the earliest days of films. I think that it is important because there is always a great deal to be learned from the best exponents of any job, and the people in these pages are undoubtedly experts in their not always easy job. The book is a record of many years of endeavour, of successes and sudden triumphs, and of millions of cinemagoers enchanted by their favourites. Between the lines of the story you can read also of the tragedies, the difficulties, the disasters, and the disappointments which we all experience, players and public alike. You will read of unknown players who suddenly became stars overnight, and of famous stars who drifted into obscurity. You will be reminded of names which you may have forgotten, or which you have heard your parents mention. Above all, you will find, as I have, that there is very little new in the entertainment world, very little which has not been done before.

Our job, the first all-important task of all comedians, is to keep you laughing. We hope to add a little humour to a world which is too often unhappy. Turning the pages of this book, I find the names of film comedians who were great stars up there on the silver screen before I was even born. I don't think I am likely to get conceited—I hope not—but if I am ever tempted, a glance at the pages of this book, with all those wonderful names coming up out of the past, will soon bring me back to earth.

Meanwhile I'll just go on, in my own way, trying to make people laugh.

AUTHOR'S FOREWORD

THIS IS A FACTUAL and not a critical account of the history and traditions of the comic film.

I have tried, within limitations, to cover the subject widely. If I have concentrated mainly on American and British films and players, I have wherever possible paid some tribute to the Continental pictures which have, in both the earlier and later days of the cinema, contributed so much to our entertainment.

Comedy Films was first published in 1954, and the original edition is now out of print. This new edition has been revised, but the period which it covers remains the same, 1894–1954, sixty years of film humour, comedians, producers, directors and their work.

CONTENTS

CONTENTS

ILLUSTRATIONS

CHAPTER ONE

The First Comedies

WHAT WAS THE first comedy film? Nobody knows for certain, but it may well have been Fred Ott's *Sneeze*, filmed in 1894 by William K. L. Dickson for Thomas Edison's Kinetoscope Company in the 'Black Maria' Kinetographic Theatre which Dickson had built for Edison in West Orange, New Jersey. Fred Ott was a member of the staff, and his appearance on the little piece of film—sneezing—probably gives him the right to be called the world's first film comedian.

Comic incidents of this kind were no novelty, even on the screen. For many years audiences in American and European towns and villages had enjoyed them in magic lantern shows which were the forerunners of film performances. Usually presented by travelling showmen, they often included moving figures, achieved by ingenious devices.

Fred Ott's *Sneeze* was never intended to be shown on a screen, but had been filmed simply for the Kinetoscope peep-show cabinet which Edison had invented. Although at the close of the century considerable research was being carried out in Britain, France, America, and Germany, in an effort to discover the secret of projected movement, Edison saw no future in projecting figures, and preferred the 'coin in the slot' principle. This had the disadvantage of allowing only one person at a time to view the moving pictures; looking through a narrow slit in a rotating shutter at a continuously running strip of film which moved in front of an electric light bulb, the spectator watched a short comedy sequence or a familiar street scene, filmed by the Edison Company.

Before tracing the history of film comedy from the first sneezing film of 1894 to the modern *Mr Magoo* cartoons it is necessary to know something about the early days of films.

The actual discovery of motion pictures as we know them has been attributed to pioneers in America, France, Britain, and Germany, and is still disputed.

On February 20, 1896, firms were first publicly projected to an audience in Britain, having already been seen in France. The occasion was the presentation by the brothers Louis and Auguste Lumière of a performance of their Cinematographe at the Marlborough Hall in Regent Street, London, on the site of the modern Polytechnic. In the first programme there was sandwiched between a short film taken at Lyons and a picture showing the arrival of the mail boat at Folkestone, a brief comic interlude entitled *Teasing the Gardener*. In this a child was seen stepping on a hose. The gardener, looking into the hose, suddenly got wet.

This little film, taken in the Lumières' garden and lasting only a few seconds on the screen, was to set the pattern for millions of feet of celluloid in the years to come, in an endeavour to keep people laughing. Every clown in every comic film was to owe something to *Teasing the Gardener*.

The fun had started. While Felicien Trewey, on behalf of the Lumière brothers, was introducing the programme at the Marlborough Hall, a London instrument maker named Robert W. Paul was demonstrating his Theatrograph projector privately. A few months later he showed his first coloured pictures, hand tinted by a lantern slide colourist.

To feed the Cinematograph, the Theatrograph, and the many rival machines which soon appeared, large numbers of new films were required. At first, familiar scenes and brief incidents were captured by the cameras; the novelty of 'the pictures' was so great that almost anything—a gale at Brighton or a lion at the zoo—was considered entertaining. The first comedies were therefore simple comic incidents enacted either by hired players or friends of the 'film manufacturer.' From the earliest days of the film up to 1910 the average moving picture took from one to fifteen minutes to show. The first films were merely brief glimpses, but people flocked to see the new marvel, to watch the endless parade of familiar scenes and everyday subjects on the screen in a local hall, a converted shop, or a circus side-show tent.

William Friese-Greene's claim to have invented the motion picture has been disputed by the champions of many other pioneers. Birt Acres, Marey, Skladanowsky, Le Prince, the

Lumières, Edison and his English assistant Kennedy Dickson, Robert W. Paul, and many others—all were in fact contributors to the final solution and the development of the invention. In October 1889 Dickson presented to Edison what was probably the world's first 'talkie.' Dickson himself was seen in the new Kinetophone peep-show cabinet, walking across a room and raising his hat, while his voice was heard to say 'Good Morning, Mr Edison. Glad to see you back. Hope you will like the Kinetophone. To show the synchronization I will lift my hat and count up to ten.'

It was four years later that Dickson built the famous 'Black Maria' studio, a dark shed mounted on a revolving platform to catch the sun. And it was here, in 1894, that the mechanic Fred Ott was filmed in his brief comic sneezing episode, a picture which was seen but not heard in hundreds of peep-show machines all over the world.

In June 1895, five months after the first Lumière show in France, Thomas Armat of Washington discovered the principle of modern film projection, and successfully demonstrated an improved machine at the Cotton States Exposition in Atlanta, Georgia, in the following September. The films which he used were those issued by Edison for his peep-show, and his projector was afterwards called the Vitascope. Soon afterwards Armat showed his pictures at Koster and Bial's music hall in Herald Square, New York, including in his programme two of Lumière's films, *Mammy Washing Her Child*, and *Teasing the Gardener*. In the same year Max Skladanowsky exhibited a programme of films at the Winter Gardens, Berlin.

In 1896 Bert Bernard took the first film of the Lord Mayor's Show in London, and a year later he filmed about 1,200 feet of stock during the passing of Queen Victoria's Diamond Jubilee Procession. This film was exhibited for five months at the Alhambra Theatre, Leicester Square, by Robert W. Paul, who started showing pictures at this famous theatre in 1896. Paul's rivals were at the Empire and the Palace, and he was constantly seeking novelty in his programme, to beat his competitors. Often he went out into the streets or the countryside to photograph everyday events and 'actualities,' which were the forerunners of the elaborate modern film and television newsreels.

Paul made film history by filming the Derby at Epsom and showing his film that same night at the Alhambra.

Topical subjects were easy to find, but what were called 'the comics'—the humorous items—required more care and attention. As people had grown accustomed to the novelty, so the comic items had to be longer. It was no longer enough to show a brief picture of a man falling into a lake. Audiences were beginning to ask 'Well, what happened to him *after* he came out?' In fact, they demanded to see the further adventures of the unfortunate man. And because Paul was a good showman with plenty of ideas he hit on the happy notion of making short comedy films on top of the flat roof of the Alhambra. With the aid of some of the scenery from the stage, and a few members of the cast and some friends, he filmed a whole series of comedy subjects high above the noisy traffic of London. The plots were thin, but the laughs were loud, and one of his first successes was *The Soldier's Courtship*, filmed in 1896, only two years after Mr Ott's simple *Sneeze*. In this comedy a soldier and a nursemaid were discovered sitting on a park bench—the roof of the Alhambra being slightly disguised. The courting couple were suddenly interrupted by the arrival of an old lady, who sat down on the seat and began to edge them off the end. The soldier and the girl, finding no space left, then rose suddenly and tipped the seat so that the old lady fell heavily onto the ground with the seat on top of her.

The whole incident was filmed without a break, the camera being set up in front of the performers as though a stage play was being filmed. Even in its infancy the film had little respect for old age, but this hilarious effort no doubt caused much laughter, for no one had seen anything quite like it before.

Paul's contract at the Alhambra had originally been for a fortnight, after which the management presumed the novelty of the animated pictures would die, leaving a space in the programme for another variety act—perhaps a Swedish acrobat or a flame swallower. However, Paul stayed on for four years, and with the help of Sir Augustus Harris of Drury Lane gave performances at Olympia and in many London theatres and music halls. Soon the Alhambra roof became cramped, and a 'stage' for filming was erected at New Southgate. Here comedies, tragedies, melodramas, and many trick or 'magic' subjects were produced, to confound and delight the millions who were now flocking to see the new wonder of the age.

As early as 1899 Paul's studio was equipped with a camera trolley, a moving stand fitted with wheels, on which the camera could be moved to achieve tracking and zooming scenes, although for some further fourteen years the static camera was generally used both in Europe and America.

*

Film shows were first given in music halls, circus and fair booths, converted shops and public halls. Later came the Bioscopes, the Electric Theatres, and then the Picture Palaces, with their bright lights, their red plush seats and their smell of stale tobacco. Much later came the cinemas. In the early days of the century 'going to the pictures' was quite an ordeal, and was regarded as hardly a suitable pastime for a well-brought-up girl.

It was France, Italy and Britain—not America—who first led the comedy race. By 1903 comedy was playing an important part in every programme, and at the Egyptian Hall in London Mr Neville Maskelyne was delighting audiences with a special comedy show made up of short films taken in Britain and France. Raymond's Bio-Tableaux was touring Britain, presenting shows to packed halls, and there was seldom a month when two or three travelling showmen did not visit each town, complete with a programme lasting from thirty to forty-five minutes, but often less—for another audience had to be packed into the hall as soon as possible.

Typical of the brief comic films which these showmen presented was *The Short-Sighted Cyclist*, in which an unfortunate man, being unable to see much further than his nose, collided with everyone and everything in his path, finally ending up in the village pond. A comedy of this type, together with some scenes of the fleet at Weymouth, a horse race, the launching of a liner, and a glimpse of railway engines being cleaned at Swindon, would probably complete the act in a music hall, where the Mammoth Bioscope Show would be at the top of the bill. Later, when motion pictures were no longer a novelty, films dropped to the bottom of the bill and remained there merely as 'chaser outs' between performances.

When it was realized that each film should have a theme, and be a sequence of events telling a story or relating action, the comic films began to develop a craziness of their own. A man would be seen running wild—perhaps in a nightshirt—dashing downhill on roller skates, through barrels and past dray carts and cabs, miraculously avoiding danger, while the audience gasped a series of 'Ooooohhs!,' knowing that soon he would finish up in the lake, or in a bin of flour, oil, soot, molasses, glue, paint, dough or treacle. These were the 'chase comic' films, which are still with us today, with variations.

As the film was no respecter of old age or dignity, audiences soon became used to the hilarious spectacle of the infirm, the blind, the rich, and the poor (but more especially the rich and haughty), the parson, and the policeman—all being caught out in ridiculous circumstances. Mothers-in-law now found themselves not only on the stage, but also on the screen. Elderly gentlemen with ear trumpets now became the object of ribald mirth, for could not all the flour, oil, soot, molasses, etc., be poured down the ear trumpet? The misfortunes of others were from the first infant flickerings a cue for hearty laughter, as absurdity was piled on top of absurdity. Meanwhile the hazards of the chase included animals, the lame and the halt, the drunk and the sober, the pursued and the pursuer. The heroine's gouty uncle, chasing the hero, would receive little sympathy either in the film or from the audience. He would almost certainly end up with his gouty foot firmly stamped on and his niece stolen from him; and he could consider himself lucky to escape the dreaded flour, oil, soot, molasses, and other devilish ingredients of the average comedy.

While these light-hearted 'comics' were being 'manufactured' (as the film trade said) in America, Britain, Italy, Norway, Sweden, Denmark, Germany, and Holland, many of the more advanced humorous pictures were being made in France, where a whole team of versatile stage clowns was engaged in making films. Onesyme, Dranem, Polycarpe, Bourbon, Zigoteau, Bataille, Marcel Levesque, Little Moritz, and Boncot were among the comedians whose films were exported in hundreds, to delight audiences who did not care—and often did not know—which country was entertaining them. Many of the funniest were from France and Italy. André Deed was one of the world's first knock-about film comedians, starring in Itala Films, and known in Britain as 'Foolshead'. His comedies combined chase, tricks, and slapstick of every description. Tweedledum, Polidor, Bloomer (domestic farce) and Tontolini (chase comic) were all Italians, and were in their day the most popular of film comedians. Gaumont of France had Calino, Simple Simon, and Leonce making one-reelers before 1914, and in England their midget comedian Bout-de-Zan scored an immediate success, and was christened 'Tiny Tim' by his London sponsors. Named after a stick of liquorice popular with French children, he appeared to be a child, but was really a dwarf of advanced years. In *Bout-de-Zan as an Author* he was seen writing a love letter on behalf of his nurse. Having substituted the time of 8 a.m. for 8 p.m. he caused a fireman to arrive at the house to see the nurse early in the morning, instead of at night. Answering the door, the terrible infant told the fireman to hide in the cellar, where a coal merchant dumped sacks of coal on him.

Charles Prince—known as Rigadin—was another early French comedian with international appeal. In Italy he was called Tarfutini, and in Britain he was 'Wiffles'. His entry into Pathé Frères' comedies had been accidental. Stopping to watch a film being made in a street outside Paris, he had been accosted by a gentleman who had said 'Excuse me, but I am Le Metteur de Scene of Pathé Frères. I am just filming a comic scene, and, if you will forgive my saying so, I have been watching you for some time. I must say that you have a wonderfully funny face—and I wonder if you will do me a favour. Will you let me film you for this one scene?'

Monsieur Prince, who had no knowledge of acting, and no particular ambition to become a film actor, shortly afterwards signed a contract with Pathé, and was for many years his country's leading film comedian.

The French comics were versatile. Dranem appeared in his first pictures as a detective, a lady's maid, a drunk, a porter, a dude, a policeman, an old woman, and a negro minstrel. Many of the films contained trick photography, which caused characters to disappear into thin air, tables to dance, the floor to swallow up the furniture, and old ladies to turn into mice and be chased by cats. It was Georges Méliès from the theatre Robert-Houdin in Paris who was the pioneer of this trick photography. He had started in 1896 to film scenes in and around Paris, and one day he found that he could not wind his camera. The film was jammed. So he cleared it, and continued to take pictures. When his film was developed he found to his surprise that the omnibus which he had first filmed had now turned into a hearse. It was a droll joke, but the explanation was simple, for while his camera was jammed the omnibus had been replaced in the street by the hearse, and had been photographed.

Intrigued by the possibility of developing tricks of this kind, Méliès began to experiment. By 1900 he had made over two hundred 'mystery' films, each a few minutes long. They were a great success all over Europe and America, where they were widely copied. People were fascinated to watch objects vanish, humans become animals, men falling into pieces, folk walking about holding their heads in their hands, and portly gentlemen flying through space with the greatest of ease, only to vanish in mid air.

A director in the same tradition was Zecca, who joined Pathé Frères in 1895 as a commentator for gramophone records, before turning to film acting and finally to directing. His *Fun After the Wedding* (1907) was a series of brief comedy sketches, gently laughing at a French suburban wedding.

While French comedians were invading British screens, English producers were not idle. In 1879 James Williamson had founded Williamson Films at Hove, Sussex, and was soon making topical and comedy subjects. In his little glass roofed studio near to Hove station he made many 'comics'. *Why the Wedding Was Put Off* was one, and *Hi! Hi! Stop!* was another —a chase comic. *The Clown Barber* (1899) featured a barber who wielded a dangerous-looking razor with awful results, cutting off a customer's head, whereupon the barber left the headless man sitting in the chair while he completed the shaving of the head on a table. His head being replaced, the customer rose, politely paid the bill, and left.

Williamson was introduced to films by George Albert Smith,

one of the most important of Britain's film pioneers, who invented the first commercially successful colour system, called Kinemacolor, which was patented in the United States. Smith rented part of St Ann's Well gardens, a public park, in Hove, where he built a stage on theatrical lines and filmed many comic and trick films from about 1899 until after the 1914 war. His *Miller and Sweep* (1913) was filmed outside a windmill, long since gone, near Brighton race course, and it was widely copied. Another early Hove film-maker was Esme Collings, who produced little pictures in his back garden and around 1896 filmed an early strip-tease subject, *Victorian Lady in Her Boudoir*, which is preserved by the British Film Institute. This was listed as suitable only for gentlemen's smoking concerts, but by modern standards can only be described as dull. Yet, in its time, it created quite a sensation.

*

In the story of the pioneers few names stand out more than that of Léon Gaumont, who in 1890 was a prosperous electrical engineer and optical dealer in Paris, with no vision of the great film empire which he was to create. Naturally interested in all photographic developments, he was attracted by experiments being carried out by Dr E. J. Marey and G. de Demeny at their physiological laboratory near Paris. Dr Marey was a physicist, and founder of the Marey Institute. His method of analysing movement was similar to that of Muybridge, for he used successive photographs on glass plates. In 1891 Demeny designed a projector to portray photographs in motion on a screen, at first using a revolving glass disc, and later an endless band of celluloid film. He called his machine the Chronophotographic projector, and it was his development which appealed to Gaumont and which brings him into our story. He set to work to make, at first in a small way, the camera and projector to which he gave the name 'Chrono'. From this small beginning was to spring the vast Gaumont Company, with its branches all over the world.

The first company was called La Société des Etablissements Gaumont, and the trade mark was a sunflower bearing in the centre the word 'Elge'. Today the sunflower remains as the Gaumont trade mark.

The first 'Chrono' projector was taken to London by Gaumont himself. In Paris in 1896 he had met Mr (later Colonel) G. C. Bromhead, and had been fired with the idea of developing a business in England, with Bromhead as his representative. In September 1898 Gaumont opened his London office at 25 Cecil Court, Charing Cross Road. He had one table, a chair, and a modest stock of photographic material. The assistant was T. A. Welsh, later to become general manager and secretary, and in 1918 partner to George Pearson in the famous producing firm of Welsh-Pearson. From such humble beginnings were fame and fortune to emerge.

Gaumont soon became well known, mainly through the mechanical perfection of his projector, which was one of the first to possess enclosed spool boxes for holding the film. It is no secret that this one projector really founded the fortunes of the Gaumont company, for it was fireproof, and there was no law until 1909 regulating the licensing of cinemas and the provision of safety measures.

In 1899 Gaumont started filming in England. A plot of land was rented at Loughborough Junction, and on this open space a wooden platform or 'stage' was built for the taking of animated pictures. Arthur Collins, of Drury Lane Theatre fame, was the stage manager (director) and the first Gaumont film player was a coster from the Old Kent Road, named Mike Savage. He appeared in the first comedy, *The Fisherman's Mishap,* and amongst other pictures which Collins produced with Bromhead were *The Pickpocket, Napoleon and the English Sailor* and *Curfew Shall Not Ring Tonight.* The cost seldom exceeded five pounds a picture, and quite a number of copies of each film were printed for sale. In those days America was buying large numbers of films from Europe, and out of 200 copies of *The Gordon Highlanders in Cairo* (eighty feet) one hundred were resold to America by an enterprising purchaser.

Wardour Street, the present centre of the British film distributing trade, was still the home of antique furniture shops. It was in Cecil Court, off Charing Cross Road, that the pioneer companies were established. Soon Cecil Court became called

'Flicker Alley'. Today, all the old firms who were there have either vanished or grown too big for such humble offices, and Wardour Street has lost its antique shops and become rich, with imposing concrete buildings whose large glass windows are bright with gaudy advertisements.

In 1904 a photographer named James Porter and a steward named Frank Lloyd were charged at Lambeth Police Court with causing an obstruction through taking cinematograph photographs—a unique case. Bromhead and Collins were also summoned, for aiding and abetting. A large crowd had assembled in Crampton Street, Newington, where Porter stood in the middle of the road with his camera, filming a tableau in the street. Lloyd, according to the evidence, was dressed as a police sergeant. Collins was 'stage managing' the production, and Bromhead was manager of the cinematograph company.

The making of the film had been interrupted by the unexpected appearance of a *real* policeman, who had taken one look at the scene—and noted the bogus police sergeant—with the result that the parties now found themselves explaining matters to Mr Hopkins, the magistrate.

Mr Hopkins: I do not see how this sort of thing could be done in the London streets.

Mr Bromhead: We have often done it with the co-operation of the magistrates. At Worthing and other places the J.P.s have assisted us.

Mr Hopkins: Here, you see, you have got a sort of play going on with a sham sergeant of your own.

Mr Bromhead: We certainly do not cause such a large crowd as the Salvation Army.

Mr Hopkins: I see what this is coming to. The next thing we shall have will be a motor accident in Piccadilly for the purpose of being taken on the cinematograph, and brought out at the Empire the same evening. Plainly, it can't be done in London.

Bromhead and Collins were each fined ten shillings and two shillings costs, and Lloyd and Porter were discharged.

At Loughborough many famous stars of the music halls appeared on the open air stage to perform for the Gaumont

Company. Harry Lauder sang 'I Love a Lassie', 'Stop Your Tickling, Jock', and other popular songs for the Gaumont 'Chronomegaphone', a primitive 'talkie' system which synchronized film with a gramophone record. Herbert Darnley, a song writer and the author of many sketches for Dan Leno, Fred Kitchen, and Fred Karno, was another who mimed in front of the camera for these novelty films.

The celebrated 'Doctor' Walford Bodie, who modestly described himself as 'The Earth's Greatest Ventriloquist, Hypnotist, Electrician, and Scientist', also appeared for Collins. He was then proprietor of Bodie's Empire Palace, Macclesfield, where he gave his own film shows as part of the bill.

In 1908 Victoria Monks, the idol of the music halls, popularly known as 'John Bull's Girl', sang and danced to the tune of her current song sensation 'Take Me Back to London Town', on flickering screens all over Britain.

Léon Gaumont himself toured the world, filming as he travelled. With his son Charles as sound engineer for the 'Chronomegaphone' he photographed native dances and tribal life along the Ganges, and went in turn to Calcutta, Bombay, and Delhi.

By 1904 the talking machine had become the improved 'Chronophone'. *The Talking Machine and Cinematograph Chronicle*, an early film trade journal, reviewed it in detail :

The Gaumont Chronophone was shown at the Grand, Fulham, recently. It was an invitation exhibition and was enthusiastically received by a large audience. A negro laughing song met with a big reception. Other examples included Carl Nebes's song from *Lohengrin*, and the drilling of a squad of German soldiers. This last was excellent, the word of command from the officer synchronizing perfectly with the movements of the men in response. The crowd on the racecourse was also highly humorous and provocative of much laughter. In every case the movements of the actors in the scenes synchronized with the sounds of their voices in the most natural manner possible. We anticipate a large measure of success for the Chronophone over here, now that it has been once introduced. We understand that the records and machines were supplied by the Gramophone Company.

The production was simple. First a wax disc was made, after which the singer was filmed in the act of singing the song, miming the words to the sound of the record. Soon the gramophone records of George Robey, Max Darewski, R. G. Knowles, Clarice Mayne, and Will Evans were added to the list. Mr Oswald Stoll described the process as 'the perfect illusion of life'. To millions who flocked to see the novelty, it brought pleasure.

In 1907 the Gaumont Company announced that although Gilbert and Sullivan's *The Mikado* was banned in Britain (for fear of upsetting the Japanese), the Lord Chamberlain had ruled that certain excerpts were permitted and could be 'displayed without let or hindrance'. Six short films featuring the most famous songs from *The Mikado* were therefore made for the 'Chronophone'. The ban referred to the stage production only, and was eventually lifted after it had been pointed out that Japanese audiences were laughing heartily at *The Mikado*.

By 1908 Gaumont had 500 employees in Britain, owned an open-air studio at Dulwich Hill, a factory and laboratory in St James's Street, and offices in Sherwood Street and Denman Street. The London Hippodrome presented the 'Chronophone' for 628 performances, and the Royal Family were given a special showing at Buckingham Palace, where the audience included the King and Queen of Spain, the Kaiser, the King of Siam, and the Czar and Czarina. In 1909 Gaumont produced his first American 'Chronophone' on similar lines.

The music hall was still the home of films, both in Britain and America, but the Gaumont 'talkies' were so popular that they were invariably at the top of the bill. Famous stage artists had for a time to take second place. But on May 23, 1906, London witnessed the opening of one of Britain's first continuous film theatres. The little building was situated opposite Liverpool Street station, and the announcement of the opening included a verse which shows the importance of comedy films in programmes of the time:

> To the world the world we show,
> We make the world to laugh,
> And teach each hemisphere to know
> How lives the other half.
>
> Elge.

29

The verse might in later years have been Chaplin's, but the signature was Léon Gaumont's way of writing his initials. The cinema—although it was not called one—was named the Daily Bioscope, and the manager's name was Salas. On the first day the programme included a hilarious comedy entitled *Lost! A Leg of Mutton!* which was described by the management in glowing terms:

Hungry Willie, who has not tasted food for some days, espies a splendid leg of mutton hanging outside a butcher's shop, and while the master's back is turned he snatches it off the hook and bolts down the street. The fun now commences, and the chase which ensues is one of the funniest yet produced. New obstacles are introduced and the subject is one long laugh from beginning to end. A screaming comedy!

A show at the Daily Bioscope lasted from twenty to thirty minutes, there was a lounge, and the auditorium was brilliantly decorated in blue and gold. Every day from noon to 9 p.m. the prices of admission were twopence and fourpence.

Gaumont's offerings in 1907 included *Father Buys a Ladder*, would could be bought outright for eight pounds, and *Towser and the Tramp* (£4 14s 6d). There was also an announcement which must have attracted many film showmen:

A thing that has been looked for and produced by us as a fitting and first class subject for the finish of picture shows. We have been to some trouble to produce such a subject and we are now successful in having turned out a beautiful picture beautifully coloured

GOOD-NIGHT

The very thing to put an artistic and pleasing finish to a picture show of any kind. Tasteful, artistic, original, pleasing. 20 feet. Price 10s.

The colouring of such announcements, as was the case with silent films for years to come, was usually achieved by hand-tinting. As the word GOOD-NIGHT appeared on the screen, flooded in red, blue, and green, the audience filed out and the pianist played the last rousing march of the evening.

The modern sub-standard projector, now used extensively in homes and schools, had its forerunner as early as 1898, when *Cassell's Magazine* reported that 'Monsieur Demeny, an ingenious Frenchman, has just brought out a small portable cinematograph for amateurs.' This gave pictures on screens from six to ten feet square. A hand crank worked the machine, which was both camera and projector.

CHAPTER TWO

The Hepworth Story

ONE OF THE leading British pioneers, whose films were for some time sold by the Gaumont Company, was Cecil M. Hepworth, the son of a well-known lecturer and magic lantern exhibitor, who had from an early age shared his father's interest in photography. When he was in his twenties young Hepworth designed an arc lamp for use in magic lanterns, which he sold on a royalty basis to a famous London optical firm. On the strength of this, Charles Urban, of the Warwick Trading Company in Cecil Court, gave him a job. Hepworth continued to experiment, perfecting many of the principles of modern film projection, and inventing a system of rapid automatic developing and processing of film stock which was far ahead of its time.

The Warwick Company, like its rival film trading houses in 'Flicker Alley', was a firm which made, bought, and sold moving pictures—by the foot. Films were treated as merchandise, to be judged by length and novelty rather than by quality, a system which has not changed even today. To young Hepworth, who was essentially an artist with a creative instinct of his own, this no doubt seemed a mercenary place—a street of traders with very little interest in making anything except money.

Hepworth had a small bank balance, due largely to his arc lamp and his developing machine. He therefore decided to leave 'Flicker Alley', and one day he went down to Thames Ditton to see if he could set up a plant where he could process films. But he was unsuccessful, and walking on to the village of Walton-on-Thames he found in Hurst Grove a small surburban villa called 'The Rosary'.

It was a modest house, set in a row of similar buildings, and the rent was £36 a year. Here, within the narrow confines of his back garden, the front sitting-room, the kitchen, bathroom, and scullery, Cecil Hepworth wrote, produced, developed, and printed for distribution a regular supply of short films. At first

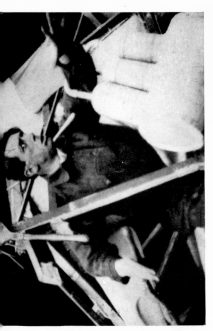

2.
*Charles Prince,
known in Britain
as Wiffles, in*
WIFFLES THE
IMPOSTER (*Pathé
Frères*, 1910)

3.
André Deed in
FOOLSHEAD TRIES
AEROPLANING
(*Italia Films,
Turin*, 1912)

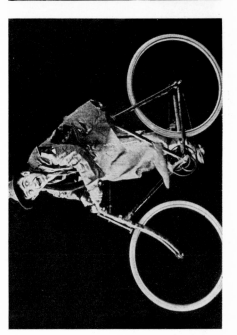

4.
TONTOLINI STEALS
A BICYCLE, *one
of the early
Italian Chase-
comic films*

5.
*John Bunny and
Flora Finch in*
A GENTLEMAN
OF FASHION
(1913)

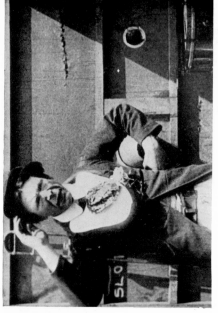

6.
Max Linder, who provided the inspiration for Charles Chaplin

7. *Fred Evans as Pimple in* PIMPLE'S WONDERFUL GRAMOPHONE (1913)

8. *Mack Sennett (right) in one of his own comedies,* BARNEY OLDFIELD'S RACE FOR LIFE. *Mabel Normand is chained to the track, while Ford*

he made pictures for a small market; later he made them for the world. The scullery housed a second-hand gas engine which provided the power, the two bedrooms were fitted out as film processing and drying rooms, and the front room became an office. The first 'studio' was the little back garden, where after a few months an eight by fifteen foot wooden platform was erected, with some upright posts to support the modest scenery, which Hepworth himself helped to paint.

It was at first experimental, and by modern standards very primitive. The early films were short comic incidents and glimpses of everyday events. When later it became necessary to introduce a theme or minor plot, Hepworth or one of his friends devised the brief story. This might require a number of players, including perhaps Hepworth and the members of his family, with some of the neighbours. Part of a film might be taken in the garden, the rest in the road outside, or in a nearby country lane. Anyone who was not appearing at that moment in front of the camera might be asked to turn the handle. Copies of each assembled film were then printed in the house, and would be sent to London for sale in 'Flicker Alley', or sold to local customers.

Hepworth produced a catalogue in which he listed his subjects by title, length, and price. When more copies of a film were required, they were processed.

The pioneer has told his own story delightfully in his autobiography 'Came the Dawn'. 'There were only two or three of us in the little company at Walton, and we did everything ourselves,' he says. 'First we thought of a story; then we painted the scenery, if it wasn't all open air, as it was usually. Then we acted and photographed it.'

Story films were only part of the output. A State visit by Queen Victoria to Dublin in 1900 was photographed, and became No. 96 in the catalogue.

History was being made and recorded on film at Walton, although it is doubtful if anyone knew it. By 1903 the business had expanded so much that a real studio could be built behind 'The Rosary'—a building with a glass roof to keep out the rain and to catch the sun. Natural light was supplemented by Westminster incandescent arc lamps. And as Hepworth progressed, he began to export his little films to the United States, where few producers had the experience or the ability to make suitable subjects for the many thousands of projectors which were now being made every year. When America began to realize the value of a strong film industry, certain American traders tried to force a 'corner' in films, but others knew the quality of the Walton product, and Hepworth now found himself invited to send a regular weekly shipment to the United States. From ten to thirty copies of each subject crossed the Atlantic, to compete successfully with the best films of the world. All the time that Hepworth was in production he held the key to the American market—which is more than can be said of others who followed him.

Most of the early Walton dramas would appear dated to modern audiences; but not one of Hepworth's films, either drama or comedy, was ever crudely made, nor was it poorly photographed. Quality was the hall-mark of Hepworth's films, and he was not afraid of good honest melodrama, or of robust but polite comedy. In one later picture, *Court Martialled* (1914), Stewart Rome was required to finger a revolver and say 'If I ever caught my wife flirting, *I would shoot her like a dog*!' At the time, this was not considered over-dramatic, for the cinema screen with its flickering heroes and heroines was itself larger than life, reflecting heroics and fantasies intended to appeal mainly to simple tastes.

Hepworth made his comedies as hilarious as possible, but he appealed particularly to family audiences, and was one of the first English producers to feature juvenile players. In a long series of *Tilly the Tomboy* films he established the reputations of Alma Taylor and Chrissie White, youngsters who started work at Walton when they were schoolgirls, and stayed on to the very end of Hepworth's production activities, as two of Britain's most charming screen heroines.

Soon Hepworth found it worth while to keep a number of his players under exclusive contract, paying them a weekly salary. So the famous Hepworth Stock Company was formed, of which not the least important member was Alma Taylor's splendid St Bernard dog, named after Admiral Sturdee. He appeared in several films, including *The Nature of the Beast*

34

(1919), which E. Temple Thurston wrote for Hepworth to film. Sturdee's rival in 1918 was 'Mac. Edwards', the beautiful collie owned by Henry Edwards and Chrissie White, who with Alma Taylor headed the list of popular players who went on working year after year at Walton. Their portraits were soon to be seen on the walls of London's Underground stations and in the foyers of hundreds of Britain's picture houses. Stewart Rome, Lionelle Howard, John MacAndrews, Tom Butt, Harry Buss, Alma Taylor and Chrissie White . . . names which were magic to a generation of picture-goers. Until 1916 there was also Violet Hopson, and later Gerald Ames, George Dewhurst, and Hugh Clifton joined the company. Their success often rivalled that of the American players, and in 1915 Alma Taylor headed a British popularity contest in which Charles Chaplin (who was included as a British player) came third. She polled 156,800 votes. In a similar contest held in America five years later the great Mary Pickford polled 158,000 votes.

Henry Edwards, who was to become one of the outstanding personalities of the British industry, made his first screen appearance with Hepworth in 1915. The pioneer had seen him on the stage in *The Man Who Stayed at Home*, and invited him down to Walton. Soon Edwards was producing, directing, and acting in the series of Turner Films made in Hepworth's studio. After 1916 he joined Hepworth's company, making his own series of feature pictures, and adding a light comedy touch which was sometimes absent in Hepworth's own productions.

During the early twenties the Edwards' films were among the biggest British successes. He made *Lily of the Alley* (the first full-length English film without sub-titles), *The Lunatic at Large*, *The Kinsman*, *Simple Simon*, *John Forrest Finds Himself*, *The Naked Man* (from Tom Gallon's novel), and *The Amazing Quest of Ernest Bliss*. These were rich in light-hearted comedy incidents, and many of his slightly more serious subjects, such as *A Welsh Singer* (Turner Films) and Temple Thurston's *The City of Beautiful Nonsense*, contained light relief. Among his several original stories, in which he also appeared, were *Doorsteps* (Turner), *Towards the Light*, and *Broken Threads*.

Chrissie White was his partner in some of his greatest successes, and, as we shall see later, she married him. Another romance was provided by lovely Ivy Close, who began her screen career by winning a *Daily Mirror* beauty contest. Judged the most beautiful girl in Britain, she married the well-known photographer Elwin Neame, and when in 1911 Hepworth saw her in a film which Neame had made, and which had been sent to Walton to be processed, he offered Ivy Close a position with the stock company. In 1914 Ivy Close Films was formed, with Hepworth acting as selling agent. The pictures were made at the little Pavilion studio on the Portsmouth Road at Esher. This studio was a converted dance hall made of glass, lying behind a row of shops at the end of a back garden. Ivy Close appeared in a series of beautifully photographed tableau pictures, and also in a number of comedies. Then she went to America for the Kalem company, to make only comedies. Her son Ronald Neame was destined to become one of Britain's leading producers, his achievements in later years including *Great Expectations*, *The Magic Box*, and *The Card*.

A description of a 1915 Hepworth comedy shows that the English 'comics' were not lacking in novelty. The film was *Simpkin's Little Swindle*, and the advertisement ran :

What would you have done to Simpkin if he had put a sponge at the bottom of your mug of beer? It was only by accident that he got caught. He had bought an alehouse from a friend who swore that the profits were fine. But the profits weren't. At the end of the week he was scratching his head for an idea that would make money out of the beer. Then suddenly, as he wiped his slate clean with a sponge, he got it. Sponge! That was it; sponges at the bottom of the mugs to soak up the beer; sponges to be squeezed out afterwards for future profit. This funny film shows how Simpkin carried out his little plot, and what happened to him for doing so.

Poor simple Simpkin, to imagine that none of his patron﹅ would find the sponges in their mugs!

In contrast, there were the more ambitious dramas, at first very melodramatic, and later more natural. In these, as in the comedies, right triumphed over evil, and the audience often cheered the hero. Yet some of the heroes started their careers as villains, as was revealed by the late Stewart Rome, who recalled that he was a dastardly blackguard in his very first picture, *Justice*.

'I began in a scene more than half-way through the film and discovered that I had done all sorts of nasty things,' he said. 'Amongst them, I had lured the heroine to a dirty old room and was expected to make love to her. The heroine was Alma Taylor. After the usual sound thrashing from that lady, I went from one crime to another until finally, in the great scene, I met my sticky end. Harry Royston, who played the injured father, escaped from prison and tracked me to my flat. We glared at each other for ten feet of film, exchanged all sorts of insulting remarks for another ten, and finished up with a fight to the death, in which everything in the room had to go—flower-pots, vases, candlesticks, chairs—a real Keystone, in fact! Royston had to finish me up by crashing a table over my head—and he did! The next thing I knew was someone shouting "Don't move!" They need not have worried.'

But if the dramas were larger than life, so was the whole magic world of the pictures. The heroes, the heroines, the villains, the kindly parents, the unscrupulous business men—all were easily recognized. Later, Hepworth's films were more guilty of quiet understatement, and although the earlier melodramas might today appear to be slightly 'ham', this was the technique of the times. Nor were his films 'artless', as no less an authority than *The Times Literary Supplement* suggested, some twenty-eight years after the last Hepworth film was made. Compared with many of the American pictures of the period, the Walton films were minor artistic triumphs, set in beautiful English scenery, using carefully composed sequences, all cleverly photographed. Some of the masterpieces of literature were filmed, and Thomas Bentley, who supervised the production of Hepworth's series of Dickens films, insisted that wherever possible the sequences should be filmed in the locations suggested by the author. Hepworth's spirit was too creative to be dismissed as 'artless'.

Not only the members of the stock company, but many of the people of Walton worked at the studios. In October 1914 a charlady who was asked to do a day's domestic washing replied 'I'll be glad to come—if I'm not acting at Hepworth's!'

The first major film was a little drama, which the pioneer filmed in 1904. Hepworth, his wife, the baby, the dog, and two actors all appeared in *Rescued by Rover*, which cost only a few pounds to make but was such an immediate success that new negatives had to be made several times, the original ones being worn out. In later years its producer was modest about this film, which has been preserved in England by the National Film Library, and has been held by many film experts to offer remarkable evidence that Hepworth was ahead of his rivals when he made it. Unfortunately, copies of equally interesting subjects made at Walton no longer exist, and the memory of those who helped to make them has dimmed. Certainly, few of the early films made at the beginning of the century in Britain created such a stir as this simple but profitable little story, which held all the ingredients of suspense, family appeal, and drama.

It was just twenty years after *Rescued by Rover* that the Walton studios—now often referred to as the cradle of British film production—were sold up, and the pioneer was forced out of business. As we shall see, the English production industry found itself by 1924 quite unable to compete with the expansion of Hollywood's big pictures. Hepworth was one of the few producers to realize that to compete in world markets he must enlarge his plant, produce on a more ambitious scale, buy good stories, and pay higher salaries. One of the players who acted for him was Ronald Colman, and although Hepworth asked the promising young actor to join his stock company, Colman was already planning to go to America. How could the little studios at Walton-on-Thames compete with this kind of thing? Many of the leading English stage actors and actresses, who had previously regarded film making as beneath their dignity, had been persuaded to travel down to Walton, where they found that filming under the Hepworth banner was not, after all, an ignoble occupation. The artistic standard was high. But now Hepworth needed more capital, to expand, and compete with America. When in the early twenties he floated a public company to make this expansion possible, he could gain hardly any support. To the disgrace of the film dealers, who were still marketing his pictures, the pioneer was allowed to face the

prospect of closed studios, while most of his precious film negatives, a wonderful record of the passing pageant of history,
were thrown on to the scrap heap.

But, as we shall see, time was to prove that Hepworth was
right. He himself had been over to America to study the situation. Although in later years he blamed no one but himself for
the failure of his company and the dispersal of his gallant band
of players, one can only wonder now why the traders of Wardour Street (who had grown too big for the cramped offices in
'Flicker Alley') did not back him. Could it be that during the
twenties they preferred to sell to English cinemas the readily
available supply of good American films, at the expense of
empty English studios? If this is so, then they have much to
answer for. Closed factories mean no technicians in the years
to follow. And so in the thirties, when the Quota production
boom started, new technicians without any real knowledge of
the industry had to be found, to be trained as they worked.

It has been suggested that Cecil Hepworth was not a good
business man. In these days, when many British producers
show an annual loss, a few of Hepworth's modest profits are
worth recalling:

	£	s.	d.
1914	9,897	17	3
1915	2,832	12	1
1916	1,332	5	9
1917	17	1	7
1918	7,339	0	3
1919	7,614	10	10
1920	10,734	16	11
1921	13,921	5	0

Even today, some British producers with no cinemas do not
make these profits. The cost of making eight feature films in the
year ending March 31, 1921, was £96,946. Hepworth's films
were consistent money makers. Yet the film trade—apart from
a few personal friends—did not support him in his policy of
expansion.

The blow was a bitter one. Several hundreds of film titles
bear testimony to his ability, from his £10,000 Hamlet, which
he made for Gaumont with Sir Johnston Forbes-Robertson, to

The Man Who Stayed at Home, Coming Thro' the Rye, and *Iris, Trelawny of the Wells, Annie Laurie, David Copperfield, Oliver Twist, The Touch of a Child, The Heart of Midlothian, Wild Heather,* and *Mr Justice Raffles.* For a decade Hepworth Picture Plays were the most popular of British films. Charmingly English, each picture frame was in itself an artistic study designed to delight the eye. Except for the Edwards series, and the many films which Florence Turner and Larry Trimble made at Walton, the feature pictures were not notably light fare, but there was a full quota of short comedy subjects, turned out regularly week after week in the best knockabout manner. And it is interesting to note that a 1921 feature comedy, *Alf's Button,* proved to be one of Hepworth's biggest triumphs.

The end of the House of Hepworth did not come until 1924. The pioneer himself did not die until 1953. As far as our own story is concerned, we must leave Cecil Hepworth and his wife in 'The Rosary', in Hurst Grove, Walton, on a summer morning long ago. They are planning a production of *Alice in Wonderland,* to be influenced by Tenniel's drawings. The famous book lies open on the table. All the years are ahead of them, for this is still 1903, and it is from this year that our story continues.

CHAPTER THREE

The Fun Continues

ONE OF BRITAIN'S first trading houses was the Walturdaw Company, founded only a month after Robert W. Paul began exhibiting his films at the Alhambra in London. James Dewhurst Walker had travelled all over Britain with Edison's 'Kinetoscope' cabinets, and he named his new company by taking the first three letters of his own name, and also of his two partners, Turner and Dawson. For their trade mark they chose a floating swan, and started at once to manufacture and market a large number of short films. They held shows in provincial theatres and music halls, where the 'celebrated Walturdaw Animated Pictures' proved a big attraction. Saturday night was often 'Walturdaw night', the bill being arranged so that the visiting projectionist and his machine were given place of honour in the programme.

Like other pioneer firms, Walturdaw at first sold copies of their films outright, at sixpence a foot. Showmen and music hall proprietors bought as many as could be printed, so that in time Walker found it more profitable to hire his films out. This move was at first condemned by his rivals, but was later adopted by every trading house. All the films manufactured by British producers were at first stocked by Walturdaw and their rivals, but Walker produced the company's own films in their studio and factory at Wembley Park.

Until recently the name of Walturdaw could still be seen in Gerrard Street, London, where the company specialized in the sale of cinema equipment. By 1914 Walker had left them to form J. D. Walker's World's Films, which in Britain handled some of the earliest products of the American Famous Players and Lasky Feature Play companies. In the United States these films were released by Paramount Pictures, then only a distributing organization.

In 1902 Walturdaw introduced their famous Cinematophone, an early synchronized disc and film system. The complete equipment consisted of a Walturdaw No. 3 projector and an Auxete Gramophone with a Parsons soundbox and a special synchronizer. The system proved highly satisfactory, almost perfect synchronization being obtained. At Wembley the company made many 'singing and talking pictures' for the Cinematophone, and between 1902 and 1905 audiences could hear many of their favourite songs from the screen, including 'Billy Brown of London Town,' 'If the Man in the Moon were a Coon,' 'Bull and Bush,' and 'Riding on Top of a Car.'

Following an injunction brought against the company to prevent the showing of a series of Gilbert and Sullivan musical films, the synchronized pictures were allowed to fade away. The synchronization had been almost as perfect as it is today, but because there was no electrical amplification, much depended upon the special gramophone and on the operator. The gramophone was contained in a cabinet fitted with a compressed air container, and the machine was electrically driven, a pump keeping the container full of air to operate with the Parsons loudspeaker, which was a new type of sound box, to which the needle was attached. The sound-box was heavy, so that the needle could not jump, as often occurred with the early sound-on-disc 'talkies' some twenty-five years later. In 1902, audiences of up to 1,500 people were able to enjoy the novelty of the Cinematophone, which sold for £72, or in attachment with the Auxetophone, for £170.

Walturdaw's films were both sound and silent, and many were comedies. In 1907 they issued an advertisement which gives us some idea of what they were offering at this time:

Grandpa's Revenge	200 ft.
Spring Cleaning	300 ft.
When We Were Boys	415 ft.
Luck in Life	550 ft.
The Female Highwayman	750 ft.
How the British Bulldog Saved the Union Jack	575 ft.

In 1900, when Walturdaw were experimenting with their sound system in London, one of the centres of the American industry, at Flatbush, New York, consisted only of three sheds. One was for dressing-rooms, one for properties, and the third was a stage. This was the famous Vitagraph studio, whose single stage was glass-roofed, and it was here in 1907 that Florence Turner, the famous 'Vitagraph Girl,' started her career as the world's first real film star. She combined her duties of wardrobe mistress, author, director, and cashier, with those of being leading lady. She was the first woman in pictures to sign a regular acting contract, and to be paid a weekly instead of a daily salary. She was twenty-one when she made her first film for Vitagraph, a little half-reel comedy called *How to Cure a Cold*. She was later given her first screen credit, in 1910, in *Florence Turner v. Jim Corbett*—a little boxing comedy in which she co-starred with the celebrated champion 'Gentleman Jim' himself.

One day, when the English producer J. Stuart Blackton was filming his *Life of Moses* at Vitagraph, a young journalist named Larry Trimble walked into the studio. Sitting together having lunch were Moses, Abraham Lincoln, Napoleon, and Florence Turner. Trimble, who was a young man with ideas, sat down and introduced himself. Soon afterwards he went to work at Vitagraph, taking with him his sheepdog Jean. In 1913 Trimble, Florence Turner and Jean all left America for England, where they joined forces with Cecil Hepworth at Walton-on-Thames to form Turner Films, whose trade mark was a picture of Jean the sheepdog.

Florence Turner was a versatile comedienne, but she did not make only comedy films. Her subjects varied from high drama to burlesque, and during the period 1913 to 1916 she was one of the most celebrated and best loved players in British films, winning several big popularity contests.

*

Meanwhile, the picture palace craze had caught on everywhere. In December 1908, patrons of the Palace Hour Picture Palace at Bristol were enjoying no less than nine films in one programme:

> Polly's Excursion
> Difficult Father-in-Law
> Lover in a Straw
> Christmas Eve Dream
> Nancy, or The Burglar's Daughter
> Venice in a Gondola

Richard the Third
Making Home Attractive
Illustrated song—'Take me on the Flip-Flap.'

At Hastings, pictures were being shown on the pier, where Payne's Bio-Photoscope was providing 'the usual array of cleverly arranged incidents of a comic order, views abroad, and coloured films, all very popular.' At the Empire Theatre, Sheffield, the chief team was Gaumont's Chronomegophone, with George Robey and Victoria Monks appearing in singing pictures. At the Grand, Newcastle, the pictures were an important part of the variety show, and nearby, at the Town Hall, the London Animated Picture Company was showing films every day. The King's Theatre, Nottingham, was celebrating in this same month its thirteenth continuous week of films with *Ma-in-Law Breaks the Record*, *Rover's Christmas*, *Gallant Guardsman*, and *The Lightning Barber*.

At Carlisle the Cinephone was making its first appearance in the city in January 1909. The wonderful singing and talking pictures had come to the Public Hall, where the attractions included *The Man and the Woman*, and *The Planter's Wife*. At the Gaiety, Aberdeen, three dramatic films (including *Love Stronger than Revenge*) were accompanied by the comic pictures *Going to Market* and *The Lost Handkerchief*. The songs featured on the Cinephone during the performance were 'My Girl's a Yorkshire Girl,' and 'For Ever and For Ever.'

During the same week, Mr Shanley's programme at the Winter Hall, Worthing, included *The Burglar and the Clock*, *Meddlesome Button*, *Don Quixote's Dream*, *Moving Day*, and ten other subjects.

In March 1909, at the Palace Theatre, London, Charles Urban and G. Albert Smith were giving the first of a series of exhibitions of natural colour films. In the west of England Albany Ward had extended his interests to include the Weymouth Picture Theatre, which was packed nightly, 'standing room only' signs being out long before eight o'clock on most evenings. The electric orchestron gave two selections, and there were also three variety acts in each show.

It seemed that everyone in Britain was going to the pictures. At Broadstairs the Grand Pavilion had become a Picture Palace.

At Bradford the skating rink in Manningham Lane was turned into the Electric Palace, providing continuous performances from early afternoon until late at night. At the Empire, Leicester Square, Bleriot sat and watched on the screen his own pioneer flight across the Channel.

In Durham there was no building in the centre of the city available for conversion into a cinema, so an old carpet factory was taken over after being gutted by fire, and became the New Picture Palace—admission 4d, 6d, 9d, and 1s. By modern standards this was cheap enough, but going to the pictures in 1909 was never expensive. At the corner of Trafalgar Road, Camberwell, the New Electric Palace could seat 180 patrons, all at 3d. The Electroscope Palace at Clapham Junction charged a penny and twopence, and each patron received a *free* printed programme. At Bristol, Glasgow, Edinburgh, Rochdale, Bedminster, and Huddersfield, where Wallace Davidson controlled picture theatres, money was reported to be turned away at every performance, simple because the houses were full.

The motion picture business was now booming all over America and Europe, and in more remote parts of the world. In Brooklyn, New York, the world's largest cinema (to seat 1,800 people) was being planned at Bedford Avenue and the Eastern Parkway, and Pathé's pictures were being shown to crowded houses on the other side of the world, in the Royal Albert Hall, Auckland. It was estimated in January 1900 that there were some 6,000 picture theatres in America, for which nine firms were producing some twenty-one new reels of film every week, to say nothing of the films which were being imported from Europe. Three of the most famous of New York's theatres, the Union Square, Harlem Opera House, and the 23rd Street theatre, had changed from vaudeville to pictures. Others were planning to change. And in other parts of the world—in India, Germany, Spain, and France—the people were responding to the international appeal of the film. In Johannesburg, Wolfram's Bioscope was showing comedies and topical pictures at the Wanderer's Hall. Soon every town of any size in South Africa would have its own Bioscope, to bring Europe and America closer to the Union.

None of the films was long, but there were always several in

45

a programme. A copy of *Father Buys an Armchair* (length 390 ft.) was available for £6 10s from J. Rosenthal of the Rosie Film Company, High Street, Croydon, Surrey. Like the other manufacturers, Mr Rosenthal had an extensive catalogue and he took care to sell films which did not date. The life of a short comedy subject might be ten or fifteen years, and there were hundreds of new films being made every month. In a single week in October 1908 the catalogues of the leading British companies contained, quite apart from the dramas, some interesting comedy titles:

Cricks and Martin, London Road, Mitcham, Surrey
>An Interrupted Bath

Sheffield Photo Co., Norfolk Street, Sheffield
>When Boys are Forbidden to Smoke
>Stolen Duck   What Little Willie Did
>Father's First Baby   Banana Skins

Hepworth, 17 Cecil Court, W.C.
>An Unfortunate Bathe
>The Unlucky Thief
>The Pet's Tea Party
>A Thoughtless Beauty
>Photographer's Flirtation

Williamson & Co., 21 Cecil Court, W.C.
>Great Bargain Sale
>Uncle Algy Proves a Good Detective

London Cinematograph Co., 154 Charing Cross Road, W.C.
>The Matinee Hat
>A Panic in the Village
>Oh! That Terrible Odour

Vitagraph Co., 25 Cecil Court, W.C.
>Female Politician
>Levitsky's Insurance Policy
>Policeman's Dream

Pathé Frères, 31 Charing Cross Road, W.C.
>My Ma-in-Law Beats the Record
>An Unfortunate Husband

Text Book of a Perfect Gentleman
Mrs. Bonney's Suitors
Flash James   The Cabman's Wife
A Well Paid Situation
Magistrate's Choice

Star Film Co., Rupert Street, W.

Burglar's Unexpected Bath
Alchemist and Demon
Oh, That Band
A Railway Passenger's Ruse

Lux Films, 68 Basinghall Street, W.C.

The Fisherman's Daughter
He Did Not Know He Was a Monk
Motorist Smugglers
Pandore's Tribulations

Kamm & Co., 27 Powell Street, Goswell Road, E.C.

Mr Hopkins in the Alps

Warwick Trading Co., Cecil Court, W.C.

Archie Goes Shopping with the Girls
All That Trouble for a Drink
First Experiment in Chemistry

Edison Manufacturing Co., Victoria Road, Willesden, N.W.

Heard Over the Phone
Comedy in Black and White
When Ruben Comes to Town
Life's a Game of Cards

Gaumont Co., Chrono House, Sherwood Street, W.

Force of Habit
The Sexton's Sleep Walk
Put Pa Among the Girls

Walturdaw Co., 3 Dane Street, High Holborn, W.C.

Step-Father's Jealousy
Invisible Button
Only a Dart
Magnetic Eye

Urban, Urbanora House, Wardour Street, W.

The Balancing Bluebottle
Quick Change Mesmerist

47

Rosie Film Co., High Street, Croydon
> What William Did
> No Good for Anything
> The Wedding that Didn't Come Off
> Percy Wanted a Moustache
> Father Buys an Armchair

Walter Tyler Ltd., 48/50 Waterloo Road, S.E.
> The Eccentric Barber
> Mr. Henpeck's Adventure with the Burglar
> Weary Willie and Tired Tim

*

In 1909 a fifteen-year-old girl whose real name was Gladys Smith, but who had already been re-named Mary Pickford by the American stage producer, David Belasco, asked film producer David Wark Griffith for a part in a picture at the American Biograph studios. Griffith thought her promising, and agreed to give her a small part in *The Lonely Villa*, in which Marion Leonard played lead. Mary was so good in this film that audiences on both sides of the Atlantic began to demand to know her name. At first she was known simply as 'Little Mary,' for the star system of later years was still unknown, and the names of the players were not revealed. In Britain, so many people asked who 'Little Mary' really was, that the London agents of the American Biograph Company hastily christened her Dorothy Nicholson, although in America she was still called 'Little Mary.' When in due course the studio was forced by public demand to announce her name and the stage name of Mary Pickford was published in the United States, the new star had a different name on each side of the Atlantic.

Three years after he had discovered her, Griffith read a short story which had been submitted by an American schoolgirl named Anita Loos. He liked it, and paid fifteen dollars for the right to film the story, which was a light comedy entitled *The New York Hat*. The picture, which was a great success, featured Mary Pickford and a young actor who had returned from Paris, where he had been studying painting. His name was Lionel Barrymore.

Within a few years Mary Pickford was famous enough to

9.
*Ford Sterling.
Keystone
Comedy King
until the
coming of
Chaplin*

10.
*Wearing his
now famous
outfit for the
first time,
Chaplin poses
for* THE KID'S
AUTO RACES AT
VENICE (1914)

11.
Chaplin in HIS
PREHISTORIC
PAST
(*Keystone,*
1914)

12.
*Mr. and Mrs.
Sidney Drew in*
HIS WIFE KNEW
ALL ABOUT IT
(*Vitagraph,*
1916)

13.
Mabel Normand, Horace McCoy (made up to look like Ford Sterling) and Keystone Cops in TILLIE'
PUNCTURED ROMANCE (191

14.
Early in 1919 *Douglas Fairbanks, Mary Pickfor Chaplin and D. W. Griffi formed the United Artist Corporation*

15.
Larry Semon in THE
BARNYARD (*Vitagraph,* 1920)

command 1,400,000 dollars from Adolph Zukor's Famous Players Company, which was probably more money than any girl of her era could earn.

*

In the autumn of 1911 Al Christie, who had established his reputation as the star and director of a series of cowboy films made in New Jersey, went to California. At the back of a roadhouse on what is now Sunset Boulevard, Hollywood, he rented a yard for the production of films. His unit was called the Nestor company, and his players included a number of comics, who appeared in the many short comedy subjects which Christie produced. Lee Moran, Eddie Lyons, Betty Compson, Billie Rhodes, Ray Gallagher, Neal Burns, Dorothy Davenport, and Eugenie Ford were the principal players, and they soon brought fame and fortune to Nestor, so that Christie was able to build a studio opposite the original plot of land. This was the first studio built in Hollywood especially for motion pictures.

By 1915, Nestor comedies and Al Christie were so well known that even Marie Tempest needed no persuasion to appear with her husband W. Grahame Browne, Eddie Lyons, and Lee Moran, in a five-reel comedy entitled—of all things—*Mrs Plum's Pudding*.

On His Wedding Day, a typical one-reeler made by Christie in the same year, showed the bridegroom being arrested for exceeding the speed limit on his way to the church. On the advice of friends he pretends to have smallpox, and so escapes just in time to dash to the church.

From 1911 onwards Nestor comedies, distributed by Universal, set the standard for most of the knockabout and domestic one-reel pictures which were to follow. Their bathing girls and their use of polite slapstick were much copied by their rivals. In later years Al Chrstie and Mack Sennett provided a wealth of laughter, in contrasting style.

In *He Fell in a Cabaret* (1915) Nestor featured Lee Moran as a young divinity student who tried to reform some people in a gay cabaret show—without much success. Comedies of the time were not always in the best of taste, and some were likely to offend minorities, who might take them seriously. Their appeal was mainly to the younger generation. In *Snatched from the Altar* Billie Rhodes appeared as a young bridegroom who is drunk on the eve of his wedding. His friends fake a wedding ceremony for him with the aid of an old maid. But next day the old maid turns up at the real service and tries to stop the ceremony.

In 1916, Al Christie left Nestor to form his own company, Christie Comedies. At first he made only one-reelers, but from 1919 he made two-reelers, with a feature film about every six months.

Equally popular were the L-K.O. comedies, featuring such stalwarts as Billie Ritchie, Fatty Voss, Gertrude Selby, Alice Howell, 'Pop' Rogers, and Louise Orth. Ritchie was an English knockabout comedian who went to America after appearing in Fred Karno's sketches on the English music halls. He was one of the 'drunks' in the box in the famous 'Mumming Birds' sketch, and in his films he wore clothes similar to those adopted by Charles Chaplin, so that some critics were quick to suggest that Chaplin was imitating Ritchie, or that Ritchie was imitating Chaplin. Certainly, Chaplin had taken over Ritchie's stage part, and learned the technique, and both comedians received the same training while with Karno. But they were not really alike.

In *A Bath House Tragedy* Ritchie and a number of other L-K.O. comics were seen careering around on a massage trolley, twenty floors up on the roof of a skyscraper. *Gertie's Joy Ride* was hardly less amusing.

Among the other American comics who were sure of a popular reception on both sides of the Atlantic were Charles Spooner, Billy Reeves, Finn and Haddie, the Tichtown Tumblers, Fay Tincher, and 'Belinda.' In *A Mixed Blessing*, Charles Spooner was seen installing a telephone in his house. Directly he has left home all his friends ring him up, and by imitating a girl's voice, arouse Mrs Spooner's jealousy. Later, through a careless message, a coffin arrives at the house instead of a birthday cake!

Belinda Makes a Bloomer showed Belinda as a maid of all work who upsets a bottle of itching powder over herself and over the other inhabitants of the house, to everyone's extreme irritation.

*

In 1909 the names of most American players were still un-revealed, and the majority of pictures were one-reelers. J. Stuart Blackton's *Life of Moses* was a five-reel drama, but only one reel was released each week. There was no comedy subject as long as this, and a typical English provincial programme during one week in April 1909 consisted of five short films of which three were comedies. The picture house was the Gem at Great Yarmouth, and the films were:

> Morgan the Pirate
> Army Socks
> Mr and Mrs Brown go Motoring
> Foolshead on the Alps
> Oxford and Cambridge Boat Race.

The first picture was American, the fourth featured Foolshead, the popular Italian comedian, and the final film was only an item included in a topical newsreel. The Gem was one of the many new picture houses to which the editor of *The Bioscope* referred in August 1909: 'The opening of so many theatres de luxe, with their comfortable seats, cosy appearance, and high-class show of films, has sounded the death-knell of the penny picture show, which will, except in the very poorest districts, soon be as dead as a door nail.'

But many of the 'penny gaffs' stayed in business for years, and during the twenties the 'theatres de luxe' became the secondary picture houses, crudely referred to as 'flea pits.'

In 1909, Barrasford's Britannia Theatre at Hoxton was announcing continuous performances, and was inviting patrons to stay as long as they liked every afternoon, admission to all parts of the house being one penny. In the evening, seats were one penny, twopence, and threepence. At many picture houses tea was served during the afternoon. At some it was free.

'Chase comics' and trick films were all the rage. Edison's *The Boots He Couldn't Lose* showed Mr Scruggles trying to get rid of a tight pair of boots which always returned. Every time he threw them away they walked back home again. *Lost in a Folding Bed, The Drunken Mattress, The Mayor's Dress Suit* and *The Haunted House* also relied on trick photography.

The Butcher Boy and the Penny Dreadful, made by Cricks and Martin at their Croydon studio, showed a butcher boy sent on his bicycle to deliver meat. On the way he buys an alluring comic paper, and becoming absorbed in it as he rides along, he upsets in turn a truck, a greengrocer's stand, a milk cart, a gang of road menders, an organ grinder and his monkey, and finally a country cart full of chickens, before arriving unharmed to deliver the meat, and still reading the comic paper.

The Wheelbarrow Race (Gaumont) was similar. In this the driver of a barrow was seen blindfolded. Obstacles in his path included steep hills, steps, a drawbridge, and the bottom of a canal. The company's claim was that the ending, which showed a large number of people injured in the journey, 'caused endless laughter.'

At Waddon, Surrey, the Cricks and Martin studio turned out a whole series of trick films entitled *the Scroggins series*. One of these possessed what must surely be the longest title in the history of films—*Scroggins Goes in for Chemistry and Discovers a Marvellous Powder*. Another was *Spring Cleaning in the House of Scroggins*.

The social comedy films were also popular. Edison's *Oh Rats!* dealt with the servant problem, evidently acute in 1909, and showed the dilemma of a good lady faced with a maid who refused to leave. When she discovered that the maid disliked rats—which she surely might have guessed—she thoughtfully released a number in the maid's room, causing consternation. Rats ran up and down the stairs, jumped up on to the kitchen table, ate up all the food, and took possession of the house. The audiences squealed with delight. *Wanted—A Son-in-Law*, *Auntie Takes the Children to the Country*, *Her Mother*, and *Father Lays Down the Law* were some of the many other domestic comedy pictures

A Hepworth film of this year is worth noting because it shows the type of short comedies which were being made at Walton for the American market. In *Beating the Bobby* a policeman was seen watching a couple of boys coming out of a tobacco shop in Walton. Seizing their cigarettes, he lit one and walked off to enjoy his smoke. The boys followed him to seek revenge, and saw him talking to a girl friend at a kitchen door. They put fireworks in his coat, and escaped over some railings just as the fireworks exploded. Later, while the policeman was seen talking to a milkman and the girl, the boys crept up and put water in the milk, which caused a dispute which ended in the policeman getting a jug of watery milk poured over him. Seeing the boys, he gave chase. But they dodged into a bush and tripped him up as he dashed past. His sweetheart then appeared and took him to the house, but the boys arrived there first, and had ruined the food which was laid out on the kitchen table. The first mouthful upset the policeman so much that he dashed outside to be sick.

Meanwhile the boys have dressed up a dummy to resemble a young lady, and they place this on a park bench, smearing glue over the unoccupied part of the seat. When the policeman (by some strange chance) walks by, the boys pull the strings of the dummy from a hiding place, so that the policeman sees a forward young lady apparently beckoning to him. He sits down on the seat, next to the dummy, whereupon the boys reveal themselves, and roar with laughter at their victim, who tries in vain to rise from the glue on the bench. But he is stuck fast, and when two of his companions hurry to the scene but are unable to detach him, they hit upon the happy idea of carrying the whole bench away to the local carpenter's shop, where the unfortunate policeman is *sawn out*. No one, apparently, thought it easier to take the carpenter to the bench, but for the sake of the extra laughs struggled down the road with the whole thing, policeman and all.

Other Hepworth comedies of this time were *A Touch of Hydrophobia*, *A Sprained Ankle*, and *A Subaltern's Joke*.

CHAPTER FOUR

Early Film Studios

1909 SAW THE START of Britain's first large chain of cinemas, the Provincial Cinematograph Theatre circuit, founded by Dr. Ralph Jupp, A. E. Newbould, and a young man named Percy Nash who had been associated with Sir Herbert Beerbohm Tree at His Majesty's theatre. Four years later, Nash was to build Elstree's first film studio at Boreham Wood. This was the Neptune studio, later the home of Ideal Films. Nash was the founder of Elstree as a film centre, for on his advice larger studios were built there later, making Elstree in the thirties a leading centre of British production. Yet as far back as 1903, long before Nash went along the country lanes at Boreham Wood to plan the site of the Neptune studio, Cherry Kearton had visited the fields on which the modern Associated British studios stand, to film bird life scenes for his early naturalist pictures.

Elstree has never been the real centre of English production, for while there are more studios there than in any other area, British production has always been dispersed around the suburbs of London. Many of the older studios are now empty, or have become warehouses or factories. The very earliest were merely open sites, like the original Gaumont 'studio' at Champion Hill, Dulwich, which was a field. Skating rinks, once the roller skating craze was over, became cinemas or studios, as at Twickenham and Walthamstow. At Esher, a glass-covered dance hall became the Pavilion studio, and nearby at Thames Ditton a glass-roofed stage, some 35 ft. by 25 ft. was used in 1913 by the Comedy Film Combine company, but by 1920 had become a film laboratory. At Kew Bridge, the Prince's studio was converted in 1919 from a theatre to form the home of Lucky Cat films, but later became a theatre.

In the heart of London, at 115a Ebury Street, Victoria, a glass-roofed stage some 90 ft. by 25 ft. housed in 1912 the British Oak Film Company, and later became the home of a £6,000 company formed to film the works of the Baroness Orczy, H. Rider Haggard, Jerome K. Jerome, and other popular writers. In Bromley Road, Catford, a studio stage was built adjoining a large house, to become in 1912 the headquarters of the Kent Film Company.

In 1913, Cherry Kearton was making films in a studio in Cranmer Court, under the railway arches at Clapham. The Leyton studio, at 588 Lea Bridge Road, was converted from an old horse tram shed, while another studio at Tuileries Street, Hackney, had originally been a gas retort house.

Film production had started at Ealing in 1902, when Will Barker began work almost on the site of the later Ealing Studios. In 1907 he built a stage there, in which a year later he was making early 'talkies' by filming an actor miming to a gramophone disc. Barker, who introduced H. B. Irving, Herbert Beerbohm Tree, and Alice Delysia to the screen at Ealing, specialized in the production of ambitious costume pictures such as *Jane Shore* and *Sixty Years a Queen*. Some thirty years later, Michael Balcon was to take over production control of the modern studio which is now separated only by a wall from Barker's first stage. But Barker made no comedies.

At Kingsbury, Herts, in the open air and in a modest studio, Walter Forde made his comedy debut for the Zodiac Company after the 1914–18 war. At Clarendon Road, Croydon, the Clarendon Film Company's studio measured 80 feet square, but was abandoned in favour of a larger corrugated-iron building with a glass roof, situated in Limes Road, Selhurst.

In 1918 the Stoll Film Company was formed, at first to distribute British and American films, and then also to produce British films. Maurice Elvey, pioneer producer and director of English pictures, was engaged as producer, and made the first Stoll Picture Productions in the converted ballroom of a house in Park Road, Surbiton. A year later the company opened new studios at Cricklewood, large enough to house three films at the same time. Here pictures were to be produced for the next twenty years, but few comedies.

The Cricks and Martin studio at Waddon was a centre for comedy films, and from here during the years 1910 and 1911 came a long series of *Charley Smiler comedies*, featuring Fred Evans. Part of a description of *Charley Smiler Joins the Boy*

Scouts indicates that they were rather naïve, and more likely to amuse the youngsters than the adults:

In due course Charley attends his first field day, and, attired in all the glory of short knickers, slouch hat, and pole, joins the corps at the cross roads. The youngsters are all lined up to clear the woods, and here Charley soon distinguishes himself by marching off in the opposite direction. The other Scouts easily clear brooks, leap banks, etc., but Smiler gets soaked at the brook, fills himself with spikes from the gorse, falls from a tree, and is hoisted over a fence into a deep pond. On returning to camp, Smiler throws down his hat and kit, and makes off.

*

In both America and Europe many ambitious young men were giving up their businesses to enter the new and still slightly despised film industry. Willam Selig of Chicago entered pictures, and in 1910 introduced Tom Mix to the screen in *Ranch Life in the Great South West*. Before this, Adolph Zukor had left the fur trade to enter the industry, first as a showman and then as a producer. William Fox gave up his job as a garment worker to become an exhibitor until 1913, and was later to found the fortunes of the great Fox Film Company. But of all these pioneers, few were to build greater empires than Carl Laemmle.

Laemmle, an immigrant boy from Germany, had seen Edison's Kinetoscope at the Chicago World's Fair in 1893, and had never forgotten the machine with the jumping photographs. Twelve years later he decided to go into the business for himself. He had been working for a clothing store in Oshkosh, Wisconsin, but he now returned to Chicago, intending to start a five and ten cent store of his own. In Chicago, however, he saw queues of people waiting outside a makeshift picture palace—a converted shop with a boarded front, an entrance on one side, an exit on the other, and a pay box in the centre.

As young Laemmle watched the constant stream of customers he decided to abandon his plans for a store, and instead to operate a ten cent picture house. He rented a tiny 'store show' called The White Front, and when it prospered he started a chain of them. To ensure that he and his rivals obtained a supply of new films, he started his own distribution organization, which in 1909 became the IMP Company—the Independent Motion Picture Company. Three years later he and his associates formed the Universal Film Manufacturing Company at 1 Union Street, New York City, but differences among his partners soon divided the new company into two groups. Laemmle moved with the Universal group to 1600 Broadway, where the organization remained for the next twelve years, their pictures being made at the old IMP studio at 11th Avenue and 43rd Street, and at Coytesville, and at Bayonee, New Jersey.

Meanwhile, the great migration to California had started. Film producers were moving westwards to the Golden State where there was a greater variety of scenery and more frequent sunshine. Laemmle and his Universal workers joined the procession, and in September 1912 he bought a site at Gower Street and Sunset Boulevard in the still quiet little village of Hollywood. There they erected a studio. So great was the demand for western films and for the many serial thrillers and comedies which Laemmle made, that at the end of two years he started to look around for a larger home. He now visualized a studio set in an estate which must be big enough for the simultaneous production of cowboy dramas, serials, animal pictures, comedies, and melodramas, all being made at once. To realize this dream his general manager Isidore Bernstein was sent off to look for a suitable estate.

Bernstein scoured the countryside for six months, before finally deciding that the 275-acre Taylor Ranch estate along the banks of the Los Angeles river was the ideal spot. Laemmle gave him the task of sketching a plan for the world's largest motion picture plant, and in his spare time the general manager worked on the problem. His daily tasks included the supervision of some twenty different units, making pictures every week.

However, the plans were imaginative and complete. Universal City, as the area was to be called, was to include a residential section and would be entirely self-contained, a film colony with living accommodation, shops, roads, even its own post office.

By the autumn of 1914 the west end of the ranch had been levelled for the erection of film stages, and grading was being completed for a network of roads. A central road a mile long ran right through the area. In the years to come thousands of motion picture stars, directors, and technicians were to drive and walk down it, on their way to fame and prosperity, or heartbreak. By October the population had reached 500, and housing was available for 425. The remaining 75 workers lived in tents along the edge of the hills, for they were the Red Indians who were shot at almost daily with blank cartridges. Real cowboys and cavalrymen, billeted in nearby bunkhouses, did the shooting.

All through the winter of 1914–15 new buildings rose. A city hall, court house, fire department, police station, café, church, arsenal, hospital, and rows of stables soon appeared. The first stages were by modern standards quite inadequate for they were roofless platforms, each 300 feet long. The Californian sunlight needed no help from arc lamps, and to diffuse the dazzling glare of the sun, huge muslin screens were hung across the actors, suspended by wires fixed to poles. Three and sometimes four companies of players would be working on one of these platforms at the same time. Directors shouted, pistols popped, lovers grasped one another, heroines swooned, and comics threw buckets of water around. Adding to the noise and the confusion were the spectators, who had paid an entrance fee to come to see the wonderful 'movies' being made. They were content to sit for hour after hour on benches above the dressing-rooms. When something exciting happened, they cheered and applauded wildly, for surely this was the greatest show on earth.

When Universal City was officially opened on March 15, 1915, over fifty films had already been made there, and huge advertisements announcing the event had been appearing for weeks in the big city newspapers. A special train was run from New York, collecting cinema owners—the folk who would buy the films—along the route. At Denver the great Buffalo Bill boarded the train. It was an age of brash showmanship, and nobody can put on a show quite like an American. A crowd of twenty thousand people watched the studio's own lady police chief Laura Oakley—later featured in many Universal pictures —present Carl Laemmle with the golden key to his realm. As the great front gates swung open, a brass band played the Star

Spangled Banner, and all the film executives, headed by the diminutive Laemmle, walked forward to be filmed for the newsreels.

During its first year the studio produced more than 250 films. Two years later, forty-two separate units were working there at the same time. And in 1916, when the first child was born in Universal City, he was christened Carl Laemmle Oelze, and was the youngest of the colony's 3,000 inhabitants. The city band had lost several hours' sleep, waiting for the infant. When the cry 'It's a boy!' was heard, the band struck up with 'Oh, You Kid' and 'Somebody's Coming to Our House'. The noise of the citizens aroused the animals in the studio zoo to such a pitch of excitement that people in the peaceful village of Hollywood, some seven miles away, were awakened just after midnight by the uproar from the zoo, the pistol shots of the cowboys, and the shouting of the revellers.

Soon Carl Laemmle was considering the possibility of installing arc lamps, to make films under cover. In England, no doubt influenced by the climate, Hepworth and his rivals had for several years used arc lamps, but in California the sunlight had been considered adequate. A new stage was soon erected, lights were installed, and another stage nearby was reserved for trick photography. At the back of the studios many permanent sets had been built, representing a fantastic collection of false western shacks, Manhattan tenements, old cathedrals, castles, oriental bazaars, side streets, and cowboy saloons. Not far away the Universal zoo housed elephants, camels, lions, leopards, monkeys, snakes, poultry, and cats and dogs, all looked after by experts.

In 1913, *Traffic in Souls* had been made, a highly successful picture about the white slave traffic. This introduced a new system of film exhibition, for the picture was shown simultaneously in thirty New York legitimate theatres. Admission prices were raised, and for the first time a film was reviewed by the dramatic critics of leading newspapers, and taken seriously. Carl Laemmle was an astute showman. Three years later he persuaded the great dancer Anna Pavlova to appear in Lois Weber's production of *The Dumb Girl of Portici*, in which

59

a juvenile player named Jack Holt made one of his first appearances.

Among Carl Laemmle's many stars of the period 1914–1918 were Harry Carey, King Baggott, Herbert Rawlinson, Ella Hall, the child star Zoe Ray, Eddie Polo, Grace Cunard, Warren Kerrigan, Dorothy Phillips, Marie Walcamp, Jack Holt, Hobart Henley, Francis Ford, Anna Little, Cleo Madison, Lois Weber, Mary Fuller, and Eric von Stroheim. Of the thousands of memorable films which were yet to come from Universal City in the twenties, thirties, and forties, perhaps the most outstanding would be *Foolish Wives, Blind Husbands, The Hunchback of Notre Dame, King of Jazz, Merry-Go-Round* with Norman Kerry, the first of the three versions of *Showboat*, and the Deanna Durbin singing pictures of the thirties.

The company which Carl Laemmle had formed had grown out of all recognition. Although the making of comedy films was never regarded as outstandingly important during the silent days at Universal, the growth and expansion of this studio is interesting because it is typical of the rise of Hollywood and the supremacy of the American film over its European rival. Even in 1916, no Universal City employee received less than twenty-five dollars a week. Star salaries varied, reaching a ceiling of 75,000 dollars a year. For everyone at Universal City the times were good, and even better days were promised. There were to be comedies with W. C. Fields, Abbott and Costello, and in the forties there was to be an alliance with the interests of J. Arthur Rank in Britain. Universal was to become New Universal, and then Universal-International. But whatever they called the company, it still owed everything to Carl Laemmle and his enterprise.

*

There were many other American pioneers besides Laemmle. In 1903, four brothers—Harry, Albert, Jack, and Sam Warner—had started showing films in a shop. Like Laemmle, Sam had been fascinated by Edison's Kinetoscope, and had taken lessons in film projection in order to earn eight dollars a week as an assistant projectionist. With his own projector and a small supply of films he now travelled all over America, and by 1906 had taken over his first converted picture house. In 1912 the Warner boys were able to form Warner's Feature Film Company, and could arrange the production of their first picture, made in a St Louis studio. With the poceeds they acquired five picture houses, and were able to move their film production unit from Brooklyn to California, where the sunshine and the rest of the movie companies seemed to be. Here the Warner Brothers were destined to be the pioneers of the modern sound film, which in the late twenties was to revolutionize the whole industry.

*

In order to prevent the widespread practice of 'pirating' copies of films the leading producers had adopted trade marks or 'brand' signs which appeared at the beginning of the film. In earlier years they were hung on the sets, and were therefore plainly obvious in each scene. Some of these trade marks still exist in a modified form, notably the golden rooster of Pathé and the heraldic sunflower of Gaumont. There was also the A.B. of the American Biograph Company, Edison's letter E in the corner, and the Barker Company's bulldog. Essanay, which gained its name by combining the first letters of the names of George K. Spoor and 'Broncho Billy' Anderson to form an S. and A., used a redskin's head for their brand. The old London Film Company at Twickenham boasted a Beefeater, and Vitagraph used the American eagle on a V.

Meanwhile in Britain the industry was not idle. In 1912 audiences were all laughing at a comical English music hall comedian named Will Evans, who had temporarily deserted the music hall stage to appear in a number of brief knock-about comedies, each lasting about twenty minutes. *Harnessing a Horse* was one, which proved to be one of the biggest money makers of the day. Nearly half of the picture theatres which showed it in Britain asked to show it again. *Building a Chicken House* was another Will Evans comedy, made at Bungalow Town, Shoreham, Sussex, by the Sunny South Film Company. In this film the laughter was provided by a roof, a ladder, a hammer, and a box of nails. In *Whitewashing a Ceiling*, not only the ceiling but also everyone and everything within range was covered in a sticky white fluid. All these were based on Evans's popular music hall sketches, and were filmed in the open air with the use of scenery, usually in a day.

Just before war was declared in 1914, Will Evans was appearing in several of the famous *Pimple pictures* with his nephews Fred and Joe. Will was not the star, for it was Fred who was 'Pimple'. Will and Joe Evans supported him, and together they made a long series of ten-minute comedies which proved tremendously successful. 'Pimple' was a clown-faced comedian with curly hair, and it is said that when he first appeared on the screen wearing a little cap perched on top of his head, the children all shouted out 'Pimple!' and so gave him his name. But few of the millions who crowded to see him realized that he was the same Fred Evans who had appeared in many less successful films, including the *Charley Smiler series* for Cricks and Martin.

Evans helped to find some of the financial backing for these little pictures, which were made mainly in the open air in and around London and the suburbs, and in a converted boat-house on Eel Pie Island, near Teddington. This was the modest studio of Folly Films, whose parent company was Phoenix Films. Every week, in fair or foul weather, a new comedy was produced; and when he was not working, perhaps on three days in each week, Fred Evans went off in his 'Pimple' outfit to make a personal appearance at a picture house.

The Folly Films were topical, drawing their subjects from life and from current film and stage successes. Whatever was in the newspapers during one week would be burlesqued in a 'Pimple' comedy during the next week. In *Pimple's Prison* our hero was seen as a governor who ran his prison in a most benevolent manner, taking his charges to the seaside for a rest and a swim. The plot was inspired by the topical question of prison reform. In *Lieutenant Pimple, King of the Cannibal Islands*, Evans was seen patriotically aiding the war effort by being a master spy on a desert island. *Pimple Enlists, Inspector Pimple, Pimple and the Stolen Plans, Pimple's Proposal, Lientenant Pimple—Gun Runner, Pimple's Wonderful Gramophone, Miss Pimple—Suffragette, Pimple Up the Pole, Pimple's Sealed Orders, Pimple the Bad Girl of the Family*, and *Pimple—*

Anarchist were all topical knockabout comedies, with plenty of action, burlesquing the events of the moment. In the latter film 'Pimple' was seen on the road to ruin, joining a gang of anarchists. The Phoenix Company explained the plot briefly: 'It falls to his lot to stage-manage the bomb which is to blow up the King of Whitechapel. Needless to say, it eventually blows up "Pimple", who finally finds himself on the telegraph wires.'

With Fred Evans was an unnamed 'Pimple, Junior', a newsboy with a round smiling face who had been asked, while filming was in progress in the streets of Twickenham, to take part. His first appearance was so successful that parts were written for him in many subsequent films.

By 1914 the one-reel comedy was an established favourite, and in addition to Folly Films there were many companies in Britain which specialized in making 'comics'. The Clarendon Company was one. In their trick film *The Kango Fire Brigade* a fire engine was seen exploding after a ridiculously slow journey to the fire. In *Mrs Scrubb's Discovery* Mary Brough, who was already a veteran of the films, was seen as a washer-woman who found that one of her customers wrote messages to her son on the cuffs of his shirt. Clarendon's *Jack Spratt series* were noted for their rather coarse treatment, but were comparable with the 'Pimple' films. In 1914 came *Jack as a Blackleg Waiter*, *Jack as a Policeman*, *Jack as a Bus Conductor* and other films in the series. Rivalry was provided by the *Captain Kettle subjects*, made at Bradford, Yorkshire. These included *The Coster's Holiday*, *Eggs is Eggs*, and *A Modern Don Juan*.

Another competitor in the comedy race was the Yorkshire Cine Company, whose comedies in 1915 included some of *The Winky series—Winky's Ruse*, *Winky and the Cannibal Chief*, *Winky Becomes a Family Man*. In *Peppering His Own Porridge* Winky persuaded an elderly colonial gentleman to impersonate his wife's uncle, only to discover that the old fellow had seized the chance to run up a large bill, which was presented to Winky for payment.

While these comedies were suitable for family entertainment, many of the films shown in the picture houses, especially those which had been produced in France and Italy, revealed women

in various stages of undress. These were advertised as DARING!
SENSATIONAL! and REVEALING! and some of them really were.
In Britain the importation of films of this nature threatened for
a while to destroy the goodwill of the entire industry. Many of
the films were catchpenny, and could do little harm. Others
were considered indecent. To prevent state censorship, which
might come at any moment, the British film trade set up in
1913 a Board of Film Censors whose purpose was to guide
producers and exhibitors, and provide a measure of safety for
the public and the trade. The so-called alarming bedroom scenes
then vanished from the screen. Later a similar move was made
in America, and the plainly pornographic film was forced out
of business, a step forward in the progress of the film. Now
whole families could safely enjoy themselves at their local
picture house, revelling in the world of make-believe, watching
the pageant of history passing before their eyes, either from
what Adrian Brunel has called the 'hard, noisy tip-up seats and
bare boards' of the cheaper prices, or the more extravagant
comfort of the plush seats of the ninepennies and shillings.

*

In 1915, Homeland Films was founded by the English music
hall comedians Jack Edge, Teddie Gerrard, Winifred Delvanti,
Charles Austin, and Billy Merson. Their pictures were made in
a little studio above the Boat House Hotel at Kew Bridge. Here
Charles Austin appeared in *the Parker series* of comedies, and
Billy Merson made his début in an ambitiously produced three-
reel comedy *A Spanish Love Spasm*, which was founded on his
popular song 'The Spaniard that Blighted My Life'. For this film
a fine pedigree bull had been discovered at a farm near Reigate,
and a cameraman was sent down to obtain scenes showing the
animal careering wildly in a corner of the enclosure. All went
well until the bull became really wild, attacking the cameraman
and driving one of its horns through the camera. It was then
decided to employ a stuffed bull, and not the real thing, for
the studio scenes.

Winifred Delvanti appeared first in *Billy's Stormy Courtship*, then with Billy Merson in *The Man in Possession*, *The
Only Man*, *The Terrible 'Tec*, *Billy the Truthful*, and *Billy*

Chuckles. With Lupino Lane she appeared in *A Wife in a Hurry*, *Hello! Who's Your Lady Friend?*, and *The Missing Link*.

Lupino Lane, a renowned member of the famous family of acrobats and dancers which had come to England from Italy in the eighteenth century, had previously played in a series of one-reel comedies for his own company, Little Nipper Films. He made his début in 1915 in *Nipper's Bank Holiday*, produced in a small studio at Clapham Park, joined the Homeland Company in 1917, and stayed with them for a year, after which he played for Hagen and Double in a series of *Kinekatures*, described as 'Film caricatures'. In these, distorting mirrors were used to make players and objects look grotesque. It was an attempt to achieve novelty, and for a while the films were fairly successful. *The Blunders of Mr Butterdun* featured Lupino Lane as the hero visiting a salesroom to buy a mysterious Babylonian ring which when rubbed (on the *Alf's Button* principle) distorted everything within sight into peculiar shapes and sizes. When this series of two-reelers began to lose novelty value, a number of one-reel *Kinekatures* was released in August 1918, of which the first was *The Haunted Hotel*.

Lupino Lane's versatility was obvious, and in a later picture entitled *Only Me* he played all the twenty-five parts himself, an effective if not an entirely original idea. Keaton—later or before?—did the same. On three different occasions, in 1923, 1925, and 1927, Lane went to America to appear in films, once to supply comedy relief in a D. W. Griffith feature, *Isn't Life Wonderful?* But British producers were guilty of neglecting his talents, and few of his pictures did him justice. Even *The Lambeth Walk*, made much later in Britain by Metro-Goldwyn-Mayer on an ambitious scale, did not do him real justice, being almost a photographed version of the stage musical 'Me and My Girl'. Both Billy Merson and Lupino Lane were much better screen comedians than their material indicated. This was also true of Bertie Wright, the brother of Huntley Wright, the renowned stage comedian. He appeared in a series of *Moonshine Comedies*, and was well known on the screen as 'Bertie'. As an amorous and over-zealous boot salesman he was to be seen in, amongst others, *Bertie Buys a Bulldog* and *Bertie's Bungles*.

The famous clown 'Whimsical Walker' was also persuaded

to appear in British comedies. He started with *The Knut and the Kernel*, then appeared for Hepworth with Alma Taylor and Chrissie White in *Tilly at the Circus*, and in *Cowboy Clem* was a cowboy visiting London to claim an inheritance. Regent Street, Piccadilly, Leicester Square, Trafalgar Square, and other familiar London backgrounds were seen in the chase sequences.

'Whimsical Walker' was of course an old man when he started filming, but Lupino Lane, Jack Edge, Billy Merson, and Fred Evans, were quite young. Could some of the youngsters have done better in America, where during the 1914 war the movie industry expanded while the British film business slumped? Lupino Lane went to Hollywood in the twenties, and did well, but few other comedians followed in the footsteps of the Chaplins and Stan Laurel.

CHAPTER FIVE

The Rise of the American Film

IN 1915, NEW YORK, with its luxurious new Strand Super Cinema in Broadway, was still the capital of the American film world. The trek to Hollywood had started, but most producers remained on the east coast. It was Chicago which was the established film centre of the middle west, and to the Selig and Essanay studios there went all the many 'movie struck' youths of the great corn belt, all anxious to make fortunes on the screen as quickly as possible.

The old Essanay 'lot' at 1339, Argyle Street, Chicago, was one of the cradles of motion picture fame. Francis X. Bushman, with Beverly Bane as his leading woman, was one of the studio's greatest assets in 1915, despite the arrival there of Charles Chaplin, who had come from the Keystone studios in New York and was intending to move on to California. Although regarded as a very good comedian, Chaplin was not yet considered to be such a powerful attraction as the handsome Bushman, who was at this time the world's most popular film hero. The Clark Gable of his era, he had been miner, racing cyclist, sculptor's model, secretary, and repertory actor, before he won a magazine competition which gained him the undisputed title of 'The Most Handsome Man in the World'. This was some title to live up to, but Bushman managed all right, sharing a dressing-room at Essanay with G. M. Anderson, the famous 'Broncho Billy' of the cowboy pictures, who had helped to form the company. While Anderson provided the action and adventure, Bushman made the hearts beat faster.

Essanay were content to leave their comedies to such experienced players as Wallace Beery, Ben Turpin, and Victor Potel. Beery often appeared in female disguise, as in *Sweedie Learns to Swim*. Meanwhile Chaplin came and went, creating a deep impression, but leaving Francis X. Bushman the undisputed king at Essanay, with a fan mail of 500 letters a day, nearly all from women. Within a few years it was Chaplin who claimed the film crown, while Bushman, despite his tremendous following and a subsequent Metro contract, slowly became less well known. A magnificent performance in *Ben-Hur* (1926) justifies his reputation, although he did nothing important later.

With the rapid development of the industry the 'chase comic' film found a rival in social comedy. In America the Vitagraph Company was the leader in the making of this new type of picture, their principal series featuring portly John Bunny.

These subjects, which began around 1910, were the stepping-stones by which films eventually passed from rough-and-tumble to straight farce, satire, polite domestic comedy and sophisticated comedy, although, as we shall see, knockabout prospered for many years, and is fortunately still with us.

John Bunny's face was probably the most famous on the screen between 1910 and 1915, when his pictures were known all over the world. The son of an English naval officer who had emigrated to America from Penzance, Cornwall, he was born in New York in 1863, but did not appear in a film until he was forty-seven, when he made his first short comedy for Vitagraph. Within three years his weekly salary had jumped from forty dollars to a thousand, and by the end of 1914 he had made more than a hundred and fifty two-reel and one-reel comedies, of which very few exist today. With him in most of these films was Flora Finch, who after his death in 1915 formed the Flora Finch Film Corporation and starred in her own pictures.

In 1912 John Bunny visited England to appear in several films at Walton, where Vitagraph had rented studio space from Hepworth. In one film he appeared as Mr Pickwick—a role which suited him admirably, for most of his comedies were devised to emphasize his grotesque size, although his comedy was never vulgar. These pictures were directed by Larry Trimble, who found conditions so pleasant at Walton that he was later able to bring Florence Turner over to form Turner Films in association with Hepworth.

Chased by Bloodhounds (1913) showed Bunny as a poultry farmer whose old clothes are given by his wife to a poor negro. During the night the negro steals some chickens, the theft being discovered by Bunny next morning during his tour of the farm.

To track down the thief, he borrows a bloodhound, which follows the foot-tracks of a neighbour, who is wearing Bunny's shoes. Soon the dog begins to follow Bunny, who is chased home in an exhausted condition, able only to flop into bed and spend a restless night dreaming that bloodhounds are chasing him all over the countryside. The nightmare is so disturbing that Bunny gets under the bed for protection, and the film ends with the ridiculous spectacle of the fat man cowering on the floor, covered in the bed-clothes, seeking protection under the bed from the bloodhounds.

Mr and Mrs Sidney Drew were two other popular players of this period. Sidney Drew joined Vitagraph in 1912, and with his wife pioneered the family social film. *When John Comes Home* depicted Mr Drew as a man who loses his memory. Going out for an evening in town, he decides to have a swim in the sea, and leaves his clothes on the beach, where his wife finds them and thinks that he has been drowned. But Sidney is very much alive, and in the meantime has absent-mindedly returned home in his bathing costume, dressed, and gone out for a walk. Buying an evening paper he discovers that his wife has inherited a fortune, which causes him to leap back into the sea, and emerge at the exact spot where his clothes were found.

Most of these comedies were satires on family life, and the Drews soon became important players at the Vitagraph studio, where members of the stock company were at first required not only to act, but also to help make and paint the scenery, provide some of the clothes, and contribute useful suggestions. John Bunny, Flora Finch, and Florence Turner were used to this, but handsome Maurice Costello protested that they were all much too important for such trivial tasks. He argued that they were picture players, not scenery shifters and technicians. After some discussion he won the argument, and it then became an established rule that players would not help to run the studio. At this time Costello was Vitagraph's leading man, their rival to Francis X. Bushman, and was considered to be one of the most handsome men in pictures. When he died at the age of seventy-three, in October 1950, he was a relatively poor man. But he was the first matinee idol of the screen, and to a genera-

69

tion which had not yet seen Ronald Colman, Richard Barthle-
mess, Gary Cooper, Valentino, Gregory Peck, and Michael
Caine, he was the perfect male.

*

While American studios were slowly winning the comedy
race, they were still offered strong competition by some
brilliantly produced subjects from France, where the standard
of film humour has always been high. In the forefront was a
gay and witty actor named Max Linder, whose name for several
years before and just after the 1914 war was almost a household
word wherever films were shown. Everybody called him 'Max',
and he was not only the first of the great international screen
comedians, but was the inspiration for Chaplin and many other
players. One of his most treasured possessions was a portrait
inscribed—'To the one and only Max, "the Professor", from his
disciple, Charles Chaplin.'[1]

Linder was born in 1885 at St Loubes, near Bordeaux, where
his parents owned vineyards. 'Can you picture me all through
my life, pulling down bunches of grapes, smelling them to see
if they were ripe?' he asked. 'If they were, I would throw them
into big metal bins. If they were not, I would get a needle and
cotton and stitch them back onto the vines.'

These were his ideas some twenty years after making his film
début in 1905. At an early age he had started a stage career
winning a first prize for comedy at the Paris Conservatoire.
He accepted several small parts in plays, and while with a
touring company in Bordeaux met Charles le Borgy, who was
then acting as secretary to the Comedie Francaise. Le Borgy
offered him advice, and tried to coach him, and soon afterwards
Linder was seen by the manager of the Varieties, and engaged.

One day while he was appearing in a comedy part he received
a letter, written on a piece of hotel notepaper, and addressed
simply to—Max. Linder tore open the envelope, expecting it
to contain the usual bill, or an advertisement. Instead, he found
a letter which was to alter his whole career—

[1] Chaplin did not become like Linder on the screen until *Monsieur
Verdoux*.

SIR, I HAVE OBSERVED YOU. IN YOUR EYES LIES A FOR-
TUNE. COME AND ACT IN FRONT OF MY CAMERAS, AND I
WILL HELP TO MAKE IT.

CHARLES PATHÉ

So Linder went to work for Pathé for a salary of thirty
francs a day, making six little films a week. The mornings were
spent filming, and the evenings were still devoted to the theatre.
The first picture was *The Collegian's First Outing*, which was
followed by *An Unexpected Meeting* and *The Skater's Début*,
in which Max afterwards revealed that he tore his trousers,
smashed a new hat, and lost a pair of gold cuff links.

Linder worked for Pathé until 1914. 'And what exciting years
they were,' he said afterwards. 'In the theatre I could hope to
be known only in France. But now these absurd films were
chasing themselves all over the world, bringing hundreds of
letters from places I had never heard of, and would probably
never see.' By 1909 he was an international figure, and was
being widely copied. In 1914 he was earning over £8,000 a
year—a lot of money in those days. Pathé had kept his word,
and together they were making a fortune.

Linder's films, at first taking less than ten minutes to show,
were at this time often hand-coloured or tinted, and contained
clever trick effects, for the French cameramen were some of
the best in the world, as they are today. Dapper, small, and dark,
Linder sported a small black moustache, and usually appeared
in evening dress or a well-tailored morning suit, carrying a cane.
In *A Rustic Idyll* he introduced a country background, as
Chaplin did later in *Sunnyside*. But this similarity was at once
refuted by Max himself. 'Chaplin has been good enough to tell
me,' he said in later years, 'that it was my films which led him
to make pictures. He called me his teacher, but I am glad
enough myself to take lessons from him.'

On the outbreak of war in 1914 Max packed up his film
clothes, and joined the army. He was badly gassed during the
early part of the war, and was later sent on a diplomatic mission
to Italy, where he played a not unimportant part in that
country's declaration of war against Austria.

Soon after this he had a serious nervous breakdown, and

71

left for Switzerland, where he recovered sufficiently to make two amusing films in the old tradition, *Max and the Clutching Hand*, and *Max Between Two Fires*. In 1916 he went to Los Angeles for six months, completing *Max Comes Across* and *Max and His Taxi*. Between 1919 and 1923 he made only three films, *Seven Years' Bad Luck*, *The Three Must-Get-Theres*, and *Be My Wife*, after which he returned to France to make *Help!* and went on to Vienna to appear in his last picture.

In *Seven Years' Bad Luck* a broken mirror was concealed by a servant who stood behind the empty frame to imitate what was done in front of the mirror. In recent years this same device has been more fully exploited by Walt Disney, the Marx Brothers, Abbott and Costello, and other comedians. And it has never failed to raise laughter.

Max Linder's end was tragic. His war experiences were said to have affected both his spirit and his mind, and in 1925 he and his wife committed suicide in a Paris hotel. Today his genius is hardly remembered, and the few copies of his films which still exist are seldom shown. Modern picturegoers have hardly heard of Max, the comedian who delighted millions, and they have little opportunity of seeing the films which he made, for most of the earlier ones were sold like any other merchandise on the open market, until the coming of film hire. Old films are invariably sold for 'junking', the chemicals being extracted from them. Sometimes they are just burned. Were it not for the enthusiasts who have from the earliest days been genuinely interested in motion pictures, very few copies of any type of film would have been preserved. It is the private collector who has over the years kept films, photographs, and catalogues, and in some of these collections the early pictures of Max Linder, John Bunny, the Drews, 'Pimple', Keaton, and their rivals, still exist. In more recent years the Museum of Modern Art in America, and the National Film Library in Britain, have bought old films for preservation and showing, and now keep copies of notable new films for future generations.

*

1915 was a vintage year for the American and British comedies. Some of their titles make interesting reading in these sophisticated days, when the cinema is more dignified, if less hilarious. *He Fell in Love with Ma-in-Law* and *The Dog Catcher's Bride* were two of the short comedies offered this year. Others were *Eggs!, Oh! That Face, Who Got Stung?, Nellie's Strategy, Slippery Sam's Wedding Day, The Butcher's Bride, Bosh!, When He Proposed, Mike and the Zeppelin Raid,* and *You Dirty Dog.* Flora Finch appeared in the Vitagraph comedy *They Loved Him So,* Sidney Drew was to be seen in *The Timid Mr Tootles,* and John Barrymore was regularly appearing in comedies such as *Are You a Mason?,* an adaptation of the stage farce.

1915 also saw Mack Swain in *From Patches to Plenty* (Keystone) in which he found a bag full of banknotes, and blossomed forth as a man about town. Syd Chaplin appeared in *That Springtime Feeling,* and Charlie Murray was in some of Mack Sennett's *Hogan* films.

In Hepworth's *All the World's a Stage,* John MacAndrews appeared as Alexander Aitchbee (H. B. Irving?), the owner of an academy of dramatic art. When he discovered that there were no pupils for his school of acting, he felt depressed. But by buying a secret mixture which made people want to become actors, he soon filled his academy with men and women who under its influence were all anxious to appear on the stage. Unfortunately, a jealous dancing mistress forced him to drink his own mixture, which made him believe he also was a great tragedian.

A good example of the photographic trick film was Davidson's *He Would Act,* in which a young man named Percy obtained a job as the leading player in a film because the star had sprained his ankle while jumping from the top of St Paul's Cathedral. In his first scene for the camera Percy had to be killed in a duel, in which he was run through with a sword several times, entirely without injury. 'The next scene is simple,' said the producer. 'You have to be run over by a steamroller.' Percy was then seen being flattened out by the steamroller, picked up, and pumped back to life with a bicycle pump. Finally, Percy was blown sky high by an explosion which carried him and the leading lady far into the air, blowing them both to small pieces. Unfortunately, when they picked themselves up they discovered that their limbs had got rather mixed. Arms, legs, heads, and clothes were all fixed to the wrong bodies.

*

Making short comedies was a profitable business. Earle W. Hammans, who became associated with films in 1915 and founded the Educational Films Corporation of America in 1919 in order to make educational pictures for schools, found little demand for them, and in 1920 he began to distribute two-reel comedies. Soon the Aladdin's lamp—no doubt at first intended to light the way to learning—became 'The Spice of the Programme', heralding in later years the approach of *Mermaid comedies*, a whole series of *Christie comedies*, *Cameo comedies*, the *Lloyd Hamilton series*, *Lupino Lane comedies*, several juvenile pictures, and a host of players who were to specialize in two-reel slapstick and knockabout hilarity.

By 1915 there were seven distinct types of screen comedy:

1. The 'Chase Comic' or ruunaway film
2. The trick photographic film
3. The knockabout picture
4. The dramatic farce
5. The domestic or social comedy
6. The satirical comedy
7. The cartoon film.

Cartoons had been popular since the earliest days of the magic lantern. In 1908 the first French cartoon film appeared, a picture only a hundred feet long entitled *Phantasmagoria*, for which Emile Cohl had made 2,000 separate drawings. By 1915 the French industry had developed the film cartoon on commercial lines, and Raoul Barre was enjoying success with his *Animated Grouch-Chaser* and his *Cartoons in a Barber's Shop*. From America came the *Arty the Artist series* produced by the Princess company. In these lightning drawings the artist appeared in the picture with the cartoons.

*

1915 was indeed a year for laughter. John Bunny was to be seen in *Private Bunny*, Roscoe (Fatty) Arbuckle was in *The Chicken Chaser* and *Love in Armour*, and was described by *The Bioscope* film trade paper as 'made of watch springs and elastic'. Then there was Kate Price, appearing with Hughie Mack in *Fair, Fat and Saucy*, and Billy Reeves could be seen in *The Substitute*, and Hank Mann in *Shaved in Mexico*. In the Kalem comedy *The Peach at the Beach*, two families—the Hams and the Hotheads—were seen on holiday. Stealing his wife's purse, Ham goes off to the beach to meet Mrs Hothead, whose fat husband is furiously jealous. While they sit together on the beach a pickpocket steals the purse from Ham's coat. To make matters worse, a cameraman with a movie camera comes along and films a scene on the beach, so that when two weeks later the Hotheads and the Hams go together to their local picture house they see on the screen the astonishing sight of Ham and Mrs Hothead sitting happily together on the beach, gazing soulfully at one another. With loud screams and shouts the Hams and the Hotheads break up the show, to tear at one another's throats, jumping over the rows of seats into battle. All is confusion and riotous excitement, as the families engage in a free-for-all which entirely ruins the performance.

Many of these comedies were enjoyed by the troops in the battle areas. Ten thousand feet of comic films were shown to the British army by Seymour Hicks and a party of actors who toured the forward battle areas with projectors. But at least one popular star—Alma Taylor—appeared in a serious war film. This was *Shooting for Women*, one of the many propaganda films which Hepworth made for the British Government. It demonstrated how the women of Britain should load revolvers, sight their rifles, and take aim and fire.

From the same studio at Walton this year came several comedies featuring Florence Turner. who had started production there with Larry Trimble. One of them was *One —— Thing After Another*, in which she appeared as a lovelorn French maid who attempts to inoculate her favourite policeman with a love germ, but by accident the contagion is spread throughout the whole family.

In June 1915 *The Bioscope* trade paper was able to report that 'Dramas have had to give way to comedies, and certain comedies are on every programme'. The *certain* comedies came from the Keystone studios, where Mack Sennett ruled. But that is another chapter.

CHAPTER SIX

The Keystone Touch

THE STORY OF Keystone Comedies and the rise of an ex-boiler-maker named Mack Sennett is one of the great romances of motion pictures. Sennett was the man who can claim to have re-invented slapstick comedy, or rather to have adapted the knockabout technique, and improved it.

Much of his success was achieved by speed of action, but fundamentally there was nothing new in what he did. The chase and the comic incident, as we have seen, were already popular on both sides of the Atlantic. What Sennett did was to add new tricks, a wealth of fresh and irreverant absurdities, and still greater pace of performance and camera. The results could not fail to increase the laughter.

Mickall Sinott was born in Denville, Quebec, in 1884. His early training had been gained as a 15s a day actor with D. W. Griffith at the Biograph studio, in New York. Here he had played unimportant parts with Flora Finch, Owen Moore, Florence Lawrence, and Mary Pickford. But by 1912 he had broken with Griffith, and had left Biograph after a brief apprenticeship as a comedy director. Griffith did not favour comic pictures, but Sennett had ideas of his own. With Adam Kessel and Charles Bauman as his backers, he formed the Keystone company, the trade mark being adapted from the sign of the old Pennsylvania railroad. Kessel and Bauman were two bookmakers whose first film-producing venture had been the production of cowboy subjects made under the brand name of Bison Films.

Cohen at Coney Island was the first Keystone comedy, with Mabel Normand from Biograph, Ford Sterling from vaudeville, and fat Fred Mace from Biograph's One Round O'Brien series. From the start the fun was fast and furious, and once the pace was set, Sennett kept things moving. For many years the untidy ramshackle studio in the Los Angeles suburb of Edendale was to be the world's great comedy centre—the citadel of slapstick. Because of Sennett's Irish ancestry and the unpainted appearance of the buildings, the studio was soon nicknamed 'The Pig Sty'.

The pictures were all burlesques. Absurd villains chased acrobatic heroes in fast automobiles down crowded streets, in and out of the traffic, over railway lines in the path of oncoming locomotives, through hayricks and farmyards full of squawking hens, into ponds and through saw-mills, before finally tumbling over docks or piers into the sea. The automobiles were often highly explosive, with doors that fell away and bodies that would continue their crazy progress without wheels, charging their way backwards or forwards in a nightmare of drunken driving, yet nearly always avoiding disaster. Miraculously, their occupants led a charmed life, being borne at high speed from one side of the road to the other, skimming trams and lorries, mixing gloriously with police patrol waggons, steamrollers, pedestrians, and other road hogs, but always ending up alive and in robust health in the Pacific, or a nice big pond.

Almost anything could happen in a Keystone comedy, and it usually did. Audiences were kept jumping about in their seats until the very last moments of the reel. Barrels would roll across the screen, upsetting pursued and pursuer. Chickens would flutter to safety, only to find another dangerous car approaching from the other direction. Beautiful but obviously dumb girls would sigh for the affection of ridiculously fat old men with gouty feet. And always there were the Keystone cops, the zany members of the world's most fantastic police force.

To publicize his absurd crew of comic policemen, Sennett used the slogan: WANTED! PLAYERS MADE OF INDIA RUBBER! APPLY TO THE KEYSTONE COMPANY! Nearly every actor who worked for Sennett was a cop at some time in his career. The chief of the motley collection was usually Ford Sterling, who spurred his ludicrous subordinates to action by waving his arms in the air and shouting into the telephone, while he danced wildly with excitement. When Sterling joined the company he was twenty-seven, and had been a circus clown, a newspaper columnist, and a vaudeville performer. For some years he was Sennett's greatest asset, but when Charles Chaplin came on the scene he was no longer the leading light, and his fame, like that of many other talented comedians, was partly eclipsed by the extraordinary ability of Chaplin.

In addition to the custard pies and the fantastic comedy pace which Sennett gave to the screen, he helped to establish many reputations. Mabel Normand, who had made her début in 1910 in the Vitagraph *Betty* comedies, left the Biograph company to become the leading lady of the Keystone troupe. When she died in 1930 she left behind her a fantastic legend which few outside Hollywood could equal. At the height of her fame she is said to have spent over £20,000 a year on clothes alone, but she gave large sums to charity and generously helped many less successful players. When a party of friends went to see her off to Europe by liner she insisted at the last moment that they must all sail with her, and she paid their fares and expenses. Like Marie Dressler in later years, she was greatly loved, and in her will she left £18,000 to her mother. But she left nothing to her husband Lew Cody, explaining that he was already one of Hollywood's wealthiest stars.

Mabel's life was not unsensational. In 1922 her friend Captain W. D. Taylor, an English film director, was murdered only an hour after she had left his house. Two years later, while she and Edna Purviance were dining out, their host—a wealthy stockbroker called Cortland Dines—was shot. The scandals ended her career. But during the happier moments of her life she brought great pleasure to millions of her admirers, and, although surrounded by luxury and wealth, was at heart a generous and kindly person. When she was advised by her doctor to take things easily she is said to have replied 'What does it matter, if I can keep people laughing?'

Edgar Kennedy and Slim Summerville were also among the first Keystone players, and in 1913 Sennett introduced a juvenile team, which were similar to Hal Roach's later *Our Gang* players. When Roscoe (Fatty) Arbuckle joined Sennett he was twenty-six, weighed sixteen stone, and for more than eight years afterwards he gained in weight and prestige, becoming one of the screen's foremost comedians. His first film was *The Sanitarium*, made for Selig. Before coming to films he had been a plumber's mate, a scene-shifter at Long Beach, and then a black-faced reciter. While singing tenor in a touring revue he fell in love with the leading lady, Minta Durfee, and married her. When Sennett saw his grotesque figure in the Selig film he hired him and his wife, offering Arbuckle five dollars a day to replace Fred Mace, who had left Keystone to make two-reel comedies for a new firm, the Apollo company of New Rochelle, near New York.

Arbuckle was teamed with Ford Sterling, and in his first year with Sennett made forty-seven comedies, directing forty more during his four years with Keystone.

It was Al Christie who had first realized the entertainment value of Arbuckle's portly figure, after the comedian had been introduced to him by a close friend, Robert Leonard. But Arbuckle stayed with Christie for only four weeks, before joining Sennett. By 1917 he was able to announce that he was 'much too lazy' to count all the Keystone films he had been in, or to calculate how many pies, pieces of crockery, sacks of flour, or quarts of ice cream had been hurled, flung, thrown or otherwise spread over his portly person.

'Outside of falling on my ear,' he said, 'being chased by bears, and surrounded by snakes, or doing 45-foot dives off the Long Wharf at Santa Monica, my film work has been fairly uneventful.'

Wil Rex, who visited the Keystone studio in March 1916, reported in *Picture-Play* magazine that the place was 'bustling with activity.' Arbuckle was supervising the construction of a set, aided by Ferris Hartmann and a dozen property men; Elgin Lessley, the cameraman, was loading his camera magazines. A dozen rough-and-ready comedians were practising falls down a stairway.

'How are you getting along with your new picture?' asked Rex.

'Slow, but sure,' replied Arbuckle. 'It's a new theme, and I want to go at it easily. I'm not trying to be too *highbrow*, but I am going to cut an awful lot of the slapstick out. If anyone gets kicked, or has a pie thrown in his face, there's going to be a reason for it.'

'How about the staircase? That looks as though something exciting was going to happen.'

'Oh, nothing much. Al St John and I are going to fall down it, but that's about all. Here, I'll show you.' As he spoke a pistol shot rang out. But Arbuckle only laughed. 'That's just Al St John shooting apples off Joe Bordeau's head. I'm going to pull that stunt in my next film.'

'How many times do you take the same scene?' asked Wil Rex.

'Until I can't do it any better. Often I use ten or fifteen thousand feet of film for a two-reel production. The average Keystone costs nearly twenty thousand dollars. Generally I take a month or more to produce a picture that runs for less than thirty minutes on the screen. In one of my films, *Fickle Fatty's Fall*, I spent just a week getting the kitchen scenes alone. I used over ten thousand feet of film just for that. In one part of the play I had to toss a pancake up and catch it behind my back. I started at nine o'clock in the morning, did it at first rehearsal, then started the camera, but didn't get it right until forty-thirty!'

During lunch, Arbuckle told Wil Rex that he had been born weighing sixteen and a half pounds, and that it had been Leon Errol who had first persuaded him to become a comedian. Errol gave him his first part, and helped him to put on his make-up.

'Where do you get your ideas?' asked Rex.

'Easy! I get a plot in my head, gather up the company, and start out. As we go, fresh ideas pop up, and we all talk it over. I certainly have a clever crowd working for me. Mabel (Normand) alone is good for a dozen new suggestions in every picture. The others aren't far behind. I take advice from everyone. Some of my greatest stuff comes from the supposed dull brains of the "supers".'

In 1917 Arbuckle was being paid several thousand dollars a week by Joseph Schenck, who teamed him in films with Buster Keaton. He spent his money lavishly, and was one of the many Hollywood stars who worked and played equally hard.

Arbuckle was that rarity, a truly jolly man, recalled his friend Buster Keaton in later years. He had no meanness, malice, or jealousy in him. Everything seemed to amuse and delight him. He was free with his advice and too free in spending and lending money. 'I could not have found a better-natured man to teach me the movie business, or a more knowledgeable one. We never had an argument. . . . The longer I worked with Roscoe the more I liked him. I respected without reservation his work both as an actor and a comedy director. He took falls no other man of his

16. *Chaplin in* SHOULDER ARMS (1918)

17. *Chaplin, Edna Purviance and Mack Swain in* THE IDLE CLASS (1921)

18. *Some Comedy Stars of the Silent Screen. Top left to right.*—Emma Clifton, Chaplin, Ford Sterling, Chester Conklin, Mary Pickford, Chrissie White, Henry Edwards, Buster Keaton, Harold Lloyd, Larry Semon, Ford Sterling, with some of the Keystone Cops, including Fatty Arbuckle on the right. Larry Semon has been called a 'minor Jewish comic', but his impact on audiences was considerable, and he is among the many forgotten, neglected players, who nevertheless made people roar with laughter during the twenties.

weight ever attempted, and had a wonderful mind for action gags, which he could devise on the spot. Roscoe loved all the world, and the whole world loved him in those days. His popularity as a performer was increasing so rapidly that soon he ranked second only to Charlie Chaplin.'

Unfortunately, Arbuckle was not able to continue the partnership or to advise and help Keaton with his career during the thirties, when Keaton fell into the trap of allowing the 'front room boys', the studio moguls, to shape his future.

It was scandal which in September 1921 ended his career. While he was entertaining friends at a party at the St Francis Hotel, San Francisco, one of the guests, Virginia Rappe, had a sudden attack of chronic pelvis illness, and died. The circumstances were unusual, and the comedian was indicted on a charge of manslaughter. The scandal now raged, and although the case had yet to be tried, public opinion fanned by a fantastic press campaign combined to hound every Arbuckle film off the screen. After a third trial Arbuckle was acquitted, but the weeks of savage rumour and the sensational headlines of the press had stirred up such feeling that no exhibitor dared to show an Arbuckle picture. The features which he had started to make were shelved, and were never exported to Europe. The Women's Freedom League of America, backed by scandal-mongers and large sections of honest public opinion, led the fight—and won easily. Arbuckle was off the screen for ever, and his photographs, having appeared throughout America under sensational headlines, were now burned.

Some years later he attempted to make a minor return to Hollywood as a director of short films, using the name of Goodrich, and for a brief minute he actually appeared once more in a film. But nobody noticed him, or even cared. The millions whom he had delighted now remembered only the scandal, and completely ignored the fact that he had been acquitted.

Arbuckle was an acute embarrassment to Hollywood, and it was unfortunate that only a year later the film colony was again shaken by scandal, when Captain Taylor, the friend of Mabel Normand, was shot. Two years later, when millionaire Cortland Dines was shot, it was Mabel's chauffeur Horace Greer who was discovered standing nearby with a pistol in his hand.

Luckily, Dines recovered, and no charge was pressed, but the damage to Mabel Normand's reputation was acute. Sennett had to withdraw his film *Molly-O*, in which she starred, and her screen career was virtually over. In February 1926 she joined the Hal Roach studio to make short comedies, but her return was not enthusiastically received. Soon she became only a legend. But to those who knew her, she was still the charming, generous, great-hearted favourite of Hollywood. Will Rogers said that she was 'the kidder, good fellow, and friend of every soul on earth, whose quiet and not-seen charity has helped many a poor soul in need.'

A later discovery was Harry Langdon, the small, pathetic, white-faced clown who was nearly always on the verge of tears. Like Stan Laurel, Langdon wandered through difficulties with innocent simplicity, constantly amazed at the strange world in which he found himself, but always emerging triumphant. Born of poor parents, he had started his career as a newsboy, and had then been a cinema attendant in Iowa, and later a property man in a third-rate vaudeville theatre. Joining a touring company, he found himself one Saturday night with the actors, stranded and unpaid. So he attached himself to a travelling medicine show, and became a performer. Langdon was a student of Chaplin, but in later years he appeared rarely on the screen, and never quite fulfilled the promise of his earlier films.

'I originally saw him doing an act called "Johnny's New Car", recalled Harold Lloyd, later. 'And I told Hal Roach that he would make a good comic for films. Hal went down to the Orpheum in Los Angeles and saw Harry, and he agreed. But they had a difference of opinion—about one hundred dollars worth—and Harry went with another producer and then landed with Sennett. After a few pictures Harry came to me and said, "Harold, I don't seem to be scoring". I had seen his comedies and thought I knew why.'

Lloyd told Langdon that he was being worked too fast, which was a habit at Mack Sennett's, where they had done the same to Chaplin. So Langdon slowed down, but in Harold Lloyd's opinion too much, and dragged his comedy.

Langdon, says Lloyd,[1] was called the baby-faced comedian,

[1] *Harold Lloyd's World of Comedy* by William Cahn.

his actions being like that of a small boy. He would start to do something, then change. Indecision and innocence were integral parts of his character. He was a fine pantomimist and had all the essentials of success, but unfortunately lacked the judgment to decide what and what not to do, so that when he came to produce his own pictures, he unfortunately failed.

Louise Fazenda—later the wife of Hollywood producer Hal Wallis—was another Sennett player who had taken up film work with Universal after a precarious early stage career. She appeared in several comedies for Sennett, but by 1925 had forsaken the indignity of custard pies to play in more ambitious feature comedies for Warners and Paramount. In 1915 Polly Moran joined Sennett, to star with Charles Murray in *The Janitor*. And before leaving Sennett to star in L-KO comedies in 1915, Alice Howell, the girl with the fuzzy hair and the penguin walk, was Keystone's popular 'scrub lady'.

The output of the Keystone studio was enormous. In 1914, the year in which Chaplin worked there, he appeared in thirty-five pictures. In several of them were the other members of the crazy gang—Charlie Murray, Edgar Kennedy, Mack Swain, Harry McCoy, Ben Turpin, and Chester Conklin, with Fatty Arbuckle and Mabel Normand.

Wallace Macdonald, who was one of the first Keystone cops, reported later that Sennett used to make his police force ride in the patrol wagon for five days in the week. 'On the sixth day, which was pay day, we all fell in the lake. Every Saturday we had to go to the park and fall in the lake. Or sometimes, just for a change, we fell in the ocean—just off the pier. It was better to fall in than be kicked in. Charlie Chaplin has kicked me into every lake in Los Angeles. Those were the good old days. No actor was too great to kick another actor, even an actor he hardly knew.'

The cops at that time included Chester Conklin, Eddie Sutherland, Eddie Kline (later both film directors), Mack Swain, Hank Mann, and Al St John, who was said to have first found fame because he could eat peas with a knife. Al was the property man when not in the picture. There was also Mabel Normand and Minta Durfee (Mrs Arbuckle) but at that time there were no bathing belles. The bathing girls came later, at a time when

Sennett decided that his comedies lacked sex appeal. Dressing some of the most attractive girls he could find in scanty but voluminous bathing costumes, Sennett daringly began to concentrate on the bathing beauties, and gave the cops a little less to do. Perhaps he thought that he could not go on throwing policemen into water week after week, and still be entertaining.

There was plenty of glamour in Hollywood, and Sennett found it. Phyllis Haver, Mildred June, Vera Steadman, Marie Prevost, Juanita Hansen, Mary Thurman, and Gloria Swanson were among the beauties who tripped down to the coast to pose for the cameras at Venice Beach, California, to the great delight of the public.

During 1914 the Keystone agents in London issued Keystone iron crosses to please young patrons and to gain publicity. The medals, stamped with pictures of the players, were offered to cinemas in Britain at wholesale prices—plain at 5s a thousand, or with a tricolour ribbon at 28s a thousand. Tens of thousands were distributed every week, for Keystone comedies were showing everywhere. There were also plenty of imitators, as a reader of *Pictures and Picturegoer* magazine reported in December 1914:

I feel that I must write and tell you about a picture I saw on Monday last. The film was a comic one, and very funny, I must admit, but it made me mad because they obviously tried to copy a Keystone. Now you know that this is impossible, for Keystones stand alone in the competition for original comedies. In this film there was a girl made up like Mabel, a fat man with a tuft on his chin (who tried to look like Ford Sterling, but failed miserably) and lastly, the most atrocious of all, there was an individual who imitated Charles Chaplin. They say that imitation is the sincerest form of flattery. If that is so, then Keystone ought to be sure of the success of their films. In my humble opinion Keystone comedies are absolutely tophole.

Around 1914–1915 everyone in the American film industry was talking about *The Clansman*, the ambitious feature film which was occupying D. W. Griffith's attention in California. In the preliminary scenes some 175 horses and 300 men had been used, and in the main sequences about 3,000 people would be employed, whole stretches of countryside being leased and closed to the public. Never had such a gigantic film been planned. Later, when *The Clansman* emerged as the epic *The Birth of a Nation*, the public were to see the most magnificent picture yet made.

Sennett, who liked to be regarded as the master producer —as indeed he was in his own field—felt that this great film was a personal challenge to his resources. He thought things over, and decided to produce a much longer comedy film than anyone had yet devised—a six-reel slapstick picture. He would have to plan it carefully, and it would be costly. But he was determined that *The Clansman* should not be the only big film on the market.

To play the leading role in his mammoth new comedy, Marie Dressler was persuaded to bring to the films her stage part in the act 'Tillie's Nightmare'. For good measure, Sennett added his new discovery, Charles Chaplin, although it was clearly understood that Marie Dressler was the star.

The film, *Tillie's Punctured Romance*, was a tremendous success. Even the four months which had been devoted to the production of this then costly experiment were not grudged, once the audiences started to laugh and applaud. The life of the picture seemed endless. Some years after its original presentation it came back as *For the Love of Tillie*, and some thirty-five years ago it came out again as *Marie's Millions*. In 1950, when the picture was showing again in London—its fifth or sixth re-issue in Britain—the public still found it funny.

In 1915 Mack Sennett was able to advertise that he had made more famous comedies 'than any other three producers'. The Keystone stars of the year included Mabel Normand, Arbuckle, Chester Conklin, Billy Walsh, and 'Dutch' Ward. The first film featuring Syd Chaplin was *Giddy, Gay and Girlish* (1,020 ft), and soon he was to appear in many more. In England, Hepworth was making *Who Stole Pa's Purse?* and *Tilly and the Nut*, which were with the many other English comedies making gallant efforts to compete with the faster and more uproarious comic action pictures which Sennett and his rivals were now churning out.

'I have had numerous bruises and injured feelings, working

85

in Mack Sennett's fun emporium,' announced Chester Conklin in 1916. 'Mr Sennett always has his plays fairly well planned before we leave the studio, and we know, in a general way, what he expects of us. Although he has little time to direct a picture himself, every once in a while he manages it. He is the key of Keystone.'

Some of the bruises were probably collected when Conklin was blown through the air by a premature explosion in the big tank. There were always plenty of explosions at Edendale, but this one went off before it was expected, and Conklin flew high in the air. He was severely shaken, but unbroken. The bottom of the tank, however, was blown clean out, and the studio was flooded with water. Not that this mattered much, because Sennett's comedians were by now used to water, and they continued work that same afternoon.

Although Sennett was probably the originator of the screen custard pie, others have claimed the honour. Whoever was responsible—and it is some responsibility—it was certainly Sennett who developed the art successfully. And an art it was, for he found that a well-aimed pie drew as many laughs as any other device. 'But for some reason,' he said in later years, 'they don't like to see a girl in a *white lawn dress* hit with pies. In fact, they don't like to see young girls pie-strewn anyway. They didn't mind more elderly women—but not girls.'

There was certainly nothing elevating about the Keystone touch. Perhaps some maiden aunts and a few school teachers saw little to laugh at when Chaplin hit someone over the head with a brick, or kicked a rival in the pants. How vulgar! But to most normal audiences it was all hilariously funny, and even if the comedy seemed crude at times, most people knew that life itself could also be crude and vulgar, although seldom as crazy as Mr Sennett depicted it.

The whole Keystone outfit was fantastic, from start to finish. Ben Turpin, who was famous for his crossed eyes, had possessed normal eyes when he started on the stage in burlesque. After an accident he reported back for work, and found that his disability was now his fortune. Later he started his film career as a property man, janitor, and comedian for Essanay, having been spotted by Chaplin, who offered him a part in *His New Job*.

Then George K. Spoor of Essanay offered him a two years' contract at twenty-five dollars a week, and he appeared with Chaplin in *His Night Out*. When S. S. Hutchinson of the American Film Company saw this film he offered Turpin one hundred dollars a week, and in 1916 the comedian was able to demand a weekly cheque of 200 dollars from Sennett. Every year his salary grew, and he stayed with Sennett until 1926. In 1921 he insured his crossed eyes for 25,000 dollars—in case they should go straight again! It was a hectic life. Charles Murray said afterwards that they hit him with pies, sat him on a hot stove, made him fall out of a high window into a tank of water, and then dragged him through a tangle of thorn bushes. After this they smeared him with paste, and set a particularly unfriendly bulldog to chase him.

By February 1918 the *Bioscope* magazine was asking, 'Why on earth can't these farce writers think of something different and occasionally amusing, instead of skidding motor cars, and manhunts on top of skyscrapers?' It was a cry in the wilderness, for Sennett was not the only one producing fantastic comedies, and audiences loved them. An important rival was Al Christie, whose 1917 subjects included *Father's Bright Idea*, *Some Kid*, *His Flirting Ways*, *Those Wedding Bells*, and in the same year Larry Semon of Vitagraph—billed as Laurence Semon—was featured with Florence Curtis, Pedro Oromando, and Joe Curtis in *Rough Toughs and Roof Tops*. Semon's popularity was soon tremendous. But if you were one of the few who didn't appreciate his acrobatic clowning, then you might have preferred the *Jerry Cub comedies*, with George Ovey, who claimed to be 'one of the few heroes of the screen who possesses the secret of being funny *quickly*'. His pictures included *Jerry and the Outlaws*, *Jerry's Big Mystery*, *Jerry's Brilliant Scheme*, and *Jerry's Romance*.

It was at the end of 1917, after the collapse of Triangle, the producers of Keystone, that Sennett decided to join Paramount as a producer and director. Many of his gang went with him, and until 1921 his films were distributed by Paramount Pictures. He later added many new names to his list, including those of Andy Clyde, Harry Langdon, and Sally Eilers. He introduced Bing Crosby to the screen after three studios had turned him down, and in 1924, 1925, and 1926, when his films were distributed in the United States by Pathé, he enjoyed prosperous years as the uncrowned king of slapstick film comedy.

By 1929 he was in financial difficulties owing to the American depression and the coming of the talkies, but somehow he managed to weather the storm. At Edendale, he could reflect, he had built Hollywood's first concrete enclosed stage. If he wanted to, he could remember with pride that he had given the world its funniest police force, a whole bevy of bathing beauties, several thousand custard pies, and a host of the most famous names of the cinema, headed by Mabel Normand and Charles Chaplin.

Altogether, it is likely that Mack Sennett created more laughter than any man of his generation. But every comedian had a trademark, which was distinctive. Thus, Chaplin was instantly recognized by his toothbrush moustache, baggy pants, and seedy clothes; Harold Lloyd became known later by his spectacles and straw hat; Buster Keaton's unsmiling face, although it hid many expressions, was unique; Ben Turpin had his crossed eyes; Stan Laurel cried; Jimmy Durante pushed his nose towards the camera; Edgar Kennedy became famous because of his 'slow burn' technique; Groucho Marx would be unthinkable without a cigar. Sennett's comedians have never been surpassed, because no one has ever moved so fast or so comically since the golden Keystone days, and no one after Sennett ever burlesqued the establishment, law and order, and conformity as he did during the years when he was the king of the world's comedians.

CHAPTER SEVEN

Chaplin—The Perfect Clown

OF ALL THE comedians whom Mack Sennett discovered for the screen, none became more famous than Charles Chaplin, the little clown with the curly hair, the baggy trousers, the bowler hat, the small moustache, the cane, and the decrepit outsize boots. This was the man described in later years by George Bernard Shaw as 'the only genius developed in motion pictures.'

He was twenty-six when he joined Sennett, taking with him many of the ideas and traditions of Fred Karno's music hall troupe, with whom he had gone to America. Ever since then he has faced criticism as well as applause. Some have alleged that even his make-up was stolen from another comedian, Billie Ritchie. Others claim that Billie Ritchie stole Chaplin's ideas. As we now know, Max Linder influenced Chaplin's early technique. Yet it was unmistakably Chaplin himself who made his own personal triumph, and because success usually brings with it responsibilities and the fierce spotlight of public opinion, this man, more than anyone else in Hollywood, has been constantly under fire. There are more fools in the world than Chaplin has portrayed.

He was born on April 16, 1889, in East Lane, Walworth, London.[1] But according to author Thomas Burke, he was born in Chester Street, which runs between Kennington Road and Lower Kennington Lane. The American *Picture Play* magazine for April 1916 announced that he was not born in London at all, but in Paris.

The son of a singer and a dancer, young Charles had to contribute towards keeping the family when his father died. His mother, who had twice before been married, danced by day, and at night earned extra money by dressmaking but was often in an asylum. They lived in a poor but neat house, and although he was later to know great wealth and security, young

[1] *My Autobiography* by Charles Chaplin (Bodley Head, London, 1964)

Charles never forgot his early days, and the struggle for the necessities of life.

When he was ten he was on the music halls, already old in ideas, having sung at smoking concerts and in public houses. He was a good clog-dancer, and was learning to be a mimic, but for all his juvenile ability the pay was poor, and his first shillings did little to swell the family budget. When he was seven he had nearly been drowned through falling into the Thames from the steps at Westminster Bridge, and soon after this he had made his film début by posing in front of a newsreel camera which was filming the Scots Guards marching though St James's Park.

In 1905 he won his first important stage role in *Jim*, and then played Billy, the boy assistant to Sherlock Holmes, in the London production of *Sherlock Holmes* with William Gillette and Irene Vanbrugh. Backstage, young Chaplin talked to Arthur Conan Doyle, and it was jokingly agreed that in future each would share the earnings of the other. Later Gillette added a curtain raiser called *The Painful Predicament of Sherlock Holmes* to the play *Clarissa* and Chaplin again played the part of Billy at the Duke of York's Theatre.

When the play closed he was out of work, and was forced by circumstances to accept an engagement in an East End music hall as 'Sam Cohen, the Jewish comedian'. He was not much of a success, and soon afterwards he started a twelve months' engagement at forty-five shillings a week, appearing in a juvenile sketch combination in *Casey's Circus*, in which he impersonated Dick Turpin and the celebrated showman 'Doctor' Walford Bodie. Here he was so successful that he joined his half-brother Sydney as a member of Fred Karno's dumb-show comedy company, playing in *The Football Match* and among other roles the part of the drunken swell in *Mumming Birds*, a comedy sketch which was known later in America as *A Night in an English Music Hall*. Others had played the part before him, including Billie Ritchie. He was paid £3 10s a week.

With Karno he learned the hard way, travelling all over Britain and going twice to America. The repertoire was varied; there were sketches about drunks, thieves, family relations, billiards champions, boxers, Turkish baths, policemen, singers who prepared to sing but somehow never started, conjurers who spoiled their own tricks, and pianists who lost the music . . . a wide variety of subjects, mixed with vulgarity.

In later years Chaplin admitted that it was not always easy to make people laugh. 'The mere fact of a hat being blown off isn't funny,' he explained. 'What is funny is to see its owner running after it, with his hair blowing about, and his coat tails flying. A man walking down a street—that isn't funny. But placed in a ridiculous and embarrassing position the human being becomes a source of laughter to his fellow creatures.'

In *Mumming Birds* Chaplin learned many of the tricks which he later introduced on the screen. He was by no means the only comedian in the show, or the one who always got the most laughs. There was another boy who also did well, and whom many people thought equally funny. His role was that of a boy in an Eton collar who fell out of the stage box in excitement. And his name was Stan Laurel.

Chaplin was playing in comic sketches in *A Night in an English Music Hall* during his second visit to America, when Alf Reeves, the manager, received the telegram which was to alter the comedian's life :

IS THERE A MAN NAMED CHAFFIN IN YOUR COMPANY OR SOMETHING LIKE THAT STOP IF SO WILL HE COM-MUNICATE WITH KESSEL AND BAUMAN 24 LONGACRE BUILDING BROADWAY

Chaplin went to see Kessel and Bauman, the owners of the Keystone Comedy Film Company, and was slightly surprised to receive an offer to go into pictures. Mack Sennett wished to engage him to take over from Ford Sterling. He thought the matter over, and paid a visit to one or two picture theatres. What he saw did not convince him that he should abandon his stage career, but he realized that at some time in the future the screen might offer him better opportunities than the music halls.

'I hate to leave the troupe,' he said. 'How do I know that pictures are going to be a successful medium for pantomime? Suppose I don't make good? I'll be stranded in a strange country.' Nevertheless, he accepted 150 dollars a week for a year's trial contract, and joined Mabel Normand, Ford Sterling, Arbuckle, and the other popular Keystone comics, making his début in 1914 as a reporter in *Making a Living*, with Virginia Kirtley, Henry Lehrman, and Alice Davenport. Afterwards he was teamed for the first time with Mabel Normand in *Mabel's Strange Predicament*, but it was in *Kid Auto Races at Venice*, his second film, that he established himself.

At first Chaplin's humour did not appeal to Sennett, who was afterwards said to have offered him money to cancel his contract. Chaplin refused, and continued to share a dressing room with Arbuckle, Mack Swain, and two other comedians. They took very little notice of the Englishman, whose first appearances on the screen were made not in his now famous disguise, but with a drooping moustache, ordinary shoes, and a battered top hat. Chaplin's personality was at first used only to carry out Sennett's comedy ideas. Most of his individual comedy was lost in the speed of each film, and in such pictures as *Cruel, Cruel Love* and *Caught in a Cabaret*, to name only two, he had little chance to prove his ability. It was not until he adopted the role of a seedy dandy and later borrowed an old pair of Ford Sterling's shoes to accentuate a comedy walk, together with a pair of Arbuckle's wide baggy pants, that he began to shine. Then it was the public which picked him out from the galaxy of comics, demanding to know who he was, asking for more.

Sennett wisely decided to give them more, and thirty short films later he suggested to Chaplin that he should play a larger part, supporting Marie Dressler in Keystone's six-reel comedy, *Tillie's Punctured Romance*. The cast was as follows:

Tillie, the Farmer's Daughter	Marie Dressler
The City Slicker	Charlie Chaplin
The City Girl Friend	Mabel Normand
Tillie's Father	Mack Swain
Café Owner	Edgar Kennedy
Film Actress	Minta Durfee (Arbuckle)
Detective	Charlie Murray
Detective	Charlie Chase
Society Guest	Harry McCoy
Society Guest	Chester Conklin

As one of the two Society Guests, Harry McCoy was made-up to look exactly like Ford Sterling. It is a common error to suppose that Sterling appeared in this film, and his name is usually included in cast lists. But actually he had left Keystone before the picture was made. The Keystone cops included Slim Summerville, Hank Mann, and Eddie Sutherland, and the part of a film actress was played by Arbuckle's wife, Minta Durfee, who is usually left out of the cast lists. Chaplin later said that he found the picture unfunny.

In America the film established Chaplin as a leading comedian. In Britain it was not released until 1916, by which time his subsequent Essanay films were being shown. He played the part of a smart man about town, dressed in natty suiting and sporting a thin pencilled moustache with a break in the middle. The toothbrush moustache which he had worn in earlier pictures was temporarily abandoned. The film showed Chaplin in an unsympathetic light, and it ended with Marie Dressler chasing him and Mabel Normand, with the aid of the cops, in motor boats and rowing boats. Finally, Marie Dressler ended up in the sea.

In April 1915, when London children were singing 'When the Moon Shines Bright on Charlie Chaplin', the *New York Herald* was able to report that 'The Chaplin craze seems to have supplanted the Pickford craze', and in this year the comedian left Mack Sennett to join the Essanay company. Once Chaplin had gone, Sennett realized that the thirty-five old films in which he had appeared were now valuable. Pictures in which he had made only a fleeting appearance were re-issued over and over again, often with new titles, until they were worn out. According to E. W. and M. M. Robson, in their book *The Film Answers Back*, one cinema in New York, the Chrystal Hall on 14th Street, played nothing but Chaplin pictures for ten years, from 1913 to 1923. There was a break for one week, when one of his best imitators was substituted as an experiment, but business was poor. Next week, when a Chaplin comedy was announced, the patrons returned. It has been estimated that over twenty-five million dollars were paid into the cinemas of the world up to 1921, just to see Chaplin's short films.

In his year with Keystone he had appeared in thirty-five films, produced at the rate of about one a week, except for the six-reeler, which had taken fourteen weeks to complete. Most of these pictures reappeared constantly under fresh titles, to confuse the public. Thus when *Making a Living* had been widely shown it was re-issued as *A Busted Johnny*, *Troubles*, and *Doing His Best*. *A Film Johnnie* became *Movie Nut* and *Million Dollar Job*. *Caught in a Cabaret* was renamed *The Waiter*, *The Jazz Waiter*, and *Faking with Society*, while *The New Janitor* turned up as *The New Porter* and *The Blundering Boob*. All around the world, over and over again, went the Keystone Chaplins. And they are still showing, although they are usually mutilated.

From Essanay, Charlie was able to demand 1,250 dollars a week. It is said that Sennett had kept the agents from rival companies away by refusing to allow them near his studio, but that one man—from Essanay—got in disguised as a cowboy 'super' and clinched the deal. In 1916 Charlie was able to leave Essanay after fourteen films, for Mutual, who paid him the princeley salary of 10,000 dollars a week, plus a cash bonus of 150,000 dollars.

Back on the Keystone lot he was succeeded by cross-eyed Ben Turpin, who now appeared in dozens of Sennett's films. Unlike many other comics of the time, Turpin did not copy Chaplin. But to be 'like Charlie Chaplin' was to ensure success, and few companies did not possess an imitator. Before he donned his famous horn-rimmed spectacles and developed his own style, Harold Lloyd was for a time in the 'Chaplin school'. Foremost among the many imitators was Billy West, appearing in *King Bee comedies* with Oliver (Babe) Hardy. A comedian named Charles Amador became Charles Aplin, and in 1925 Chaplin sued him, and obtained a judgment. France and England had several imitators, and in Germany there was a Charlie Kaplin. But Charlie thrived on imitation, and went from strength to strength, simply because there was nobody quite like him.

The Essanay company gave him more scope than Sennett had done, and as partners he had Edna Purviance and, before he went to Keystone, Ben Turpin. Charlie was now responsible for more of the actual production, and the laughs were louder. As a boxer with a horse-shoe in his glove, or even as a young woman flirting with a middle-aged man, he kept audiences eagerly asking for more. *His New Job, The Champion, Work, The Tramp, By the Sea, In the Park,* and *Police* were all titles which Fred Karno might have given to his famous music hall sketches. English humour had conquered the American screen. The ageless tradition of the clown, the buffoon, the silent mimic, had captured the new medium.

In all he made fourteen films for Essanay, for which he received some ten times the salary that Sennett had paid him.[1] The old custard pie technique was by no means forgotten. There was often a chase, some drunken stumbling, and comic officialdom to be guyed. There were gouty feet to be trodden on or caught in revolving doors, some heavily bearded villains to leer at the beauties, and plenty of action with the cane, which was useful for balancing, and for moving drunken bodies out of the path. Large jellies and trifles still sailed through the air. But Chaplin himself was getting a little more serious, slightly more mature. And more entertaining.

Not that he ever wanted to play Hamlet. But it was probably *Carmen* (1916), his burlesque of the opera, which made him think of making a more serious type of picture, in which the laughs could be balanced with the tears, the light tempered with the shade. The Essanay company, however, would not consider his suggestion. They were making too much money out of laughs to risk losing any on tears. So Charlie decided to wait.

But from this time onwards he tended to slow up the knock-about and began to develop into a player with better timing and a purpose behind everything he did. Although he would always point his moral with the aid of comedy, his pictures were never again made solely to make people laugh. In most of them there were to be tears, in some of them slight bitterness. The tramp who emerged from the slap-happy studio at Edendale was not an Englishman or an American. His theme was universal, as was his appeal. It was, and still is, as readily understood in Cairo or Tokyo as in Boston or Maine. Fundamentally, the peoples of the world are very much alike. And Chaplin knew

[1] A fifteenth picture, *Triple Trouble* was made for Essanay in 1918, when he had left Mutual and before he went to First National.

this, because he was and is at heart an international moralist, an entertainer capable of catching the hopes and fears, the sorrows and joys, of the ordinary person, sometimes with only a gesture, the movement of a hand, or the shuffle of his feet.

In May 1915 *The Bioscope* film trade paper reported in Britain that 'so strong is the grip of the Chaplin comedies that last week numerous halls in the Liverpool district adopted the expediency of giving special performances, at which the films exhibited consisted exclusively of the Chaplin productions.'

In 1916 he left Essanay to join Mutual, for whom his first picture was *The Floorwalker*, with Edna Purviance. In all his twelve short Mutual films, and in those which came later, he appeared as a little man who might have come from any city, in any country. In *The Immigrant* (1917) he depicted a number of homeless people of different nationalities travelling to America in the steerage of a liner. He showed the Statute of Liberty in the background, and in the next scene depicted the passengers being ruthlessly herded together behind ropes. It was laughable, but it was also an expression of social condition. Chaplin had started his crusade.

The Mutual pictures included *The Fireman, The Vagabond, One A.M., The Count, The Pawnshop, Behind the Screen, Easy Street, The Cure,* and *The Adventurer*. Many of these were based on familiar themes. *The Rink* was similar to Max Linder's skating film, although there must be a limit to the amount of antics that can be accomplished on skates. In *The Pawnshop* there were two hilarious minutes in which Chaplin passed dishes through a clothes wringer to dry them, then dried a cup in the same way, and finally his hands.

The modern generation rarely sees an early Chaplin film in its original form. Sequences have been cut out, and the original titles lost. The addition of wholly irrelevant commentaries, explaining what Charlie may do next, often spoils the picture. Sound effects are added, which do nothing to help the comedy. But worst of all is the commentary, all too frequent, which 'guys' the classic comedy film, so that the picture is spoiled. In spite of these defects many of the old Chaplin films are still in great demand, and are likely to remain so as long as people retain their sense of humour. *Easy Street* (1917) con-

slie Henson and Alma Taylor in ALF'S
BUTTON (*Hepworth,* 1921)

20. *George Robey in* THE PREHISTORIC
MAN (*Stolls,* 1924)

Buster Keaton and Florence Turner in
COLLEGE (1927)

22. *Walter Forde with a friend in*
WALTER WANTS WORK (1921)

25. Harold Lloyd in FEET FIRST (1930)

23.
Harold Lloyd
with Jobyna
Ralson in THE
KID BROTHER
(1927)

24.
Chaplin in THE
CIRCUS (1928)

sidered by many to be the best of the Mutual series, is, with *The Cure*, one of the most popular of all. During 1948, Wallace Heaton, with one of the biggest hiring libraries of sub-standard films in Britain, kept sixteen copies of *Easy Street* in circulation, and seldom had a copy on their shelves.

Late in 1917 Chaplin left Mutual to sign a new contract with the First National Corporation. The three years with Keystone, Essanay, and Mutual, had established him as the most popular comedian in the world. He was the idol of everybody who could go to the pictures, and in such theatres as the New Gallery Kinema, London—considered to be the smartest picture house in the metropolis—his short comedies were given more prominence than the feature attractions. In the noisier districts of London's Commercial Road, Canning Town, and Mile End, the appeal of Chaplin was terrific. To Englishmen, and especially to Londoners, he has always been the foremost comedian on the screen, a household name remembered when the name of the last Prime Minister might be forgotten, the name of the President of France ignored.

In France, during the horrors of the 1914 war, his name was a byword with the troops. Home and beauty were typified by the wife, a hot bath, and Charlie Chaplin—who represented all the gaiety and good feeling of the world to the ordinary Allied soldier. When a Chaplin film arrived at the front it offered entertainment to the troops which few actors could surpass. The officer commanding the 6th Divisional Supply Column in France wrote to the Essanay company:

Gentlemen,

I have to thank you for your letter of September 11th, forwarded to me today, and for the gift of films. It is impossible to make you realize how much they were appreciated, and I truly wish you could have heard the cheer that went up when Chaplin appeared on the screen. The posters—i.e. cardboard figures of Chaplin, were carried off during the night to the trenches, and have been the subject of great attention by the enemy.

W. Murphy,
Major, A.S.C.

Soon Chaplin was able to build his own studio—described as a 'snug and unobtrusive little affair', and stated to have cost him up to £20,000. It was erected on a site bought for some 30,000 dollars, in the best residential district of Hollywood, a mile away from the existing studio centre. The initial ceremony of turning the first earth on his five acres of land was performed by Charlie himself, in the presence of Syd, and a few members of the company. Both brothers took off their coats and began to dig. Then Charlie carted away some earth in a wheelbarrow, and an army of workmen swarmed in.

For the little man from Walworth the moment was important. From now on he was relatively independent, working for himself, and at last free to express himself. Under his contract with First National he made eight films, in addition to *The Bond*, which was produced for the Liberty Loan Committee and was issued free. The titles were *A Dog's Life*, *Shoulder Arms*, *Sunnyside*, *A Day's Pleasure*, *The Kid*, *The Idle Class*, *Pay Day*, and *The Pilgrim*. Neither *Sunnyside* nor *A Day's Pleasure* were considered in 1919 to be among Chaplin's best films. His position was by now being contested by the frequent appearance of his rivals Larry Sermon, Arbuckle, Harold Lloyd, and Buster Keaton. But with the coming of *The Kid* (1921) his supremacy was assured.

Pay Day (1922) was the last two-reeler. Only the less popular comedians were now to be seen exclusively in two-reelers. After this came *The Pilgrim* (four reels), in which he was seen as a convict escaping from prison. After exchanging his clothes for those of a parson who was swimming, Charlie walked up the road, only to meet an elderly couple—who asked him to marry them. Escaping to a town, he was greeted warmly by the good folk, who were all collected together to meet the visiting parson. In the pulpit Charlie brilliantly told the story of David and Goliath, entirely in pantomime.

Now that wealth had come his way, he could afford to be generous; 150,000 dollars went to the War Loan, and with Sir Harry Lauder he gave his services for a special short half-reel comedy, the proceeds going to the Loan. He was now making an immense amount of money, and so were the men who marketed and showed his pictures. The British rights in

The Idle Class (1921) were sold for the record sum of £50,000, but British cinema owners were at first reluctant to pay what they considered high rental charges for the picture.

Shoulder Arms was filmed in 1918, but was not shown in America until three weeks before the armistice. It was felt that the troops might not like the humour, being so familiar with the reality. Five reels had been planned, but they were finally cut down to three. There was really no danger of the troops being offended, and it was generally considered to be Chaplin's best picture. As an awkward recruit unable to stand in line because of his extraordinary feet, Charlie reached new heights of comedy. Every humorous war picture of later years was to be influenced by *Shoulder Arms*. When at last the shouts of his fearful sergeant had died away, the new recruit was seen asleep in the barrack room, fitfully dreaming that he was already in the front line trenches.

The grim nightmare was comic, yet the settings were realistic and the atmosphere wholly convincing. Charlie's method of opening a bottle was to hold it above the trench until a bullet shattered the top. When every other soldier received his mail from home, he got nothing. But at last his parcel arrived, a cheese so old and ripe that he sought the safety of a gas mask before hurling it far away into the enemy lines.

Peace came at last at the end of the nightmare, with Charlie dreaming that he was sinking to sleep below the water line of a flooded trench, breathing bubbles through a tin funnel. Only a sergeant's head and feet, with a frog sitting on one boot, could be seen above the water level.

Shoulder Arms ended with a sniping expedition into No Man's Land. Disguised as a tree, Charlie was invisible to all but a wandering dog, and when chased up a drain pipe by the enemy, he lost his trousers. Finally came the moment in his dream when he captured the Kaiser, the Crown Prince, and Von Hindenburg, all at once. Brother Sydney was the Kaiser, but there were objections to this part of the picture, and some cinemas did not show it. The ending was even more sensational, showing the Allied leaders giving a magnificent banquet to Charlie, at which the President of France made a speech. As Charlie rose to reply, the King of England crept up to steal a souvenir button from the hero's coat! Needless to say, the general public did *not* see this sequence.

Shoulder Arms and the other films which Chaplin made between 1918 and 1923 for First National represented the fruits of the experience he had gained with Sennett, Essanay, and Mutual, and showed that the comedian was ready for bigger things. In 1921 came *The Kid*, still considered to be one of the outstanding motion pictures of all time. It started melodramatically with the words 'Her only sin was motherhood . . .' followed by a scene showing a woman leaving a child on a front doorstep. Then came Charlie the tramp, pausing to remove a fingerless glove, and carefully selecting a cigarette stub from the old sardine tin which he used as a case.

The child star of *The Kid* was Jackie Coogan, and the story continued in a rambling fashion, production being almost on a day-to-day basis, without script or scenario. A dream sequence entitled 'Fairyland' showed the tramp and the child in heaven, a happily decorated slum street in which even the policemen flew around with white wings. In order to earn money to keep the boy, the tramp became a glazier, sending the youngster round the houses to break the windows which he could then repair. Later, in *The Gold Rush* (1925) Chaplin provided a variation on this theme by sweeping snow from one house in front of another, then moving on to offer his services at the house where the snow was piled up.

The Kid brought sudden fame to little Jackie Coogan, who had made his stage début when not quite two by escaping from his father's dressing room clad only in a petticoat, to make an unexpected entrance on the stage. Three years later Chaplin saw him and engaged him for the film. According to tradition, the five-year-old boy winked at the famous comedian in a hotel lobby.

By the time he was ten Coogan had made about £230,000, including £100,000 paid in advance for four future films. When in the autumn of 1924 he went to Greece, he was acclaimed in every country he passed through. American children had subscribed a million dollars to send a mercy cargo of milk and food to the children of Greece, and Jackie Coogan was chosen to deliver it. At Southampton he was received in state by the mayor, and in London enthusiastic crowds greeted him. The harbour of Piraeus, the port of Athens, was beflagged and decorated with hundreds of posters bidding *Zito* (Welcome) to the young ambassador. In Athens he was presented with the Golden Cross of the Order of Jerusalem and the Silver Cross of the Order of George. To the world this boy was Young America, yet within a few years he had slipped from stardom and was no longer even a box-office attraction. When he grew up, people lost interest in him. Of all his many films, *Peck's Bad Boy*, *Trouble*, *Oliver Twist*, and *Circus Days*, in which he gave excellent performances, only *The Kid* is remembered. A child star is seldom an adult star. In later years Shirley Temple, Freddie Bartholomew, and for a while Jackie Cooper were to know how hard it is to live down a juvenile reputation, and claim attention as an adult.

Early in 1919 Chaplin joined Mary Pickford, her husband Douglas Fairbanks, and D. W. Griffith, to form the United Artists Corporation. Each was to produce pictures for distribution through their new organization. It was no longer necessary for Chaplin to make many films—certainly not at the rate to which he was accustomed. In future his pictures could be bigger, but less frequent.

It was not until 1921 that Charlie returned to Europe, when he visited England, France, and Germany. In Paris he found a little café, where he had enjoyed coffee some years before, but it was now closed. There could be little time to remember the past, for Chaplin was the man of the moment. When Max Linder told him that people knew him as Charlot, and his brother Sydney as Julot, Chaplin roared with laughter and insisted on being called Charlot all day. Later he had to be rescued by gendarmes from a howling mob of admirers, all shouting 'Vive Charlot!'

In Paris he met Dudley Field Malone, Waldo Francis, and Georges Carpentier, and went to see Versailles with Carpentier and Sir Philip Sassoon. When he attended the French première of *The Kid* he found his box decorated with American and British flags, and afterwards he received the Medal of the Beaux Arts. Back at the Crillon Hotel awaiting his return were Douglas Fairbanks and Mary Pickford, with General Pershing.

In England Chaplin had stayed at Lympne in Kent, with Sir Philip Sassoon. When his host asked him to attend the unveiling of the village war memorial Chaplin had hesitated, thinking that a comedian would be out of place at such a ceremony. Nevertheless, he attended the service, to the great delight of the villagers.

A week was spent in Essex with H. G. Wells, of whose novel *The History of Mr Polly* Chaplin said, 'Some day I am going to do it in pictures.' But *Mr Polly* did not appear on the screen for nearly thirty years, and it was then John Mills and not Chaplin who made it. Charlie, however, was quite right—he would have made an excellent Mr Polly. It was strange that several of the critics who praised John Mills in the film pointed out that he was almost 'Chaplinesque' in certain sequences.

James Barrie, Thomas Burke, and Rebecca West were among the celebrities whom he met with H. G. Wells. He showed them how to play baseball, and discussed with St John Ervine the possibility of making talking pictures. Chaplin expressed his opinion that speech would spoil the art of pantomime, and that talk was totally unnecessary to films.

When he returned to England from France the 'plane was held up by fog over the Channel, and was two hours late at Croydon. Sir Philip Sassoon had arranged for Chaplin to meet the Prime Minister, David Lloyd George, and because of the delay Chaplin was rather worried. There was a crowd at the airport, where the police cleared a gangway for Chaplin to reach his car. Directly he was in the car, it started off, but instead of going to the Ritz Hotel, Chaplin found himself nearing the Clapham district. When he asked the driver where they were going the man in front pulled off a false moustache and announced: 'I am Castleton Knight. You remember me. You promised to visit my theatre. My patrons were all told about it, and they expected you. You didn't keep your promise, so I have kidnapped you.'

To have kidnapped Charlie Chaplin under the noses of the police at Croydon, was no mean achievement. Castleton Knight was the enterprising manager of the Majestic Theatre at Clapham. He had driven a large car up to the airport, and had announced to the police that he was collecting Mr Chaplin.

Luckily, Chaplin thought it was a good joke, and at once agreed to appear on the stage of the Majestic. He made a short speech to a delighted audience, and went on in the car to his hotel.

The European tour had started at Southampton, where he had been greeted by the mayor and a civic reception. In his book *My Wonderful Visit*, he later described the welcome at Waterloo Station:

The barriers are broken. They are coming on all sides. Policemen are elbowing and pushing. Girls are shrieking—'Charlie! Charlie! There he is! Good luck to you, Charlie! God bless you!'

He did not like the hysterical adoration of the crowds. And in his first four days in London he received 73,000 letters, of which 671 were from relatives in Britain, of whom he knew nothing. Most of them claimed to be cousins, but nine different women said they were his mother. Almost all the writers asked to be set up in business, to meet him, or to go on the films.

After being introduced by Edward Knoblock to E. V. Lucas, Chaplin accepted an invitation to dinner at the Garrick Club, where he sat next to J. M. Barrie, who suggested that *Peter Pan* ought to be filmed. They continued the discussion in Barrie's flat until three o'clock in the morning.

In Germany Chaplin was almost unknown, for only *The Rink* had been shown there. On his first evening in Berlin he went to a leading restaurant, but, not being in evening clothes, was placed in a corner at a small table, where he sat meekly eating his dinner, with only a poor view of the crowded room. As he was leaving, a man from a more important table jumped up and walked quickly to greet him. It was Alf Kaufman, the European representative of Paramount Pictures, who at once persuaded Chaplin to join his table, where his wife was sitting with Pola Negri.

'Negri is a wonderful person,' said Chaplin afterwards. 'Young, vivacious, beautiful. She speaks no English—she is Polish, you know, not German, even though she has played in German pictures. We became very good friends, and I dined with the same party every one of the three nights in Berlin.

Negri is coming to America in January to make pictures in California. She will be a revelation.'

She certanly was a revelation, and so was Ernst Lubitsch, the German director of her films, whom Chaplin also met. But because Lubitsch knew no English, and Chaplin could speak very little German, conversation was difficult.

In an interview with George P. West in 1923 Chaplin revealed that the now familiar tramp outfit helped him to express the conception of the average man, whom he sought to represent on the screen. 'The derby (bowler), too small, is striving for dignity,' he explained. 'The moustache is vanity. The tightly buttoned coat and the stick and his whole manner are a gesture towards gallantry and dash and "front." He is trying to meet the world bravely, to put up a bluff, and he knows that, too. He knows it so well that he can laugh at himself, and pity himself a little.'

It was in this year that Chaplin decided to realize his ambition and make a serious film. *A Woman of Paris* was the result, an almost tragic story of two young people forbidden to marry. Edna Purviance and Adolphe Menjou were the stars, and Chaplin himself appeared for a brief second, walking almost unnoticed across the screen.

He tried most of his films out 'on the dog,' as he used to say, arranging to show his latest picture unannounced in a normal cinema programme. Then he would sit in the audience and watch, and listen to what people said, and note where they laughed. If they laughed he was happy, but if they did not then he cut out the sequence. There was not very much that he had to cut, once he had completed his film.

In 1925 came *The Gold Rush*, 'the picture I want to be remembered by,' said Chaplin at the time. The famous log cabin scenes, together with the dancing figures and the eating of his boots, are memorable. The picture was the first comedy which he made entirely on his own account, and it took a year to complete, and cost over 800,000 dollars.

It was two years before he made his next, *The Circus*. Whether cooking an egg, being chased into the sawdust ring, or swallowing a horse pill because the horse blew down the tube first—the little man was always in trouble. But the pathos paid handsome dividends, and during its first week of showing in New York 105,000 people paid £14,500 to see the film.

In *The Circus* (1928) Chaplin appeared as a man in search of a job. Unknowingly he becomes the accomplice of a pickpocket, and is soon wanted by the police. When a policeman sees him, he runs off to hide in a circus, where he is engaged as an odd-job man. But he is so clumsy that he is dismissed. When the circus men go on strike he is re-engaged, and falls in love with the daughter of the owner—a love which he is too shy to reveal.

With the coming of talking films, Chaplin's future hung in the balance. But two years later he decided to challenge the new technique by making a silent comedy with recorded music. This he called *City Lights*, described as a 'comedy romance in panto-mime'. Although in 1930 all Hollywood was making noisy sing-ing and dancing pictures, he decided to keep his film silent, except for an original musical score and sound effects.

When a reporter from a Hollywood magazine asked Chaplin what he thought of sound films, he was reported to have re-plied: 'Talkies? You can say I detest them! They come to ruin the world's most ancient art, the art of pantomime. They anni-hilate the great beauty of silence.'

City Lights probably represents the highest achievements of the silent film, which by 1928 had reached perfection as a method of telling a story without speech. It is the tale of a tramp who falls in love with a blind flower girl. She mistakes him for a wealthy man, and through his devotion regains her sight. Pathos and hilarious knockabout comedy are carefully mixed, the highlights being a night club sequence in which Chaplin eats spaghetti and streamers, a brilliant dancing boxing match set to music, and a delightful supporting performance by Harry Myers as the millionaire who knows Chaplin only when he is drunk. The boxing match, one of the funniest sequences ever filmed, is timed with masterly precision. It would be impossible to see it without laughing. The final close-up, in which the flower girl (Virginia Cherrill) realizes that the pathetic little tramp is her benefactor, is one of the most poignant of film scenes.

Nineteen years after its first release in Britain, *City Lights* was revived and generally released to delight a new generation. Silence had indeed proved golden, for the Chaplin of 1930 proved to be a greater comedian than any of his later rivals. The evidence was contained in a nineteen-year-old film.

'A comedy is only as funny as its gags'—in this one sentence Larry Semon had held the whole key to the success of comic films. And because both Chaplin and Semon were *clowns*, their gags were visual. *City Lights*, like every Chaplin film, had plenty. The tramp watches a man walk past him smoking a cigar, jumps into a Rolls-Royce, and follows the wealthy one down the street. When the man throws the cigar end onto the sidewalk, the tramp stops the car and makes for it. But from out of the shadows comes another tramp, who gets there first. Whereupon Charlie dashes up, pushes the intruder over, snatches the cigar end, and drives off in his car. The scene fades out on the dazed intruder, watching with amazement the spectacle of a cigar butt collector driving around in a Rolls-Royce. When analysed, every comedy sequence in this film is a gag, or a collection of gags.

In 1936 came *Modern Times*, the story of a worker in the twentieth century machine age. It was a silent film, except for a gibberish song, sung by Chaplin himself to the tune of 'Titina.' The message behind *Modern Times* was more obvious than it had been in his previous films. The absurdity of the mechanical era was paraded for everyone to see. The moral behind the laughs was clear, as it was in *The Great Dictator*, which ridiculed not only Hitler and Mussolini, but all dictatorship, in every form. Man's inhumanity to man was clearly shown. And if there was slightly less to laugh at than there had been in *The Cure* and *Easy Street*, this was because by the time the picture was shown dictatorship was hardly a laughing matter, Hitler and Mussolini being at war with half the world.

Monsieur Verdoux, (1947), proved to be an even more serious picture. Now that he had talked on the screen, in *The Great Dictator*, it was obvious that his new film would rely greatly on dialogue. But in place of the baggy pants and shabby coat, he now wore the smart morning clothes and silk hat of a French Bluebeard—a murderer who disposed of his wives with finesse. Murder is a strange subject for a jest, and it was perhaps not surprising that many members of the public could not readily appreciate the chilly atmosphere of the new picture. Yet even in this unusual story the brilliantly polished performance of Chaplin the actor did much to overcome the opposition. He held the screen completely, his timing was a delight, and his diction was as perfect as every gesture that he made.

Monsieur Verdoux was not a success. In some states in America it was boycotted, the Catholic War Veterans and other organizations protested that it was unsocial and unpleasant, and pickets were placed outside the theatres which showed it. The fact that in one scene in the film Chaplin had made a veiled plea for the cause of Christianity was ignored. Sections of the press attacked the picture vigorously. Chaplin's private life, which had claimed the attention of the more scurrilous American newspapers for some years, was again laid bare.

Partly because of the press reports, and what they had heard about it, large sections of the public stayed away from *Monsieur Verdoux*. Many believed that it might be too 'highbrow' for them. They could not visualize a Chaplin who did not make them rock with laughter. After all, that is what he had always done in the past. But in Europe the film was more successful, the press being more enthusiastic, and the public, particularly in Britain, being anxious to see Chaplin, whatever film he had made.

*

To appreciate something of the purpose of Chaplin the crusader, as opposed to Chaplin the clown, it is necessary to recall part of his final speech from *The Great Dictator*:

I should like to help everyone, if that were possible—Jew and Gentile—black and white. We should all want to help one another. We should want to live by each other's happiness, not by each other's misery.

If Chaplin has done nothing else, he deserves the applause of the people of the world for expressing this creed through a medium which has influenced thoughts and actions since the earliest flickerings of the magic lantern. No one else—except perhaps D. W. Griffith—had ever used the screen in order to spread such a simple Christian doctrine. Of all the great thinkers and politicians of the world, it was left to a clown—a baggy-trousered comedian from Walworth and Kennington—to remind people that they should live together in peace and happiness. Hollywood and sections of the American public might later resent the doctrines of Chaplin, might fling mud at his private life, and label him a Communist—or anything else unfashionable—but the average man can find little wrong with the expression of such sentiments. All too seldom are they expressed, except in half-empty churches.

It was in 1916 that Chester Conklin had said 'Without a doubt, the one person who has been most successful in making people laugh is Charlie Chaplin. His recent contract, which is said to bring him nearly seven times the income of the President of the United States, proves his success. He is the most successful public-tickler in the world.'

It is likely that future generations will think of Chaplin as a master clown, and not as a humanitarian. For while there are many preachers in the world, all teaching their own creeds and beliefs, in thousands of languages, there are very few really great clowns. And the language of the clown is international.

CHAPTER EIGHT

Harold Lloyd

FOR MANY YEARS Harold Lloyd was one of Chaplin's keenest competitors for the title of King of the Film Comedians.

A pair of horn-rimmed spectacles brought him success, and they also helped to save his life. The year was 1919, and Lloyd had been asked to pose for a publicity photograph for one of his films, lighting a cigarette from a dummy 'bomb.' The studio property department produced the 'bomb'—an innocent looking small black metal object with a length of fuse. The experts explained that it was quite harmless, and that there was no danger. But in actual fact it was extremely dangerous, being a high-explosive bomb which had been mixed with the dummy 'bombs' by mistake.

As soon as the camera was set up and the photographer had arranged a chair for Harold Lloyd, the bomb was lit. The fuse was long, and the small curl of smoke looked most effective as the comedian placed a cigarette in his mouth and raised the bomb to his lips.

'One moment,' said the photographer, moving round to alter his camera lens. Harold Lloyd lowered his hand from his face to adjust his spectacles, and at that moment the bomb exploded. It shattered the windows, blew a hole in the roof, and knocked the photographer unconscious. Harold Lloyd was thrown to the floor, his face covered by his hands, his mind an agony of pain and shock. Technicians ran to help him, and rushed him to hospital, where he was given an anaesthetic and put to bed with his face and eyes bandaged over. For three days he lay quite still, in mortal fear that he would be blind. On the third day the doctor warned him that his right eye might be affected, but when the bandages were removed he opened both eyes and to his great relief he saw the nurses in the room, and the trees in the hospital grounds. Gratefully, he thanked God for his good fortune.

Harold Lloyd started life in the little village of Burckard,

Nebraska, where his father was a salesman. There were only three hundred people in the community, and the school was so small that it could never have held all the youngsters who in later years claimed that they grew up with Harold Lloyd.

Quite early in life he fell in love with the theatre, for he discovered that in exchange for showing people to their seats and opening doors he not only earned pocket money, but also saw the shows for nothing. When he was twelve he graduated to the Orpheum theatre in Omaha, where he was head boy usher, and it was here that he met John Lane Connor, the leading man in the Burwood Travelling Stock company. The actor had asked him where he could find lodgings in the town, and young Harold had dashed home to his mother and persuaded her to let him have a room. Two weeks later, Connor was looking for a boy to play a small part in his show, and naturally thought of young Harold, who made his début for Connor as Little Abe, the lame boy in Thomas Hardy's *Tess of the D'Urbervilles*. He was almost unnoticed, but his father was delighted, and when a few months later he was awarded two thousand dollars in an accident damage suit, he invested it in a theatrical training for young Harold.

The boy went to San Diego Dramatic School, which Connor had founded some years before, and here he studied acting while attending the nearby high school. One day the Edison company came out to San Diego to take some moving pictures. The whole town was alive with excitement, and crowds flocked to see the company's two stars, Laura Sawyer and Ben Wilson. When it was rumoured among the youngsters at the dramatic school that local talent was to be recruited, Harold pestered Connor until he was persuaded to ask the film director to give the boy a chance, playing a crowd scene in the film. 'I got three bucks for the day's work,' he said afterwards. 'They dressed me up as a half-naked Indian, and as soon as I had painted myself brown, it started to rain.'

Harold thought nothing more about films, and went on tour with a travelling stock company, struggling for several years in tenth-rate parts in company with Charlie Ruggles, Florence Reed, and William Desmond. It took him many years to realize that he was not likely to make a good dramatic actor. 'You'll make a better comedian than an Irving,' said Ruggles one day, and left Harold Lloyd to think it over.

The next town in the tour was Balboa, where the Edison company owned a film studio, and Harold determined to go along and see if anyone remembered him. He had made one or two friends among the film technicians, and they might want some actors.

Unfortunately, no one remembered him. But as the company wanted some crowd players he was put on the pay-roll and received three dollars a week for three weeks, appearing in crowd scenes. It was long enough for him to realize that film making was a fascinating business. At the end of the third week he drew his salary, packed his bag, and bought a ticket for Los Angeles—and Hollywood.

Hollywood was young and growing, but it could still offer plenty of work and opportunity to the right people. Harold Lloyd, however, found that nobody wanted to give him a chance. It was almost impossible to get past the studio gates. But eventually he succeeded in 'crashing' the Universal studios by walking through the closely guarded gateway with a number of extras returning from lunch. Harold had smeared make-up on his face, and was at last inside the gates.

Once there, he was determined to stay. He managed to attach himself to J. Farrell Macdonald, a leading director of cowboy films. For several months young Harold earned from three to five dollars a day playing tough parts in cowboy films starring J. Warren Kerrigan, then one of the most popular of film actors. It was while appearing in *Samson* that Lloyd met another small-part actor who had also been engaged for cowboy pictures. His name was Hal Roach, and they spent many hours together discussing the film industry and their precarious way of living. For one part of the film, in which a number of actors had to appear as hairy Philistines, Harold Lloyd and Hal Roach were asked to help with the make-up. While Lloyd covered each man with liquid glue, Hal Roach came up behind with a large bunch of hair, ready to sprinkle it generously over the actors. It took two days to get the stuff off, but both Lloyd and Roach escaped being Philistines, and drew extra money for their make-up services.

One day, Hal Roach announced that he had been left a few thousand dollars—a small fortune to the two young men. He felt sure that he could produce a few short comedies which would make him some more money, so he decided to become a film producer on his own. It naturally followed that the first name on the pay-roll was that of Harold Lloyd—at three dollars a day.

A room was hired in the old Bradbury Mansion in Court Street Hill, Los Angeles, and here Roach established his office. His studio was the open back-yard behind the house, and here for several years he and Lloyd turned out a regular series of one-reel slapstick comedy films amidst a jumble of bickering and quarrelling.

'Think of a crazy get-up,' Hal Roach had said. 'If you can build up a character on Charlie Chaplin lines I'll pay you not three but five dollars!'

'So 'Willie Work' was born—Harold Lloyd's first comedy character, a nondescript fellow with a cat-like moustache, baggy pants, a broad-shouldered coat, and a tiny hat. As soon as Roach had completed the latest 'Willie Work' comedy they sent it off on the train to one of the film companies in New York, but the cans of film came back so fast that they jokingly declared that someone was turning them back halfway, at Kansas City.

Hal Roach was not satisfied with 'Willie Work,' and he kept on thinking of crazy situations to improve the films. One day he decided that Harold should get into bed with a skunk. Harold objected, but Roach assured him that it was as tame as a kitten. Directly Harold got into bed, the skunk bit him, much to the amusement of Hal Roach, who thought it was a funnier scene than any they had filmed for weeks.

'Willie Work' was not a great success, but although money was running out, Roach decided to spend everything he had on a final attempt. He sat up all night discussing ideas with Harold Lloyd and Jane Novak, who was to be the leading lady. Every comic situation which they had proved successful was now adapted for this final effort.

To the surprise of everyone, the film was a success. The American Pathé company not only liked it, but offered Roach a contract if he would sign up his three leading players, Harold

Lloyd, Roy Stewart, and Jane Novak, to make some more. But on the same day that the contract was drafted Harold discovered that Roy Stewart was being offered more money, and he went at once to Hal Roach and demanded a rise. Roach had to refuse, because he couldn't afford it. But Harold Lloyd felt pig-headed about the whole business, and feeling that he wasn't getting anywhere, went and joined Mack Sennett's Keystone company.

The Keystone gang at this time included Fatty Arbuckle, Chester Conklin, and Ford Sterling—three of the most important comedians on the screen. They thought Lloyd's 'Willie Work' films rather poor, and the new arrival soon realized that he was only a very unimportant comedian in the prosperous Keystone studio.

Feeling depressed one afternoon, Harold was summoned to the telephone, and there was Hal Roach on the line with an offer of fifty dollars a week, if only he would return. Harold threw off his Keystone cop's uniform and rushed straight back to his old partner. He knew that it had been a mistake ever to leave the Hal Roach company, where he was at least regarded as important, and where, if they were lucky, they might yet make a success of his films.

The American Pathé company had some new ideas. They still wanted a character based partly on Chaplin lines, but with a new name and some different clothes. With a coat cut from a woman's tailored costume, a pair of narrow trousers, a clipped vest, and a small collar and spindly moustache, 'Willie Work' became 'Lonesome Luke.' It was as simple as that.[1]

Lloyd's partner in many of these early films was a dark-eyed beauty of fifteen named Bebe Daniels. For nearly four years she acted with him, spending many of her evenings with him at local dancing contests, where they won several cups from such famous partners as Gloria Swanson and Wallace Beery, and Wallace Reid and his wife, Dorothy Davenport. The dance hall owners encouraged the stars to win, because it was a good advertisement.

When Bebe Daniels joined Harold Lloyd she looked even

[1] From January 1916 onwards, Lloyd made nearly a hundred 'Lonesome Luke' one-reel films for the Rolin company, distributed by Pathé, making from one to three pictures a week.

younger than her fifteen years. Dressed in one of her aunt's dresses, Bebe had walked over to the reconstructed house which served as a studio. With dignity, but secretly terrified that the big safety-pin at her waist would come undone, she asked if she could appear in the Harold Lloyd films.

'We wanted a blonde,' said the manager.

'I could wear a blonde wig,' suggested Bebe, persuading them to give her a chance, which they never regretted. When after four years Bebe Daniels left Hal Roach to join Cecil B. de Mille, blonde Mildred Davies was given a contract to play opposite Lloyd, although she was still attending high school. She made her début in 1919 in *From Hand to Mouth*, and later, during the making of *Why Worry?*, she accepted Harold's proposal of marriage. Two years after this she gave up acting, to devote her attention to her family. 'One funny person in the family is enough,' she said.

'Lonesome Luke' was quite a success, but Harold resented the criticism that he was like Chaplin. He wanted to be himself, to create laughs without absurd clothes. He therefore went to the Pathé offices in New York, and outlined his plan to become a screen country bumpkin—a rustic lost in the big wicked city. The humour, he suggested, would come from the incidents and the story, not from the absurd clothes.

The Pathé company were not impressed with the idea, for although they admitted that 'Lonesome Luke' was not exactly a sensation, he was making good money for them, and it would be taking a risk to start again with a new character. So Harold Lloyd returned to Los Angeles without convincing them. But to show Hal Roach what he meant, he took him out shopping, in search of a pair of spectacles. Horn rims were just coming into fashion with young men, and he thought they would suit his 'country cousin' character. All he wanted was a large pair of spectacles, to circle his eyes without covering his eyebrows. After visiting several shops he found the ideal pair in an optician's shop in Spring Street, Los Angeles.

The year was 1917, a memorable one for Harold Lloyd. Back in Roach's office he took a hammer and knocked out the lenses, to avoid the reflection of the studio lights. Then he looked at himself in the mirror, assumed an expression of country simplicity, and started out on his new career.

He never needed to look back, nor did he lose his original pair of spectacles, for when they were first broken he mended them with glue, and in later years they were carefully locked away. When he realized that they were beyond repair he ordered a new pair from New York, and received by return twenty pairs, together with his cheque. 'The advertisement you have given to tortoise-shell rims leaves us still very much in your debt,' explained the accompanying letter.[1]

From the one- and two-reeler stage, Lloyd soon developed into a feature comedian. *Never Weaken* and *A Sailor-Made Man* (4 reels) were followed a year later by his biggest success to date, a five-reel comedy entitled *Grandma's Boy*. When Chaplin saw this he wrote to Harold Lloyd, saying that the film was an inspiration to him to do his own very best work, to be contented with nothing else but the best for himself.

The Lloyd recipe for laughs was based on the old theme of the weak and innocent young man meeting difficulties in a big world full of sophisticated and clever people. By appealing to the young, he captured the imagination of the majority of cinema patrons, and provided wholesome family entertainment, with a generous sprinkling of thrills. His 'Willie Work' and 'Lonesome Luke'—known in Britain as 'Winkle'—had made way for a more polished performer with a strong screen personality. Soon the name of Harold Lloyd began to be a big attraction in the cinemas of the world.

Doctor Jack (in Britain, *Doctor's Orders*), *Safety Last*, *Why Worry?*, *College Days*, *The Kid Brother*, *For Heaven's Sake*, and *Speedy* followed in rapid succession, making Harold Lloyd into one of Hollywood's richest and most successful stars. There were nearly always adventurous escapades—hectic skyscraper thrills in which Harold was suspended high above the roaring traffic, with only a clock face or a torn window awning between himself and certain death.

[1] In 1920, Pathé announced that it had signed Lloyd to a contract worth more than 1,500,000 dollars in one first year, claiming he was 'the highest-priced actor in the world'.

These illusions, which he had first used some years before in a one-reeler called *High and Dizzy*, were filmed above a tunnel in Los Angeles. The sets were built on a small hill above the tunnel, so that an impression of great height could be obtained, with real traffic moving on the busy street below. Lloyd himself was seldom more than a few feet above earth, but the illusion was completely convincing.

When one of Harold Lloyd's first silent picture successes, *Bumping into Broadway* was shown in New York in 1919, many people thought a new comedian had arrived. 'They didn't realize the hell I had gone through,' he recalls. 'They didn't realize that I had been on the stage since I was twelve years old; that I had worked in repertory companies and had gone through one-reelers; that I had done 'Willie Work' and 'Lonesome Luke' before I arrived at my glass character. They thought I was just a new comedian, born overnight. The hell I was! I had gone through a tremendous schooling, and had hard knocks to find out what I should and shouldn't do.'

In the middle of making his last silent film, *Welcome Danger*, the talkie boom started. Always a clever showman, he decided at once that he must turn it into a sound film, and was thus able to offer the public one of the first all-talking feature comedies. There was great curiosity to hear the favourite stars talk, although it was noticeable that the dialogue in the comedies tended to hold up the visual active humour. The outstanding feature of this first talkie was a fantastic night spent in a Chinese bandit's cellar—with fireworks, and all the thrills of the old comic chase.

Feet First and *Movie Crazy* came next, reviving several of his own personal experiences in Hollywood. In one sequence he accidentally puts on a magician's coat, from which—as he is dancing at a crowded party—there emerge rabbits and white mice. The same idea was used later by Gracie Fields and Sydney Howard in *Shipyard Sally*.

The Cat's Paw, *The Milky Way*, and in 1938 *Professor Beware*, showed that Lloyd had lost none of his magic touch. Unlike Chaplin he was never a true clown, and aspired to be nothing more than a family comedian. Vulgarity never intruded in a

Harold Lloyd film, and although he made no claim to immortality, his simple recipe—laughs, thrills, an ingenuous romance, and then more laughs—made him a tremendous box-office attraction, and one of the wealthiest of the stars.

During the first years of the second world war he produced two films for R.K.O.-Radio, but he did not appear in them. Danny Kaye, however, appeared in an adaptation of the earlier Lloyd comedy *The Milky Way*. Then, in 1947, Harold Lloyd started work on a new starring film, *The Sin of Harold Diddlebock*, which continued the adventures of the young college boy of *The Freshman* (British title, *College Days*). The new film made use of part of the last reel of the earlier silent film. Diddlebock, having scored the winning try in a big football game, is offered a job in an advertising agency after he has completed his studies at college. Three years later Harold, still clutching his passing-out diploma, presents himself at the city office where the advertising tycoon who offered him the job sits in regal splendour. But the advertising man has forgotten all about his extravagant offer and barely recognizes Harold. However, he offers him a job in the book-keeping department, and here we see Harold some twenty years later, still a minor book-keeping clerk. After his twenty years' service he is presented with a gold watch, the 2,000 dollars he has saved, and a pink ticket telling him that he is fired. His subsequent adventures with a lion lead him once more out on to the fire-escape and the narrow ledge high above the busy traffic.

In Britain the picture was re-titled *Mad Wednesday*, and was not shown until 1951. Preston Sturges had written and directed it, and the large cast included Jimmy Conlin, Raymond Walburn, Franklyn Pangborn, Lionel Stander, and Edgar Kennedy. The revival of *Movie Crazy* in 1950 had confirmed the belief that the amazing adventures of Harold Lloyd were still as entertaining as ever, particularly by modern film standards. If *Mad Wednesday* was not quite as amusing as *Movie Crazy*, it was still one of the few genuinely comic pictures of its year. The many millions of admirers of yesterday's Harold Lloyd wondered what one of the older silent pictures, such as *Speedy*, or *The Kid Brother*, would look like today. The release of *Harold*

117

Lloyd's World of Comedy, made up from excerpts from some of these early triumphs, was a great success. According to the critic James Agee, Lloyd was the ideal film comedian. 'If plain laughter is any criterion,' he said, 'few people have equalled him, and nobody has ever beaten him.'

CHAPTER NINE

The Roaring Twenties

T H E E N D O F hostilities in 1918 had found America on top of the film world, and likely to stay there. Hollywood was now a vigorous and thriving industrial centre, concentrating on the mass production of the world's most entertaining motion pictures. Competition from Europe was negligible, but within the American market itself it was fierce, for every producer, distributor, and exhibitor was by now a fully qualified show-man, influencing enormous numbers of people. The markets of the world were still wide open, and in tens of thousands of towns and villages in America, Europe, Asia, and Africa, cinemas were being built. People who had never read a serious book, or who were unable to read, joined the queues of white, black, brown, and yellow folk, waiting for the local picture house to open. It was a tremendous responsibility, this making of films. But Hollywood as a whole did not seek to enlighten, a task which was felt to belong to the schools, the churches, and the writers. Hollywood felt that its job was to entertain, and this it did remarkably well.

During the first year of the United Artists Corporation, Douglas Fairbanks made two pictures, D. W. Griffith made two, Mary Pickford made one, but Chaplin made nothing. When his picture *The Kid* was ready for showing it compared very favourably at the box-office with Fairbanks' semi-dramatic *The Mark of Zorro* and *The Three Musketeers*. From now onwards Chaplin concentrated only on feature productions, which appeared infrequently, but with great commercial success.

In retrospect, the period 1920–1929 appears to have been the golden age of Hollywood. For the American comedians, whose ideas had matured since the war, it was especially a vintage period. Chaplin, Harold Lloyd, frozen-faced Buster Keaton, Eddie Cantor, Monty Banks, and dozens of other comics pro-vided—with expert assistance—most of the laughs. The drama was left to such great names as Norma Talmadge, Pauline

Frederick, Mae Marsh, Mary Pickford, Lon Chaney, Lillian Gish, Richard Barthelmess, Dustin and William Farnum, Blanche Sweet, Nazimova, John Barrymore, Thomas Meighan, Alice Terry, Valentino, and Gloria Swanson. These were the big dramatic stars of the American films, with Milton Sills, Clive Brook, Ronald Colman, Garbo, and Clara Bow rising to become the greatest attractions of the international screen. By the middle twenties Ramon Novarro, Gary Cooper, Emil Jannings, and John Gilbert were heading the popularity lists. The fact that the serious players heavily outnumbered the comedians placed the latter at an advantage, for only one out of every forty feature films was a comedy, and for this reason it was doubly welcome. It was always essential to provide a balanced programme, and to do this every astute cinema proprietor needed to hire a short comedy as a 'fill up'. If his bill lasted for only three days of each week, as it usually did, then two new comedy pictures had to be booked each week, with the inevitable topical newsreel and cartoon to add weight to the programme.

Those concerned with the making of short films found the demand encouraging. Mack Sennett and his rivals could claim that the middle twenties were their most prosperous years. There were as yet no 'double feature' programmes to crowd two-reelers off the screen. People might queue up without a murmur to see Gloria Swanson or Garbo, but they would soon complain if there wasn't a 'comic' in the programme.

Sennett's *Married Life*, one of the many pictures which he made in the twenties, was a supporting film based on a sure formula. Ben Turpin and Ford Sterling were the stars—players whose names outside a picture house would attract almost as many patrons as Valentino, or Clara Bow. In this picture Ben and Ford were seen walking down the corridor of a hospital, congratulating themselves on having gained their freedom. They have just been discharged from the alcoholic ward. Unknown to them, another patient is being given gas in a nearby ward, but when the doctor is suddenly called away, the patient starts to swell, and is soon floating high into the air, round the room, and finally out of the door into the passage. Here the floating patient is seen by Ben and Ford, who realize with horror that they are not properly cured, and must return at once to the alcoholic ward for further treatment.

But even Sennett could not produce all the comedies which were demanded by the exhibitors. Roscoe 'Fatty' Arbuckle was at the height of his form in two-reelers at the beginning of the era, Larry Semon was one of the most popular acrobatic clowns, and Eddie Lyons and Lee Moran of Universal fame were teamed in many vigorous and amusing two-reelers, such as *The Model Husbands*, *Poker, Police, and Promises*, and *Shot Suited*. Later these two made several feature films.

In Britain, where few comedians were making short pictures, Walter Forde was during the twenties one of the most popular of English screen comics. With a Harrow-type straw hat and horn-rimmed glasses, he made dozens of comedies. His career had started when he was only two months old, being thrown once nightly through a window during the production of a stage drama called *When Lights are Low*. His father trained him in tumbling, eccentric dancing, singing, the piano (at which he became an expert), and juggling. After working in an insurance office he went on the stage, and in 1921 he signed a contract to appear in six short pictures for an English company, Thespian Films. In 1922 he played a dual role in *Walter's Trying Frolics* (Zodiac Films), appearing as Lord Gadabout, a monocled man about town, and also as a motor salesman. In *Walter Makes a Movie*, his fifth for Zodiac, he was seen planning and producing a comedy picture. Altogether he made some fifty-one one- and two-reelers, and later became a film editor, being responsible for the editing of several major productions, including *The Volga Boatmen*, and *The King of Kings*. In England his direction some ten years later of *Lord Richard in the Pantry*, *Bed and Breakfast*, *Third Time Lucky*, and *Jack's the Boy* proved highly successful. The British silent feature films in which he appeared in the late twenties included *Wait and See*, *What Next?*, *Would You Believe It?*, and *You'd Be Surprised*. They were among the best English comedy subjects of the twenties, although some considered that Forde was influenced partly by Harold Lloyd. *Would You Believe It?* first ran for twenty-two consecutive weeks at the Tivoli cinema, London—a record run for a British film during the difficult mid-twenties, when English films were rare, and often of doubtful entertainment value.

During the making of *Wait and See* at the Nettlefold Studios, Walton, Walter Forde revealed that the straw hat which he was wearing was the original one which had appeared in all his old short comedies. It had accompanied him to America, and, although yellow with age, it would not be replaced while he appeared on the screen. And it never was.

Almost every family cinema in America and Europe was now showing Hal Roach's short *Our Gang comedies*. The idea was born when Roach decided to feature a little negro boy in *Sunshine Sammy comedies*. The boy had first appeared for Roach in some of the Harold Lloyd comedies, and it was decided to give him juvenile support and some animals in this new series. The *Sunshine Sammy comedies* soon became the *Our Gang comedies*. Hal Roach called them his 'rascals', but the kids themselves called the bunch 'the Gang', and the name stuck. The first players included Mickey Daniels, Joe Cobb, Jack Davis, Jackie Condon, Mary Kornman, and Little Farina (Allan Hoskins). Joe Cobb was 'Fatty', and little Mary Kornman was introduced to Roach by her father, who was Harold Lloyd's still-cameraman. Mickey Daniels was so popular that he was given a special part by Lloyd in *Doctor Jack* (*Doctor's Orders*) and *Safety Last*, and Jack Davis was the small brother of Mildred Davis. These were the first permanent members of the *Our Gang comedies*, but the personnel altered many times during the next fifteen years. The antics of the children delighted or infuriated audiences all over the world.

In 1921 few comedians were more popular than Italian Monty Banks, who had emigrated to America when he was seventeen, leaving his native name of Bianchi behind him. At first he appeared with Arbuckle, and then he starred in many two-reelers and a number of feature films, including *Fresh Air*, *Keep Smiling*, *A Concrete Mix-Up*, *Atta Boy*, *Horse Shoes*, *Flying Luck*, and *Play Safe*. In 1928 he arrived in Britain to direct and star in *Adam's Apple* and several other films. When he was asked by Basil Dean to direct *Queen of Hearts* he met Gracie Fields, and married her. Returning to America he appeared infrequently in supporting roles, as in *A Bell for Adano*, but always with distinction.

In *Fresh Air*, Monty Banks was seen as a townsman out in the country for exercise and sport. As a fisherman he was no success, for the fish chased him away from the river; and when he tried shooting rabbits they laughed at him. Finally, when a bear appeared, he nearly had a fit. This film was shown with Chaplin's *The Kid* at a party given by King George the Fifth and Queen Mary. In London the picture was later advertised as 'the comedy at which two Kings and three Queens and 500 guests laughed so heartily at Sandringham'.

Monty Banks proved that making comedies could be a strenuous business. For one film he was attached by a rope to a car, and pulled down the face of a cliff, ending up in hospital. On another occasion he was lying in bed behind the upper storey of a dummy house for a film sequence, when a fire-engine backed by accident into the lower part, throwing him 20 feet down, on to the engine. It was, he said, all in the day's work for a knockabout comedian.

*

Influenced by what they saw on the screen, millions of men and women were now buying clothes and goods which they saw in their favourite American pictures. Rudolph Valentino had but to wear long 'sideboards' to have large sections of the male youth of America and Europe apeing him. The enormous cinema public was now reading all about the world's great sweethearts, their private lives, their loves, scandals, clothes, swimming pools, and automobiles. Nothing was sacred in the harsh spotlight of film fame. Hollywood was constantly in the news, the activities of its leading personalities being watched with interest by millons. 'Conceit is rampant among your film makers, and good sense is almost non-existent,' George Bernard Shaw told Hollywood in 1925. 'That is where Mr Chaplin scores; but Mr Harold Lloyd seems so far to be the only rival intelligent enough to follow his example.'

*

Meanwhile, Britain had fallen sadly behind America in the comedy race. But in April 1920 a minor move in the right direc-

tion was made with the formation of Minerva Films, whose
original directors, R. F. Power, C. Aubrey Smith, A. A. Milne,
Nigel Playfair, and Leslie Howard, were later joined by Lionel
Philips and director Adrian Brunel. Several short comedies by
A. A. Milne were filmed, including *The Bump*, *Bookworms*, *£5
Reward*, and *Twice Two*. The players included C. Aubrey Smith,
later to become the Grand Old Man of Hollywood, the greatly
loved Leslie Howard, Barbara Hoffe, Faith Celli, Ivan Samson,
Jeff Barlow, Pauline Johnson, Lewis Ransom, and Mrs Hayden
Coffin. The policy of the distinguished company was (as if pro-
testing against slapstick comedy) to make films which were
'funny without being vulgar'. A two-reel comedy, they claimed,
need not be a rude farce, and could still be amusing. There was
little wrong with Minerva Films, except that they had very
little money, and therefore made few pictures. Perhaps the films
were inclined to be slow, but they did not receive the backing
they deserved, for at this time few people were interested in
British pictures. A gallant attempt therefore faded out.

In 1920 came Cecil Hepworth's *Alf's Button*, adapted from
the successful play by W. A. Darlington. Because of its topical
nature and Leslie Henson's popularity it was a great triumph
for Hepworth. Supporting Henson were Alma Taylor, Gwynne
Herbert, Eileen Dennes, Jean Cadell, James Carew, Gerald Ames,
and John MacAndrews. It was one of Hepworth's biggest financial successes, and it came at the end of his career as a producer.
When he was no longer at Walton, a relatively poor man ignored
by the industry, the film was still being shown to enthusiastic
audiences.

Giving his reasons why *Alf's Button* was one of the best
pictures he had shown, Mr T. Wright of the Scala theatre,
Nottingham, said (in the *Bioscope* trade paper for March 10,
1921) that apart from the box-office results, it was a magnificent British picture, full of comedy, with witty and clever
sub-titles which were devoid of slang—'which spoils so many
American films from a British point of view'. This was of course
only a personal opinion.

Although Hepworth's stars were among the most popular,
they were not present at the Leeds Kinema Ball in 1920, when
the British screen was represented by Malvina Longfellow.

James Knight, Marjorie Villis, Stewart Rome, and Gregory Scott. At this dance a signed portrait of Malvina Longfellow was sold for £500 in aid of charity, and later the star auctioned a prize for a further £100. The most popular English male stars of the early twenties were Ivor Novello, Henry Edwards and Stewart Rome. Of these, only Henry Edwards occasionally played light roles, as in *The Lunatic at Large* (Hepworth 1921) in which he was seen as the lunatic, escaping over the wall of a mental home by means of a ladder. Having reached the top he pulls the ladder up after him, and descends to freedom on the other side. He now runs round to an open back gate, through which he carries the ladder to replace it where he had originally found it, in the grounds.

Three hundred and seventy-nine cinemas in Britain reserved playing dates for this film directly it had been shown to the film trade, although no contracts had yet been signed. Henry Edwards had no equal among the British players of this period. But there were few of them.

*

'Is Chaplin coming back?' asked the *Kinematograph Weekly* of January 6, 1921. 'Charlie Chaplin has been the subject of more rumours during 1920 than any other figure in the industry. It has been variously declared that he has lost his powers, that he has become so obsessed with Socialist theories as to be indifferent to money making, and that he has been superseded by Harold Lloyd, Larry Semon, and half-a-dozen other comedians.'

To silence the critics came *The Kid* and a revival of *Shoulder Arms*. Meanwhile his rivals were concentrating on two-reelers, to meet the increasing demand for laughter. Larry Semon appeared for Vitagraph in *The Sportsman*, and Florence Turner made a series of one- and two-reel burlesques, *Girls Will be Boys*, *Matrimony*, *Old Dials for New*, and *Stenographers First*. Will Rogers was hailed by the London *Daily Mail* as 'the finest comedian in the world' for his work in Goldwyn's *Almost a Husband* and *Water, Water, Everywhere!*, and Mack Sennett's lovelies had a very modest rival in Britain—the Tom Aitken Bathing Beauties. There was also an English series of *Pip and*

Squeak cartoons, and an Elstree-made feature entitled *The Adventures of Mr Pickwick*, with Bransby Williams and Mary Brough. Harry Myers appeared in one of the year's most successful American comedies, *A Yankee at the Court of King Arthur*, but Fatty Arbuckle's *The Life of the Party* did not reach Britain. The scandal had already ended his career.

British pictures were now relatively few and far between. Apart from some comedies featuring George Robey, which were infrequent, the Stoll studios at Cricklewood were concentrating on dramas, their *Sherlock Holmes series* directed by Maurice Elvey with Eille Norwood being popular in America. Stewart Rome had left Hepworth after returning from the war, and had joined Broadwest, following an unusual lawsuit in which Hepworth sought to restrain the actor from using the film name which he had given him. Rome, whose real name was Ryott, won the case, and in the following year starred in five dramas for Broadwest. For an actor of his looks and ability the prospects were good. If British studios were making anything, they preferred to make dramas or melodramas.

In the early twenties there were twenty-seven major studios in Britain, although many were small and made few pictures:

1. Alliance Film Corporation, St Margarets, Twickenham.
   One studio 142 ft. × 91 ft.
2. Astra Films, Hoe Street, Walthamstow.
   One studio 212 ft. × 86 ft.
   Producer: Kenelm Foss
3. Barkers Studio, Ealing Green, W.5.
   Three studios.
4. British Actors' Film Co., Melbourne Road, Bushey.
   Two studios, 100 ft. × 60 ft., 60 ft. × 40 ft.
5. British and Colonial, Hoe Street, Walthamstow.
   One studio 212 ft. × 86 ft.
6. British Art Films, Princes Studio, Kew Bridge.
   One studio 120 ft. × 50 ft.
7. British Famous Films, High Road, Whetstone, N.20.
   One studio 2,480 sq. ft.
8. Broadwest Film Co., Wood Street, Walthamstow.
   180 ft. × 70 ft.
9. Broadwest Windsor studio, Bromley Road, Catford.
   120 ft. × 60 ft.
10. Dallas Cairns Film Co., Watcomb Hall, Torquay.
    One studio 120 ft. × 60 ft.

11. I. B. Davidson studio, 588 Lea Bridge Road, Leyton, E.10.
    Producer: A. E. Coleby.
12. Famous Players-Lasky British Studios, Poole Street, Islington.
    16,000 sq. ft.
13. Gaumont Studio, 59 Lime Grove, Shepherds Bush, W.12.
    One studio 102 ft. × 43 ft.
14. Harma-Clarendon Studio, 16 Limes Road, Croydon.
    Two studios, 90 ft. × 40 ft., 80 ft. × 30 ft.
15. Ideal Films, Boreham Wood, Elstree.
    One studio 5,200 sq. ft.
16. Progress Film Co., Bungalow Town, Shoreham-by-Sea.
    50 ft. × 50 ft. under glass. One open air stage.
17. Stoll Studios, Temple Road, Cricklewood.
18. Stoll Studios, Regent Studios, Surbiton.
19. Hepworth Picture Plays, Hurst Grove, Walton-on-Thames.
    Two studios.
20. Beaconsfield Studios, Candlemass Lane, Beaconsfield.
    One studio.
21. Master Films, Weir House, Broom Road, Teddington.
    One studio.
22. Torquay and Paignton Photoplays, Public Hall, Paignton, South
    Devon.
    One studio.
23. British and Oriental Films, Thornton House, Thornton Road,
    Clapham Park, S.W.12.
24. Welsh-Pearson Studios, 41/45 Craven Park, Willesden, N.W.
25. Pavilion Studios, Portsmouth Road, Esher.
    One studio.
26. Samuelson Film Company, Worton Hall, Isleworth.
    One studio.
27. New Agency Film Co., 115a Ebury Street, S.W.1.
    One studio.

In 1921 Syd Chaplin, whose career had been partly over-
shadowed by his more successful half-brother, had temporarily
deserted the screen, but this year saw the re-issue of what many
regarded as his best picture, a Keystone comedy made in 1916,
entitled *The Submarine Pirate*. This was described as 'three reels
of crazy absurdity', and it was calculated to keep audiences
rocking in their seats. It was the type of picture which English
studios could never attempt, for in Britain the producers seemed
unwilling to explore the art of absurd comedy, or to find the
gag-men who could create it. Syd Chaplin was seen as a waiter
who secretly preferred to be a juggler. Overhearing a plot to

capture a bullion ship with the aid of a submarine, Syd buys an admiral's second-hand uniform, and takes over command of the submarine. He succeeds in sinking the bullion ship with a torpedo, but a gunboat arrives, and sinks him. The film ended with a scene showing Syd swimming for dear life under water, swallowing a fish, and finally meeting a shark, which bites off his head.

During the making of this film the story called for Syd Chaplin to be chased by the Keystone cops along the edge of several roofs, twelve storeys from ground level, on to an iron girder suspended between two tall buildings, from where the comedian had to slide down a rope on to a passing car. There was no faking, for Mack Sennett required his stars to risk their lives, if necessary. But it cost him ninety dollars to insure Chaplin and each of the Keystone cops for the two minutes during which the camera was turning.

One Glorious Day (1922) had been intended as a starring vehicle for Arbuckle, but when he left the screen the part was given to Will Rogers. It was the tale of a spirit which comes to earth to inhabit the body of a professor. A commercial failure, the film amusingly and satirically debunked fake spiritualism and politics.

In August 1923 came Harold Lloyd's *Doctor Jack* (*Doctor's Orders*), advertised as 'one solid hour of unparalleled mirth'. Lloyd played a country doctor who believes that putting a little sunshine into his patients does them more good than tonic. His unorthodox prescriptions include the latest jazz music for a saxophone player suffering from gout, visits from a neglectful son to a lonely old mother, and sudden excitement for a pampered heiress. His patients have their temperatures taken with sticks of barley sugar, the pulse is timed with a bunch of keys, and a small boy is cured of an illness by being told that the school has been burned down. The patients all get better, and everyone in the village loves the young doctor. 'With the exception of Charlie Chaplin, this film is unbeatable,' said the *Kinematograph Weekly*.

There were plenty of supporting comedies. Max Fleischer's *Out of the Inkwell cartoons*, in which a pen drew lightning caricatures, took from 2,500 to 3,000 little drawings for each brief film, and set audiences asking 'How is it done?'. George Robey in *The Prehistoric Man* (Stolls) showed the 'Prime Minister of Mirth' in a stone-age world of monsters and bearskins, and raised reasonably hearty guffaws of laughter. Unfortunately, Robey did not receive much encouragement in British studios, who were hardly in a position to spend money on elaborate comedies, and seemed loath to make two-reelers. With the armistice, British studios found themselves quite unable to contest the rivalry of Hollywood, and in 1922 only 1½ per cent of the British pictures offered to America were eventually shown in the United States. No less than 426 films were put up for sale, but only six were accepted. And of these not one was a comedy.

The comics who might have appeared in British films had either gone to America, or were simply not offered an opportunity. The English music-hall, traditionally the home of British comedy, had for long been rich in pantomime, but few in British studios thought it worth while to seek new comedians from the halls—or anywhere else. The days of 'Pimple' were over, and another clever clown, Lupino Lane, who had done well in the few British films offered him, had been given so little encouragement that he soon went to America.

Britain's film exports to the United States in 1922 included *This Freedom* (Ideal), *Strangling Threads* (Hepworth), and *The Sign of Four* (Stolls). A half-million-dollar company was formed in New York to handle the Hepworth product. Yet, generally speaking, British films did not move with the times, perhaps because they lacked the money which backed the Hollywood product. British film distributors seldom helped to finance English studios. The films therefore usually lacked the showmanship and vigour of their American rivals. A glance at some of the film titles of the time shows how solid the English fare could be:

The Monkey's Paw, Through Fire and Water, In the Blood, Becket, Comin' Thro' the Rye, The Prodigal Son, Guy Fawkes, Fires of Fate, Doctor Fu Manchu, Heartstrings, Bonnie Prince Charlie.

The last film was a Gaumont picture, starring Gladys Cooper and Ivor Novello. Hugh Miller, who was also in the cast, recalled later that amongst the players it was jokingly called *Bonnie Prince Cardboard*.

The stars of these pictures—Stewart Rome, Betty Balfour, Clive Brook, Victor McLaglen, Matheson Lang, Sir Frank Benson, and Alma Taylor, were all accomplished players. Yet in the world market their films could not compete with such subjects as *Robin Hood*, *The Covered Wagon*, *Scaramouche*, *Down to the Sea in Ships*, *If Winter Comes*, and *Tol'able David*. The few English comedies—George Robey in *The Rest Cure* and some shorts based on the W. W. Jacobs stories—seemed dismally inadequate beside Harold Lloyd's *Safety Last*, Larry Semon's *The Barnyard*, *Home Sweet Home*, and *That's Him*, to name only four of the hundreds of comic pictures from Hollywood.

The box-office champion, however, was not a human, but a cat. Every errand boy in America and Europe was now whistling or singing:

> Felix kept on walking—
> Kept on walking still,
> With his hands behind him
> You will always find him . . .

On the screen Pat Sullivan's comic *Felix the Cat cartoons* had few serious rivals. The G. B. Samuelson company at Worton Hall, Isleworth, produced a brief series of *Tom Webster cartoons*, featuring the popular cartoonist's drawing of Tishy the horse, Jimmy Wilde, Inman, and other sporting characters, but the animation was far from perfect. Felix walked alone, along a path paved with dollars.

In 1923 came Lupino Lane in *A Friendly Husband*, one of the several amusing films which he made in America for Fox Films. In Britain Henry Edwards married his screen partner, beautiful Chrissie White. They were the most popular team in British pictures, and could be seen this year with Mary Brough and Annie Esmond in a delightful light comedy called *Tit for Tat*. Henry Edwards, who had played opposite Ethel Barrymore on the New York stage, and was to return to Broadway during the second world war, had now established a reputation for what he called 'simple love stories, with humour and a few tears'. This recipe, which was to be used in later years by Herbert Wilcox and Anna Neagle, proved highly successful. 'Tedwards,' as he was affectionately called by the industry, continued to appear in and to direct films until the thirties, until in the forties he was playing heavier supporting character roles with equal distinction.

Although 1923 was not rich in British comedies there were some compensations. George Dewhurst, who had been a member of Hepworth's stock company, produced for Gaumont the brightest of his five versions of *A Sister to Assist 'Er*, with Mary Brough, Pollie Emery, John MacAndrews, and Mrs Fred Emney. Syd Walker, who had worked with Karno when Chaplin joined the company as a beginner, now started work in *Old Bill Through the Ages*, based on Captain Bruce Bairnsfather's cartoon creation 'Old Bill'. He was seen in a variety of disguises, in Georgian days, with Shakespeare, signing Magna Carta, as William the Conqueror, in the role of an Elizabethan courtier, and as 'Old Bill' the soldier in the trenches in the 1914 war. Betty Balfour added a touch of glamour to *Life, Love, and Laughter* and *Squibs' Honeymoon*, one of the *Squibs series* which British audiences found pleasantly amusing.

But the year—as were all these years—was notable for American triumphs. Chaplin had nothing new, but *A Dog's Life* was revived. Harold Lloyd had stolen much of the applause with his *Why Worry?* and *Safety Last*. Now came Charles Ray in *Alias Julius Caesar*. Ray had made his name in country comedies, and, like Harold Lloyd, he had been typed as a simple, slightly gawky, easily embarrassed youth. He was to be seen standing around looking bashful, shifting uneasily from one foot to the other. When he became tired of these roles he left the Ince studios, with whom he had worked since 1912, and invested a large personal fortune in an ambitious and costly production called *The Courtship of Miles Standish* (1923). Unfortunately the picture was a failure, and Charles Ray was unable to reclaim the unique position which he had held as a country-boy comedian, although he made a return to comedy in *Percy* (1925) under the direction of Roy William Neill.

In *Polly of the Follies*, Constance Talmadge, to whom Griffith had given her first great chance in *Intolerance*, was seen at her best in one of the silent back-stage comedies. The story, by Anita Loos, showed her as a stage-struck country girl who gets her chance with the famous Ziegfeld Follies, but upsets the show so much that the curtain descends suddenly on her brief and inglorious career.

That America possessed the pick of the leading players can be seen from this list of only a few of the many actors and actresses who were working in leading American studios during the particular month of August 1923:

Pickford Fairbanks Studios, Hollywood
    Mary Pickford
    Douglas Fairbanks
    Evelyn Brent

Goldwyn Studios, Culver City, California
    James Kirkwood
    Claire Windsor
    Mae Busch
    Conrad Nagel
    William Haines
    Eleanor Boardman
    Eric von Stroheim
    Kathleen Key
    Aileen Pringle

Inspiration Pictures, New York City
    Richard Barthelmess
    Dorothy Mackaill
    Lillian Gish
    Dorothy Gish

Vitagraph Studios, Talmadge Avenue, Hollywood
    Alice Calhoun
    Cullen Landis
    Percy Marmont
    Larry Semon

Paramount Studios
    Dorothy Dalton
    Glenn Hunter
    James Rennie
    Elsie Ferguson
    Alice Brady
    Nita Naldi

Lasky Studios, Vine Street, Hollywood
>Pola Negri
>Gloria Swanson
>Bebe Daniels
>William Boyd
>Antonio Moreno
>Lois Wilson
>Jack Holt
>Agnes Ayres
>Lila Lee
>Richard Dix
>Charles De Roche
>Lewis Stone

Mayer Studios, 3800 Mission Road, Los Angeles
>Earle Williams
>René Adorée
>Pat O'Malley
>Stuart Holmes
>Doris Pawn
>Gaston Glass

United Studios, Hollywood
>Norma Talmadge
>Jack Mulhall
>Conway Tearle
>Wallace Beery
>Constance Talmadge
>John Harron
>Betty Francisco

Mack Sennett Studios, Edendale, California
>Mabel Normand
>Ben Turpin
>Kathryn McGuire
>Mildred June
>Billy Bevan

Metro Studios, Hollywood
>Alice Terry
>Ramon Novarro
>Barbara La Marr
>Clara Kimball Young
>Rod La Rocque
>Malcolm MacGregor

Universal City, California
> Hoot Gibson
> Gladys Walton
> Norman Kerry
> Reginald Denny
> Virginia Valli
> Lon Chaney
> Mary Philbin

Griffith Studios, Mamaroneck, New York
> Ivor Novello
> Mae Marsh
> Carol Dempster

Fox Studios, Western Avenue, Hollywood
> Tom Mix
> Shirley Mason
> Buck Jones
> John Gilbert
> Ruth Dwyer

Distinctive Productions, New York
> Alice Joyce
> George Arliss
> Edith Roberts
> Alfred Lunt

Hal Roach Studios, Culver City
> Harold Lloyd
> Ruth Roland
> Jobyna Ralston
> Marie Mosquini
> Snub Pollard
> Paul Parrott

Of course, this by no means exhausts the list of studios, or the players who were to be found inside them during August 1923. It merely shows where some people were working.

*

Foremost among the leading comedy personalities of the twenties was Johnny Hines, who had made his screen début in 1915, and had risen to popularity in the *Torchy series* of two-reelers, light comedy subjects about the average American boy next door. Soon afterwards he appeared very successfully for First National in feature comedies, such as *Chinatown Charlie*. Co-starring with Mary Astor in the middle twenties at First National was Ben Lyon, who alternated between light comedy and straight leading man roles.

At the Goldwyn studio at Culver City lovely Helene Chadwick was co-starring during 1920, 1921, and 1922 with handsome Richard Dix, a light comedian before he went to Paramount to play similar roles, and finally to appear in westerns and character roles.

Another popular player of the early twenties was Douglas MacLean, who had been civil engineer, bank clerk, reporter, and salesman, before appearing in small parts, then in leading roles in cowboy pictures. His chance came when he played opposite Mary Pickford in *Captain Kidd Junior*, but his success in this led him to believe that he had a future as a light comedian. Finding that no one agreed with him, he financed his own picture, *Going Up*. The phenomenal success of this revealed that he was one of the best light comedians on the screen. His many pictures included *Soft Cushions*, *Seven Keys to Baldpate*, *Introduce Me!*, *That's My Baby*, *Ladies First*, and *Let it Rain*. His films were polite farces, and his leading lady was Sue Carol, later Mrs Alan Ladd.

Wallace Reid, who died from drugs in the early twenties, was one of the greatest of the light comedy stars, although he was also a fine straight actor. His pictures included *Excuse My Dust* and *The Roaring Road*, and among his most popular leading ladies were Bebe Daniels, Wanda Hawley, Lois Wilson, and Lila Lee.

The 'smart Allick' of comedies of college life, William Haines, owed his screen career entirely to chance. He was stopped in the street one day by a Goldwyn talent scout, and was entered for a 'new faces' screen contest, which he won. He went on a trip to Hollywood with Eleanor Boardman, and made his début in *Three Wise Fools* in 1923. Between 1925 and 1931 he was star of many Metro-Goldwyn-Mayer comedies, and Joan Crawford appeared several times with him. He suited the medium of talking pictures as easily as he had mastered silent films, and in the thirties appeared with success in *The Girl Said No* (1930),

Way Out West, Are You Listening (M.G.M.), *Let's Go, Fast Life,* and *Young and Beautiful* (1934).

Constance Talmadge, who had left Vitagraph to join Griffith at Triangle in 1916, and had migrated by way of *Intolerance* to Selznick Pictures, for whom she had appeared in dozens of comedies—*A Pair of Silk Stockings, Good Night Paul, Up the River with Sadie*—to name only a few, had in the twenties joined First National, with whom she stayed until the coming of sound films. But she never made a talkie, retiring with great wealth while she was still young and beautiful. Her sister Norma Talmadge married Joseph Schenck, and her other sister Natalie married Buster Keaton, making Keaton and his producer brothers-in-law. But Keaton did not mention his wife by name in his autobiography, *My Wonderful World of Slapstick*.

Dorothy Gish was another great name not usually associated with comedy. She had scored a triumph in Griffith's *Hearts of the World* (1918), wearing a black wig. Now, supervised by the watchful eye of Griffith, and still with the same wig over her fair hair, she made several comedies for New Art Productions, distributed by Paramount (1918–21). The first was *Battling Jane*, a domestic comedy with a war background. Then she returned to Griffith drama with her sister Lillian, appeared in *Orphans of the Storm* (1922), and some years later arrived in Britain to appear with Nelson Keys in *Tip Toes*.

Another success in comedy roles was Laura La Plante, who had started her career in a series of *Bringing Up Father comedies* made by Al Christie for Universal (1920), based on the popular comic strip by George McManus. She played the fluffy daughter of Jiggs. Then she went into Christie comedies for Educational Pictures, with smiling Bobby Vernon, before joining Carl Laemmle at Universal City to appear as leading woman in cowboy films with Hoot Gibson. When Gladys Walton left the screen Laura La Plante took her place in feature comedies with Reginald Denny—*Sporting Youth, Dangerous Innocence,* and *The Teaser*—and after starring in *The Cat and the Canary, Love Thrill, Thanks for the Buggy Ride,* and *Show Boat,* made some twelve further films in Hollywood and joined the First National–Warner Brothers studios at Teddington, England, where she appeared in several pictures during the thirties.

Also making pictures at Teddington during the thirties was Bebe Daniels, who had been Harold Lloyd's leading lady when still in her early 'teens. She had starred in many pictures for Paramount during the twenties, including *Brewster's Millions, She's a Sheik, Take Me Home*, and later made *Rio Rita, Love Comes Along, Reaching for the Moon, Forty-Second Street*, and some twenty more subjects before becoming one of Britain's most popular radio comediennes.

Then there was blonde Marion Davies, who deserted costume drama for frolicsome farce during the twenties, and was for ten years one of the greatest attractions of the screen—and Colleen Moore, the prototype of the 'flapper' of the roaring twenties, to be seen in *Sally, Irene, Why Be Good?, Orchids and Ermine, Naughty But Nice*, and *Footlights and Fools*.[1]

This leads us inevitably to Clara Bow—the 'It' girl, whose red hair and big brown eyes had won her a beauty contest while she was still at school. When Elinor Glyn called her the 'It' girl, her fortune was assured. Every little girl in the twenties—or nearly every little girl—wanted to have 'It', and Clara Bow demonstrated her sex appeal to good effect in *Kid Boots, It, Hula, Red Hair, The Fleet's In*, and *The Wild Party*, making her talkie début in *Dangerous Curves*, followed by *The Saturday Night Kid, Paramount on Parade*, and *True to the Navy*, although the silent days were her best.

Then there were Marie Prevost and Phyllis Haver, former bathing beauties who shone equally well in drama or frothy comedies. Marie Prevost followed in the footsteps of Bebe Daniels and Gloria Swanson, and was first featured with Charles Ray. Phyllis Haver was a cinema pianist before she went on the screen, to appear in *Up in Mabel's Room, Fig Leaves, Hard Boiled*, and *The Nervous Wreck*—gay titles, but surprisingly innocent comedies.

Finally, there was another 'It' girl—blonde Alice White, the 'baby vamp' heroine who had started her career as a typist in a film publicity office, but inevitably found herself on the

---

[1] William Randolph Hearst, the newspaper magnate, formed Metropolitan Pictures, distributed by M.G.M., to star his friend, Miss Davies, in pictures selected by her. The company is said to have lost several million dollars.

screen, displaying her charms in *Gentlemen Prefer Blondes*, *Broadway Babies*, *Hot Stuff*, *The Girl from Woolworths*, *Playing Around*, *A Showgirl in Hollywood*, *Man Crazy*, and *Sweethearts on Parade*.

Gloria Swanson, Constance Talmadge, Lillian Gish, Dorothy Gish, Laura La Plante, Bebe Daniels, Marion Davies, Clara Bow, Marie Prevost, Mae Murray, Phyllis Haver, and Alice White . . . what memories these names conjure up, to those who can look back to the golden age of the roaring twenties. They could give a lesson in feminine glamour to many a film star of and fifties and sixties.

Then there was Bessie Love, who had made her screen début with Triangle and remained at Culver City when Triangle was merged with Goldwyn, when she quit the screen for the stage. It was not until the coming of talkies that she returned, invited by Bryan Foy to make some short films for Vitaphone. Her act was a stage act, but when Metro-Goldwyn-Mayer saw her they at once offered her a contract to appear in *Broadway Melody*, and later this charming little lady appeared in *The Hollywood Revue*, *The Girl in the Show*, *Chasing Rainbows*, and *Good News*, all for M.G.M.

These were only a few of the great stars of the screen who were making comedy films during the twenties. Another was Douglas Fairbanks, who, for all his early acrobatics in feature films, was in fact a comedian first, part cowboy second, and a costume player third, although he will probably be best remembered for his ambitious historical films, *The Thief of Bagdad*, *The Three Musketeers*, *Robin Hood*, *The Gaucho*, *The Mark of Zorro*, *Don Q*, *The Black Pirate*, and *The Iron Mask*. Even in costume, Fairbanks was essentially a comedian.

*

British producers found it impossible to compete with this sort of opposition. Worried by the apathy of the public towards all but the few outstanding English films, they started a British National Film League. The Prince of Wales, supported by a distinguished company which included Sir Arthur Conan Doyle, Sir Edward Marshall Hall, and Mr Ramsey MacDonald, spoke at a luncheon to inaugurate the League. Exhibitors were persuaded to present British Film Weeks all over the country, and to ensure that there were plenty of pictures available several of the film renters brought up from their vaults a number of *old* British films, which were dusted and put out again with the few new pictures, to back up the 'Show a British Picture' campaign. Weighed down by mediocrity, the League collapsed, and by 1924 most of the English studios had closed or were on the verge of closing, while many of Britain's best players were on their way to Hollywood, or already there. Of the few stars who resisted all Hollywood offers, Betty Balfour shone the most brightly. In 1924 she easily won first place in a British film star popularity contest organized by the *Daily News*. But it was Fairbanks, Harold Lloyd, Buster Keaton, Valentino, Gloria Swanson, Laura La Plante, and the other great names of Hollywood that the British public flocked to see.

To help revive the industry the British Government decided in 1925 to fix a quota law, by which every exhibitor was bound to show a proportion of one British picture in every ten. This quota was to rise on a sliding scale, until by June 1929 it was estimated that one in every four films shown in British cinemas would be made in England. Quantity, not Quality, was thus assured.

The Quota was needed, for only thirty-four films had been made in Britain in 1925, including the semi-documentary *Ypres*, *The Unknown* (Percy Marmont), *Human Destinies* (Clive Brook), *The Rugged Path* (Stewart Rome), *The Rat* (Ivor Novello), and *Bulldog Drummond's Third Round* (Jack Buchanan). The English laughter was provided almost exclusively by Sydney Fairbrother in a series of *Mrs May comedies*, two-reelers made on a modest budget. Typical of the heavy fare was *The Presumption of Stanley Hay, M.P.* (Stolls), which must have worried some of the poster artists, and could hardly appeal—on title value— with *Oh Doctor!* (Reginald Denny) or *Seven Chances* (Buster Keaton). Who would see the Stoll film when there was Chaplin to be seen in *The Gold Rush*, Glenn Hunter appearing in *Merton of the Movies*, and in the best dramatic traditions of Hollywood, *The Iron Horse* and *Raffles*? The 1924 films were still showing— some of the magnificent costume pictures including *The Arab*, *Abraham Lincoln*, *Beau Brummell*, and *The Thief of Bagdad*. No wonder Britain needed a Quota!

CHAPTER TEN

The End of Visual Comedy

IT WAS Roscoe Arbuckle who introduced Buster Keaton to the screen, after seeing him in a vaudeville show. The son of Joe H. Keaton, a famous acrobatic comedian, Buster was of Irish and Scots descent. He was born in a farmhouse near the show grounds at Pickway, Kansas, on October 4, 1895, and was first carried on to the stage when he was only three months old. When he was about three his father gave him a costume to match his own, with bald wig and whiskers, and he then joined the act as one of the three Keatons. His father threw him all over the stage, fell down on him, walked over him, and pushed him around.

Buster, who had been given his name by the great Harry Houdini, soon showed considerable skill as an acrobatic comedian. His comic appeal, when allied to his tumbling, was so great that he was offered the leading role in a Schubert revue at the New York Winter Garden. He was then only twenty-one, but he turned down the offer, with its certain 750 dollars a week, to accept 200 dollars a week playing in motion pictures, supporting Arbuckle in two-reel comedies for Joseph Schenck Productions. His first film was *The Butcher Boy* (1917). Soon he was to be hit with pies, covered with flour, bitten by dogs, dropped into barrels of molasses, and to suffer a thousand other indignities in the cause of screen comedy. In *A Reckless Romeo* he appeared with Corrine Parquet and Alice Lake; in *The Rough House* and *His Wedding Night* he was with Josephine Stevens, and in *Oh Doctor!* and *Coney Island* he starred with Alice Lake. All these were 1917 comedies. He was making a name for himself when the war came. Joining the army, he found himself in the 159th Infantry Regiment of the 40th Division, and went to France.

Corporal Keaton was on the Somme when the armistice was signed, and soon he was home again, making two more films with Arbuckle, which brought his salary up to 500 dollars a week. Now he adopted his famous 'dead pan' technique, the frozen face which was to make him one of the most famous figures on the screen. *The Saphead* (Metro, 1920) was his first feature picture, still played straight, without the 'dead pan'. This was a five-reeler adapted from Bronson Howard's play *The Henrietta*, dealing with the adventures of Bertie van Alstyre, whose father was fabulously wealthy, but who was regarded as a fool. The *Bioscope* trade paper reported in January 1922 that 'Nothing funnier can be imagined than Buster Keaton's Bertie.'

In 1923 Keaton married Natalie Talmadge. His two-reelers now included *Neighbours*, *The High Sign*, *One Week*, *The Electric Horse*, *Convict 13*, *The Scarecrow*, *The Haunted House*, *The Frozen North* and *Cops*. While these were showing all over the world, his new feature films were gaining him vast popularity. *The Three Ages* (1923) introduced the new 'frozen face' technique. After this came *Our Hospitality* (Metro), *Sherlock Junior*, *The Navigator* (M.G.M.), *Seven Chances*, *College* (United Artists), *The General* (United Artists), *Steamboat Bill, Junior* (United Artists), and *The Cameraman* (M.G.M.).

In 1921 Buster Keaton had broken his right leg after catching his trousers in an escalator. Only once after this did he use a 'double' to appear instead of him in a film stunt. This was when he hired Lee Barnes, the champion pole vaulter, to vault into a second-floor window. In *The Paleface* Keaton had to drop 85 feet from a suspension bridge into a net, and while making *Sherlock, Jr.* he had to ride a motor-cycle while sitting on the handlebars. He hit both cameras, knocked down the director, and collided with a car. For *Hard Luck* (1921) he was required to dive from a 50 foot platform, missing a swimming pool by a few yards, to crash through a 'marble' tiled pavement made of paper, covered with wax. He dived, but his head and shoulders were seriously cut. He never used a stunt-man or stand-in, and in *Sherlock Jr.* he broke his neck.

'Not only can Keaton leap across bridge boards without coming to harm, but he gives proof in the leap of a dazzling elasticity,' says J. P. Lebel, in his biography of the comedian. 'His legs work like vigorous springs and endow him with an astounding bounce as well as a force and stability in the initial preparation. In *The General* he leaps from the truck attached to his locomotive to the tender, and from the tender to his driver's cabin with a graceful curve that brings him with an almost tele-guided precision to his destination. The unequal length of the successive leaps proves that the certainty of his trajectory owes nothing to tricks, and everything to his muscular mastery.'

At the height of his career, Keaton made a great deal of money. 'In 1924 I built a beautiful three-bedroomed home in Beverly Hills for my own family,' he says in his autobiography *My Wonderful World of Slapstick*. 'After living in our modest Hollywood house a short while, I borrowed 50,000 dollars from Joe Schenck to buy a home of my own. After living in it for six months, I resold it for 85,000 dollars. Then I bought another house for 55,000 dollars, living in that one for six months, and sold it for 85,000 dollars. I used some of my profits to help Mom buy a large home for the family. My 1924 house cost only 33,000 dollars, but it was on a large lot, had a swimming pool, and was ideal for the four of us. I was so sure of this that I wouldn't let my wife see it until I was ready to move in. I wanted to surprise her. When the great day came for her to look it over we brought along Mrs Bernice Mannix, whose husband Eddie was then Joe Schenck's studio manager. My wife took one look at the house and announced that it was too small. "In the first place," she said, "it has no room for the governess. Where would she sleep?" Our Jim was then three years old . . . The house I finally built in Beverly for the four of us was large enough to satisfy anyone. It was a two-story mansion with five bedrooms, two additional bedrooms for the servants, and a three-room apartment over the garage for the gardener and his wife, who worked as our upstairs maid. This made six servants with a cook, butler, chauffeur, and governess. It stood on three and a half acres of beautiful lawn. The land and the house together cost me 200,000 dollars, and we spent another 100,000 dollars furnishing it . . . By that time I was getting 2,000 dollars a week, plus 25 per cent of my pictures' profits, which brought me an additional 100,000 dollars a year.'

Keaton was essentially a visual comedian, an acrobatic clown, ideally suited to silent pictures. His films were always full of good visual gags, as in *The Cameraman* (1928), in which he was

142

seen as a newsreel photographer who grabs his chance of a 'scoop' when a fire-engine dashes down the street by jumping on to the moving vehicle, only to discover that it is bound for the depot, having already been to the fire.

The comedian was so brilliant in his silent pictures that it is sad to record that he was not an equal success in sound films. His art was essentially pantomimic, requiring no dialogue. Almost every word of the several Keaton sound films was a waste of breath. Every minute of Keaton in a silent picture is a joy. His best films are generally considered to be *Our Hospitality*, *Go West*, *The Cameraman*, and *The General*—all silent.

Keaton revealed his own recipe for screen comedy in 1930: 'The best way to get a laugh is to create a genuine thrill and then relieve the tension with comedy. Getting laughs depends on the element of surprise, and surprises are harder and harder to get as audiences, seeing more pictures, become more and more comedy-wise. But when you take a genuine thrill, build up to it, and then turn it into a ridiculous situation, you always get that surprise element.'

According to Maurice Bardeche and Robert Brasillach, in their book *History of the Film*, the drama in every Keaton picture lay in the relationship between the comedian and a machine or monster. Thus, in *The General* (1926) he appeared as Johnnie Gray, a locomotive driver who has been refused enlistment in the Southern Army during the American Civil War, but gets his chance in 1862 when his weird old locomotive helps him to rescue his girl from the Northern troops, thus earning the gratitude of the general of the Southern Army. Similarly, in *The Navigator* he was seen on board a liner, making coffee in pots large enough to serve five hundred passengers, while in *Steamboat Bill, Junior* he struggled against another monster—a flood tide. In *Go West*, a burlesque of William S. Hart in cowboy pictures, he faced a menacing herd of cattle. This formula, that of the little man versus the great big world, was used exclusively by Chaplin and Harold Lloyd, and was to be an essential ingredient of Frank Capra films.

With the coming of sound, Buster Keaton's appeal slowly waned. His pictures were spoiled by speech, which was superfluous to his brand of comedy. It was not that talking pictures were funnier—indeed, they were not. It was just that overnight, as we shall see, the whole technique changed. The position can best be shown by comparing a Keaton silent, say *The Cameraman* (1928), with almost any talking comedy film of the 1930 period. *The Cameraman* is extremely funny, and does not appear to be technically dated. The 1930 film, no matter what the title, is not only dated, but relatively unamusing.

The Keaton talkies included *Spite Marriage* (1929) (called in Britain *A Romeo in Pyjamas*), *Free and Easy* (1930), *Dough Boys* (1930) (known in Britain as *Forward March*), *Sidewalks of New York* (1931), *The Passionate Plumber*, and *Speak Easily* (1932). There was also *The Hollywood Revue of 1929*,[1] and *What! No Beer?* (1933). In several of these films Keaton was teamed with Jimmy Durante and Polly Moran. Some were financially successful, and contained many amusing moments. But it was unfortunate that the talkies had arrived—unfortunate, that is, for Keaton's admirers. In *Dough Boys*, directed by Edward Sedgwick, Keaton appeared as a millionaire conscript who goes to the 1914 war, and, in spite of himself, wins honour. In London the *Bioscope* trade paper reported: 'There is no lack of inventive humour, though perhaps it will again be noted that the humour depends chiefly on what Mr Keaton does and rarely on what he says.' The paper, however, found the picture a 'screamingly funny farcical war story,' with the settings 'realistic to a degree beyond the demands of farcical comedy'. This realism was always a feature of Keaton's comedies, just as his strange and handsome, mask-like features hid a hundred expressions, a mobility of eyes and mind and thought which no words, smiles, grimaces or winks could have captured. 'I wasn't even aware of it myself,' he said, when told he had a reputation for impassivity, because he never smiled. 'I just concentrated on what I was doing.'

As we have seen, Arbuckle was no longer there to guide him, and the result of his unhappy experience in talkies, and an unsuccessful first marriage, led to severe bouts of alcoholism.

'In 1928,' he says, 'I made the worst mistake of my career. Against my better judgment I let Joe Schenck talk me into

[1] A 13-reel monster talkie which featured all the M.G.M. stars, including Keaton, Lionel Barrymore, and Joan Crawford, but not Garbo.

giving up my own studio to make pictures at the booming Metro-Goldwyn-Mayer lot in Culver City. Even then it was the studio of stars, and had under contract John Gilbert, Marion Davies, Wallace Beery, Lon Chaney, Lionel Barrymore, William Haines and Greta Garbo. Marie Dressler, the greatest comedienne I ever saw (until Lucille Ball appeared) was also under contract there but only as a featured player . . . It seemed to me I would be lost making pictures in such a big studio.'

He was right. Chaplin and Lloyd warned him, and he tried to arrange for Paramount to distribute his films, but Adolph Zukor was already taking the Lloyd comedies and had been informed by the all-powerful moguls that 'Buster Keaton is the exclusive property of Metro-Goldwyn-Mayer.'

The result, as we have seen, was disastrous for Keaton. After 1933 he left M.G.M. and then went to France to star in an undistinguished comedy for Paramount. In 1934 he visited England, to star in a comedy called *The Invader*. It was an unhappy failure, chiefly owing to the lack of a good story, and the unambitious standard of production. The *Kinematograph Weekly* summed it up:

Feeble slapstick comedy, just a slipshod symposium of threadbare knockabout gags, resurrected from the silent two-reeler. Buster Keaton does the best possible in the circumstances, but in the end suffers overwhelming defeat in his tireless battle with shoddy material. The staging is cheap, and the direction obviously handicapped. It is impossible to assess the entertainment value of this film—there is none. The director, who has made good pictures since this was produced, has clearly been unable to fight against his material. Buster Keaton finds it impossible to raise a laugh, so feeble is the story and the gags.

How tragic, that a British studio could do this to such a fine comedian as Buster Keaton. But it was at a bad time in Keaton's career, and he was often drunk. The man with the unsmiling face returned to Hollywood, to appear without distinction in a number of short films, to write scripts, to become a television star, and to make brief but always welcomed appearances in *Hollywood Cavalcade*, *Sunset Boulevard*, Chaplin's *Limelight*,

It's A Mad, Mad World, and *A Funny Thing Happened on the Way to the Forum*.[1]

*

Towards the end of the first world war and in the early twenties few comedians were more popular in short pictures than white-faced Larry Semon.

The son of a magician, young Larry had shown considerable talent as a child, and was sent to art school to become a cartoonist on the New York *Sun*. His evenings were spent in amateur dramatic circles, and at this time he began directing comedies at the Vitagraph company's studio. Later he was persuaded to appear in them, at first in one-reelers and then in two-reelers. He was at once a tremendous attraction. In 1922, when he was earning a hundred thousand dollars a year for stopping custard pies and falling off ladders into flour bins, Semon is reported to have said 'A comedy is only as funny as its gags. The comic is of secondary importance. I have thirty-two members of my company in stock, including property men, technical men, cameramen, assistant directors, and actors. I expect them not only to be ready to do any doggone thing I ask them to do, but to eat, sleep, think, and read gags.'

Some of Larry Semon's outstanding feature films were *Stop, Look and Listen* (1926), *The Perfect Clown* (1925), and *Spuds* (1927). With Oliver Hardy as the Tin Man, he had played the part of the Straw Man in *The Wizard of Oz* (1925), and married his leading lady, Dorothy Dwan.

At one time Larry Semon was worth some 250,000 dollars, but when he died of pneumonia in 1928 at the comparatively early age of thirty-eight he was bankrupt, with assets of less than sixty pounds and debts of over £100,000. Clown-faced, agile, and usually wearing a bowler hat, Semon was considered by many to be as funny as Chaplin, and like many comedians he wanted to be a serious actor. In his latter films he achieved his ambition, with some success, appearing as a featured player in Paramount pictures.

Semon carried in the pocket of his short high pants a small

[1] It should be appreciated that all of Keaton's earlier and best pictures were those made under his personal direction or individual control. These are his films which continue to be shown.

black leather note-book. This was all the script he ever used when making a knockabout picture. Every night he wrote in it each new idea, fresh joke, or variation on an old visual theme. It was his precious gag book, and wherever it is now, the screen is the poorer for the absence of Larry Semon and his note-book.

*

1925 was probably the peak year for American short comedies. 'The industry is an infant no longer,' announced producer Adolph Zukor. 'It is a lusty child.'

Fortunately, it was still a silent child, for if all the comedians engaged in making short films at this time had been required to talk, Hollywood would have been a Babel. In addition to the many leading brands of short comedies, cinema proprietors were being offered well over a hundred less popular varieties. They all helped to swell the programmes of the world. There were the *Bobby Ray series*, the *Plum Centre comedies*, *Monte Weeks comedies*, the *Chester Conklin comedies*, the *Hank Mann series*, *Frank E. Nicholson's Variety Pictures*, and from the California studios on Gower Street, Hollywood, came comedy shorts featuring Cliff Bowes, Dot Farley, Al Alt, Jack Richardson, Charles Delany, Al St John, Eddie Gribbon, and Bill Franey. Even this did not exhaust the list. The *Molly May series*, the *Make Me Laugh comedies*, the *Mutt and Jeff cartoons*, the *Telephone Girl comedies*, and the *Go Getters series* were among dozens of offerings with which British, French, and Italian producers did not even attempt to compete. Monkeys, pet dogs, and whole families of children appeared in the 'comics.' Sunny McKeen, born in 1925, was only eighteen months old when he first appeared as 'Snookums' in the Stern Brothers comedies. He made thirty short films, and when he was four was reputed to be earning £4,000 a year.

The cost of making these short films had risen considerably since the earlier days. Lloyd Hamilton, who had been the 'Ham' of the *Ham and Bud series* for Kalem in 1914 was appearing in *Sunshine comedies* for Fox in the early twenties. 'Making people laugh is harder than making them cry, especially these days,' he said. 'This is due to the rapid change and advancement in people's tastes for comedy, and the constant demand for something new. It takes a large amount of money, a long time, and a great deal of thought and hard work to make a successful comedy. I remember the time I used to make a *Ham and Bud* in four or five days. Recently I was ninety-eight days making a *Sunshine comedy* for the Fox programme. The cost was forty times as much.'

Both D. W. Griffith and Mack Sennett thought very highly of Lloyd Hamilton, and he had been offered the opportunity of appearing as comedy relief in Griffith's *One Exciting Night* (1922)—as a black-faced comic, but unfortunately contracts could not be adjusted. A droll lanky fellow, six feet tall, he had made his screen début in 1914 under the direction of Marshall Neilan, and became a favourite after the success of the *Ham and Bud series*. His routine was rigorous:

'Comedy work doesn't end when the comedian finishes his scenes,' he said. 'He has to figure out new business for the days to come. The dressing room, or some secluded spot, is where I head for when not actually filming, and there I try to think. I must be quiet and alone. One of my best gags came to me the other day as I was sitting in a four-wheeled chariot that had been used by Theda Bara. Only recently we figured out a splendid gag for a mule that was supposed to be led out on to a spring-board, but it had to be abandoned because no mule was silly ass enough to do it. We tried several, but they all stopped dead when they saw the water below them, and turned it down.'

*

Although there were now few British comedies, there was always George Robey, whose arched eyebrows appeared in Stoll's *George Robey's Day Off*, a full-length feature based on the comedian's book, which told how, as an overworked and tired comic, he went for a little peace and quiet to stay in a country retreat called Little Slocum. Here the whole population, including the brass band, turned out to greet him. Strictly speaking, this was not Robey's first film, but it was his first feature picture, and it was good enough to encourage Stoll's to make some more. The next was *Widow Twankee*, in which Robey played his famous music hall part of a dame, and then came *The Prehistoric Man*, set in caves fitted with telephones. Robey's fruity vulgarity did not sparkle in silent films, and *Don Quixote*, produced by Maurice Elvey with Jerrold Robertson in the lead, was only partly successful. Later he appeared in a talkie version with Chaliapin. According to Robey, a man reading his evening paper in a tramcar was heard to say: 'Blimey! Here's George Robey going to act in a film with Charlie Chaplin! Won't that be a beano?'

One of Robey's early sound films was *The Temperance Fête*, by Herbert Jenkins. Then came *Marry Me*, with Renate Muller, Harry Green, Ian Hunter, and Maurice Evans, a version of *Chu Chin Chow*, *Birds of a Feather*, *Men of Yesterday*, and *The Trojan Brothers*.

*

If 1925 had been a slack year for British films, the next year was worse. America made 650 feature films, and some 1,400 short subjects, of which at least half were comedies, but the English studios produced only eighteen feature films in all, of which four could be classed as major productions. It was hardly surprising that the announcement of the opening of new studios at Elstree was regarded in British film circles as the event of the year. England's dwindling dramas included the Herbert Wilcox triumph *Nell Gwynn* (Dorothy Gish), *The Chinese Bungalow* (Matheson Lang), *The Flag Lieutenant* (Henry Edwards), *The Lodger* (Ivor Novello), and *The Triumph of the Rat* (Novello).

The comedies consisted of *Blinkeyes* and *Somebody's Darling* (Betty Balfour), and a series of two-reelers by Eliot Stannard with the radio comedian John Henry, Mabel Poulton, and Mary Brough, entitled *John Henry Calling*. During the twenties Betty Balfour and Mary Brough appeared in more British films than any other players.

There was also a series of short burlesque films, produced in satirical mood by Adrian Brunel. He depicted the adventures of the great travellers, Mr and Mrs Sherry Keating, Mr Rosita Fords, and their native guide Oompapa, in *Crossing the Great Sagrada*.[1] Then he made *The Pathetic Gazette*, a burlesque of the inevitable topical newsreel, which earned him the title of 'the Leacock of

[1] A burlesque based on the activities of naturalist Cherry Kearton, and the traveller Rosita Forbes.

the Screen,' and incidentally led to a contract from Gainsborough Pictures for five further burlesques. There followed *A
Typical Budget, Cut it Out* (a satire on film censorship), *Battling
Bruiser, The Blunderland of Big Game*, and *So This is Jollygood*,
a lament on the troubles of films, featuring the popular star
Rhubarb Vaselino. Unfortunately, no other British films of the
time possessed this satirical touch, and although these little
pictures drew loud laughter, the industry as a whole gave Adrian
Brunel very little encouragement. Wardour Street executives
were not creative enough to see further than the lorry loads of
film which were arriving in the street every day, fresh from
America. These were making so much money for the traders
that they did not need to think about British pictures. And
Brunel (who received more encouragement than most creative
film makers) was expected not only to make films on a shoe-
string, but also to produce them in his own back garden.

*

One of the features of silent comedy films was the use
of the explanatory sub-title. In dramatic stories the title writer
would be content with a mere CAME THE DAWN or NEXT MORN-
ING, but in comedy subjects it appeared essential that the sub-
title must also be facetious. During the twenties the art of
writing witty sub-titles was developed to a fine art in America,
where specialists were employed in producing lines which were
guaranteed to raise laughter :

> They always had pork on Sundays, so Charlie made a pig of himself.
> So desperate that he could blow his brains out—if he had any.
> Mrs Onion, who would repeat anything. . . .
> Her face was her fortune, so she had an overdraft.
> She had an awful fright, but she married him.
> So dumb that he kept her mum. . . .

The titles were often amusing, but sometimes they were
merely crude. Occasionally they were so American that English
audiences did not understand them, and the British distributors
had to substitute new sub-titles. Many pictures, including the
earlier Max Linder comedies, scorned the written word, and let
the action tell the story. Sometimes little sketches on the title

card illustrated the words. At their best the titles could be funny, but at their worst they were almost nauseating. Chaplin's captions were cut to a minimum in later years—an essential LATER or BACK FROM EOROPE serving to link sequences and denote the passage of time in *City Lights*, which remains an example of the highest art of the silent screen.

In the midst of the British film depression the London *Daily Express* announced that it would spend £50,000 on the production of a film—to encourage English pictures. Michael Balcon of Gainsborough Pictures said 'It is a sporting offer . . . and we will be glad to take up the challenge in a sporting spirit, and make a picture ourselves in parallel competition with the *Daily Express* film.' Unfortunately the *Daily Express* film did not materialize, but Lord Beaverbrook himself gave considerable support to the home industry.

If the average picturegoer wished to see an exciting cowboy picture, a spectacular historical romance, or needed a good laugh, he or she went to see an American film. To keep audiences laughing there was Harry Langdon (with Joan Crawford) in *Tramp, Tramp, Tramp*, Lupino Lane in *The Fighting Dude* and *Maid in Morocco*, George Sidney and Charlie Murray in *The Cohens and Kellys*, and Anita Loos' *Gentlemen Prefer Blondes*, with Alice White, Ruth Taylor, Ford Sterling, and Mack Swain. Then there was Syd Chaplin in *Oh, What a Nurse!*, Buster Keaton in *Go West*, Wallace Beery and Raymond Hatton in *Behind the Front*, and Reginald Denny in *What Happened to Jones?* Syd Chaplin, who was regarded by many as second only to his more famous brother, had been recommended by Charles for the title role in *Charley's Aunt* (1925), which he had played on the English stage. The picture was a great success, and continued to be shown for years. A cinema owner in South Wales found that his patrons liked it so much that he booked it in advance for a special Christmas season, once a year—for five years. A year later Syd Chaplin made *Oh, What a Nurse!*, followed by *The Better 'Ole* and *The Man on the Box*, all for Warners. Then he visited England to appear with Betty Balfour in *A Little Bit of Fluff* and *The Missing Link*.

For good measure Hollywood offered a series of *Jerry cartoons*, drawn by Bilby and Griffith, while the *Al Christie comedies* of the time featured Bobby Vernon, Neal Burns, Dorothy Devore, Vera Steadman, Walter Hiers, Jimmy Adams, and Billy Dooley. Typical of the hundreds of two-reelers of this period was *A Bankrupt Honeymoon* (Fox) in which Harold Goodwin, learning that his fortune had vanished, embarked with a taxi-driver on an 'eat while you ride' motor restaurant enterprise. The scheme led to the bride's father, an omnibus magnate, offering a vast sum for the control of the company, and the fitting-out of a double-deck omnibus as a restaurant. For all the ingenuity of the comedies of this class, and the increasing amount of money which was being spent on them, the pace was noticeably slower than it had been a few years previously.

Hollywood was now paying fantastic salaries. In 1926 Harold Lloyd was stated to be America's highest-paid player, earning an average of £8,300 a week. Chaplin was said to come next, with £6,300, while Douglas Fairbanks was paid £5,000. Gloria Swanson, Mary Pickford, Norma Talmadge, and Tom Mix were all in the £4,000 a week class, after which there was a drop to Thomas Meighan, who was reckoned to receive £2,500 a week. Remembering that taxes were low in 1926, and that dollars and pounds were worth considerably more than they are today, it will be seen that there was plenty of money in Hollywood, for those at the top. Many of the weekly salaries were to be increased, and some were to fall during the next ten years, but in 1926 the other highly paid stars included:

Weekly Salary £	
2,100	Marion Davies (comedy and drama)
1,900	Lillian Gish
1,700	Colleen Moore (mostly comedy)
900	Buster Keaton (comedy)
	Pola Negri
	Corinne Griffith
	Betty Compson
	Buck Jones
630	Lewis Stone
	Wallace Beery (comedy and drama)
	Mae Murray
500	Adolphe Menjou
	Reginald Denny (light comedy)

Weekly Salary
£

450	Richard Dix (light comedy)
	John Gilbert
	Ramon Novarro
	Ernest Torrence (comedy and drama)
	Bebe Daniels (comedy and drama)
	Francis X. Bushman
	Antonio Moreno
360	Ronald Colman
310	Norma Shearer (sometimes comedy)
	Rod La Rocque
	Alice Terry
	Conrad Nagel
290	Louise Fazenda (comedy)
	Billie Dove (comedy and drama)
250	Clive Brook
210	Charles Murray (comedy)
	Chester Conklin (comedy)
	Laura La Plante (comedy)
170	Mary Philbin
160	Clara Bow (comedy)
	George O'Brien
105	Vilma Banky
85	Greta Nissen
	Greta Garbo (a newcomer)
75	Lillian Rich
65	Dolores Costello
	William Boyd

*

In 1926 Eddie Cantor entered films when Jesse L. Lasky
bought the rights in the successful Broadway musical show *Kid
Boots* for 61,000 dollars, with the proviso that Cantor and no
one else should star in the film. Billie Dove, Natalie Kingston
and Clara Bow were signed up in support, the film taking a
modest six weeks to complete, a whole week being devoted
to an acrobatic stunt in which Cantor did not appear.

Cantor's second film was *Special Delivery* (1927), which he
wrote himself. *Kid Boots* had earned a small fortune, and the
popularity of the little man with the big eyes and the still bigger
smile was now assured. He was a hard worker and had come far
from the early days, when he had run away from school to
become a Wall Street messenger boy. Discharged because his

153

clowning made the other boys laugh during working hours, young Eddie had joined a juvenile revue, and had become a singing waiter at Coney Island before touring American vaudeville theatres with a team of jugglers.

When Cantor entered the motion picture world he was at once a star, soon to become one of the most highly paid comedians in the industry. In the thirties his *Kid Millions*, *Strike Me Pink*, and *Roman Scandals* were to make him immensely popular, and when he temporarily deserted the screen for the American radio, his became one of the best-known voices in the Western hemisphere.

1926 also saw the release of *When the Wife's Away*, *Sunnyside Up*, and *Bardelys the Magnificent*, starring George K. Arthur, an English actor who had run away from school at Rugby to enlist when only sixteen in the Argyll and Sutherland Highlanders, with whom he served throughout the 1914 war. Although trained as an accountant, he decided that he would, in his own words, rather 'figure in a cast than cast up figures,' and in 1919 he made his film début in Liverpool, in a comedy made by the Success Film Company. While in *Charley's Aunt* at the Surrey Theatre, London, he was seen by film director Harold Shaw and engaged for the leading part in the Stoll picture *Kipps*, which led to further offers, and in 1924 he joined the queue for Hollywood.

At first he was unsuccessful, but in a San Francisco café he chanced to meet a film director who was almost as poor as himself—a man of whom he had never heard, named Joseph von Sternberg. On borrowed capital, and very cheaply, they made *The Salvation Hunters* (1925) which was at once acclaimed an artistic masterpiece. This brought a number of offers for Arthur, but although *The Salvation Hunters* had been a dramatic study of low life, Hollywood now wanted the actor to be a comedian. *When the Wife's Away*, *Tillie the Toiler*, and *Spring Fever* were among his later comedies, and during the talkie period he appeared in many pictures, including *Oliver Twist*, *Looking Forward*, *Blind Adventure*, and *Riptide*, after co-starring with Karl Dane in a number of silent feature comedies for Metro-Goldwyn-Mayer. It will probably be for his performance in *The Salvation Hunters*, however, that George K. Arthur will be remembered.

Hollywood films were now arriving in Britain in such numbers that companies had to wait their turn for the privilege of showing them in London's few leading cinemas. H. F. Kessler-Howes, writing in the *Kinematograph Weekly* in January 1926, deplored the fact that in London film circles a picture was considered to have only a week's life. The Tivoli cinema had announced its intention of 'reviving' Harold Lloyd's *College Days* (*The Freshman*) on January 26 after its release on January 4th. Within a few years the merging of cinemas throughout Britain into three main powerful groups was to make the potential life of a film even shorter than in the twenties.

*

In 1926 Frank Capra, who was later to direct *Mr Deeds Goes to Town* and other notable social comedies, was engaged by Mack Sennett as a gag writer. Later he joined forces with Harry Langdon, who had been making two-reelers for Sennett, and together they made three features, of which *The Strong Man* was the most amusing. In this, Langdon appeared as a Belgian soldier in the 1914 war, and was seen capturing a German with the aid of a peashooter, only to be captured in turn by the enemy. Peace declared, Langdon and the German both go to America, where the German becomes a professional strong man. Langdon, who is his assistant, searches New York for a girl whom he has never seen, but with whom he has exchanged letters during the war. In the end, after several hilarious adventures, he finds her.

After completing *The Strong Man*, Langdon and Capra quarrelled and parted. The comedian's subsequent pictures were not wholly successful, and after attempting a come-back with Oliver Hardy in *Elephants Never Forget*, he gradually faded from the screen. Capra, on the other hand, went from strength to strength, as we shall see. In *Three's a Crowd* (1927) Langdon was seen as a tenement boy working for a wagon owner. Living alone, he dreams of having a wife and family. Fate ordains that he should find a beautiful girl, lost in the snow with her baby. He takes them back to his shack, where he cares for them, falling deeply but bashfully in love with the girl. However, he is quite unable to tell her of his devotion, and on Christmas

Eve, just as he is preparing to play Santa Claus, the girl's husband arrives to claim his family, and Harry Langdon is left alone. The plot might be said to owe something to *The Gold Rush* (1925), but Langdon was not the only comedian to be influenced by Chaplin.

It was becoming increasingly difficult to think of original ideas for comedies. Earl W. Hammans, who was by 1927 one of America's leading producers of short comedies, thought that the two-reel 'comic' was the most difficult type of picture to make. 'In dramas you can use the same themes over and over again,' he said, 'but with comedies you cannot. It is like telling a funny story. You may get a laugh first time, but if you keep on repeating the story it falls flat. Therefore, if comedies are to be successful, they must constantly offer something different. One of our most prominent directors claims that laughs in a film are worth 330 dollars apiece.'

The lack of new gags and fresh material was especially noticeable in British comedies. There were only two screen comedians in England who could claim to include new gags, original themes, and speed of action in their pictures. These were Walter Forde and Lupino Lane, and both possessed a thorough knowledge of American methods. George Robey and Nelson Keys can hardly be counted, because their film appearances were infrequent, and they remained essentially stage comedians.

Nelson Keys, however, deserves special mention as a versatile character comedian, who might have been offered more opportunity by British studios. On or off the stage and screen he was an amusing personality. On one occasion he was filming by day at Welwyn, and at night was appearing in a London revue, for which his son John Paddy Carstairs had written some of the lyrics. 'Bunch' Keys—as he was always known—was usually detained at the studios until the last moment, and had to dash to the nearby railway station to catch the train for London and the theatre. Often he was still wearing his film make-up. On this particular evening he was observed by a passenger to be removing his beard in the corridor of the train. This seemed very sinister to the passenger, who kept careful watch. He was not surprised to see the little man putting on another weird disguise—the make-up for his first entrance on the stage. The suspicions of the passenger were now confirmed. A dangerous criminal was making his escape from prison! He immediately summoned the guard, and when the train arrived at London there were two detectives waiting on the platform to meet Nelson Keys, who stepped from the train heavily disguised. They refused to believe his story. No actor with a dressing-room at the theatre would make-up in a train. So 'Bunch' took them all in a taxi to the theatre, and proved that he was innocent.

One of the few English producers who offered modest encouragement to players and directors was the millionaire Archibald Nettlefold, who had bought the studios at Walton-on-Thames after the Hepworth crash. Archibald Nettlefold Productions continued to make pictures throughout the twenties and thirties, and in the fifties the production company at the same Nettlefold Studios was Nettlefold Films Ltd. One of the first moves that Archibald Nettlefold made when he took over the studios was to invite Cecil Hepworth to return and direct for him *The House of Marney*, with Alma Taylor, John Longden, James Carew, and Gibb McLaughlin. Later Nettlefold produced the highly successful Walter Forde feature comedies, generally considered to be among the funniest British films of the twenties.

*

While most of Britain's producers had been marking time, and hoping for a return to prosperity, events of unusual interest were taking place in a small film studio at Clapham. Here, during 1926 and 1927, pioneer sound-on-film (not disc) talkies were made by Lee de Forest Phono-films. Miles Mander directed several of the films, in which Owen Nares, Mary Clare, Malcolm Keen, and Dorothy Boyd appeared. One year later an experimental sound-on-film picture was completed in Berlin at the Weissenee studio, featuring the English actor Arthur Chesney, the brother of Edmund Gwenn. By then the sound system known as British Acoustic had been perfected in Britain by Doctor O. K. Kolb of the Gaumont Company, on a principle devised by two Danish inventors, A. Petersen and A. Poulsen.

At exactly the same time, in America, the Warner-Vitaphone and Fox Movietone rival sound systems were the object of simultaneous research. An increasing number of people were interested in making sure that the movies talked. After years of service, the silent picture was already doomed. The revolution which was to follow was to alter the whole technique of motion pictures, and to turn the industry upside down. The career of nearly every player, especially of the comedians, would soon hang in the balance.

Meanwhile, the silent pictures were still drawing the crowds, and amongst the most popular of the stars of the two-reelers were Laurel and Hardy. Stan Laurel (Arthur Stanley Jefferson) had gone to America from England in 1910, to understudy Charles Chaplin in the stage sketch 'A Night in an English Music Hall'. In 1917 he had entered films with Hal Roach, appearing in an amusing series of burlesques of other pictures— *The Egg*, *Mud and Sand*, *Rob 'Em Good*, *When Knights were Cold*, and *White Wings*. In 1926 he teamed up with Oliver (Babe) Hardy, and together they started work on a series of two-reel comedies for Hal Roach.

The partners soon found themselves the most popular pair of comedians on the screen. Their two-reelers were almost the only short comedies to be accepted entirely on their merits, and to justify advertising outside cinemas. When in 1931 they appeared in their first feature film, critic Hannen Swaffer regretted the move. *Jailbirds*, however, was a great success, the forerunner of many other Laurel and Hardy features.

*

The end of the silent film era saw a partial recovery in British studios. There were two new companies working at Elstree, apart from the small Ideal Films studio and British International Pictures, who had taken over from British National. Walthamstow and Beaconsfield were active again, and the Alliance studios at Twickenham were planning a comparatively ambitious programme. At Elstree, Herbert Wilcox had started work on his *Tip-Toes* with Dorothy Gish, Will Rogers, and Nelson Keys. And Harry Tate was making a series of short subjects based on his music hall sketches—*Fishing*, *Motoring*, *Golfing*, *In His*

Office, and *Peacehaven*. The British dramas still outnumbered the comedies by twenty to one, the outstanding English offerings being *The Battles of Coronel and Falkland Islands*, *Downhill*, *London*, *Poppies of Flanders*, and *The Emden*.

To producer Michael Balcon the future of British films looked encouraging. Announcing the plans of Piccadilly Pictures at the end of 1926 he was able to say: 'To my mind things never looked better in this country for the independent producer, who, by studying in the arrangement of his programme the one thing that matters—i.e. audience appeal—by the choice of ·a wide variety of subjects makes his goods of such a nature that no enterprising showman can afford to lose them.'

Most of the best films still came from Hollywood, which was now producing eighty-five per cent of the world's motion pictures. In the United States alone ninety million people went to the cinema every week. The American studios were as rich as the British studios were poor, simply because money earned from the Hollywood pictures went back into production. History proves that Britain's studios have suffered because they have been neglected by the middle-men, the renters, distributors, and shop-keepers, who could have backed Hepworth, but allowed English studios to become empty derelict stages year after year. When in 1951 Sir Laurence Olivier pointed this out to the British film industry, the traders of Wardour Street did not like it.

But distributors were coining money from the last few of the American silent films. *Love*, with Greta Garbo and John Gilbert (later made as a talkie and called *Anna Karenina*), *Sunrise*, with Janet Gaynor, Cecil B. de Mille's magnificent *The King of Kings*, Emil Jannings in *The Way of All Flesh*, and Corinne Griffith and Victor Varconi in *The Divine Lady*. These were some of the dramas. The comedies included Wallace Beery and Raymond Hatton in *We're in the Navy Now*, Charles Murray and Chester Conklin in *McFadden's Flats*, Larry Semon in *Spuds*, Buster Keaton in *College*, Monty Banks in *Atta Boy*, Bebe Daniels in *A Kiss in a Taxi*, and George Sidney in *Millionaires*. Chaplin's *Shoulder Arms* was re-issued, and played for a month at the Capitol cinema in London's Haymarket.

The short comedies from Hollywood included the Hal Roach,

Mack Sennett, and Educational series, featuring Lupino Lane, 'Our Gang', the Juveniles, Big Boy, Franklyn Pangborn, Al St John, Lige Conley, Lionel Barrymore, Ben Turpin, Charley Bowers, Mabel Normand, and Ethel Clayton.

Against this formidable opposition Nelson Keys battled bravely in *When Knights were Bold*, directed by Tim Whelan at Elstree. 'The production is elaborate,' said *The Bioscope*, 'Nelson Keys plays Sir Guy with spirit and fully brings out the satire of the situation. An amusing and well played comedy.' But unfortunately it was one against many.

Blissfully unconscious that the noise was soon to start, Chaplin was planning his new picture. Nearly four years were to pass before it would be ready for showing. It was to be the last great silent film of the era, one of the most amusing comedies ever made.

26.
English audiences did not at first like American film accents. Peter Lawford was then a child actor

27.
But all the world liked Maurice Chevalier, seen here with Jeanette Macdonald in THE LOVE PARADE (1929)

28.
W. C. Fields as Wilkins Micawber in DAVID COPPER-FIELD (1935) *with Freddie Bartholomew as David*

29. *Some British Comedy Players of the Thirties. Top left to right.*—Cicely Courtne[
Jack Hulbert, Gordon Harker, Ralph Lynn, Tom Walls, Margaret Rutherford, Robe[
Hare, Alfred Drayton, Sydney Howard

CHAPTER ELEVEN

All Talking!

Under all speech that is good for anything there lies a silence that is better. Silence is deep as eternity; speech is shallow as time.

THOMAS CARLYLE.

WHEN IN 1926 the Warner Brothers exhibited their synchronized film *Don Juan*, starring John Barrymore, the interest which this aroused led them to look for a subject to exploit the perfection of their sound system. Financial disaster was threatening the company. Only astute showmanship could save the day.

The solution was found on the American stage, where the Jewish actor Al Jolson had achieved a considerable reputation as a black-faced coon singer of sentimental songs. On October 6, 1926, the Warner Brothers let loose upon an unsuspecting world their film *The Jazz Singer*, in which the star Al Jolson sang one synchronized song. This was 'Mammy', but not only the song but also several lines of dialogue were recorded for the film. Jolson was heard to say 'Come on Ma, listen to this . . .' and then he began to sing the melody which was to set the whole entertainment world upside-down, and make every film actor and actress start singing or chattering.

As a film *The Jazz Singer* was a poor effort, but as a novelty it was unique. The song and the few words of dialogue carried it to immediate success. The Warners netted a profit of over a million pounds, and immediately embarked on a sequel, *The Singing Fool*. This grossed even more money, and from the moment that Jolson opened his mouth to sing 'Sonny Boy', there could be little doubt that the novelty had come to stay. The silent picture was doomed.

The first Warner 'talkies' were made at the old Vitagraph studios at Flatbush, Brooklyn, New York. The word 'Vitaphone' came out of 'Vitagraph'. It was here that John Bunny, Flora Finch, the Drews, Maurice Costello, and Florence Turner had acted. A glass-roofed building which had been painted over when arc lamps were introduced had now become the studio of the Vitaphone company, the subsidiary organization which the Warners used to make and market their sound films. Draperies and sacking had been hastily hung from the beams to muffle the many intruding noises.

At first Hollywood was not convinced that the talkies had come to stay. Syd Chaplin in *The Better 'Ole*, with a synchronized musical score, supported by a programme of Vitaphone musical short films, was playing to packed houses late in 1927. But the critics considered that the 'canned music' was no improvement on the orchestral accompaniment to which they were accustomed. The musicians naturally agreed. And many film magnates regarded the new sound films as freaks—novelties which would soon fade. After all, they pointed out, it had happened before. There had been Hepworth's Vivaphone system, and the Gaumont and Walturdaw synchronized pictures, which were really only novelties. The public had always returned to the silent picture.

But according to the Warners, their new sound films were responsible for an immense rise in cinema attendances. Later it was claimed that while fifty-seven million Americans went to the movies in 1927, no less than ninety-five million went in 1929. For almost a year the Warners led the field, their only serious competitor being Fox Films, whose early musical shorts, synchronized newsreels, and 1927 feature film *What Price Glory?* made good use of a sound-on-film recording system which was to attain a high standard of perfection. The immediate success of their Movietone newsreel did almost as much as Al Jolson to convince cinema proprietors in America and Europe that the crowds who queued to see and hear the novelty would come back again—if the pictures were good. To show the Movietone newsreels the cinema proprietors had to install sound apparatus, and where this had been installed in one district it was inevitable that it must soon come to the next town. Patrons were all taking about the *sounds* which could now be heard on the newsreels—and the Fox company took good care to introduce into each weekly reel not only plenty of news, but also plenty of noise. By the end of 1927 all the leading producers

162

of America had obtained licences from the recording companies, in order to produce sound films.

Warner Brothers were now faced with considerable competition, but in addition to their feature films they were turning out four Vitaphone short pictures every week. For these almost every vaudeville comedian, singer, and dancer was pressed into service. Finally, a two-reel short entitled *Lights of New York* was expanded into five reels, and for a modest 60,000 dollars the world's first all-talking picture was completed, some two months before Al Jolson's *The Singing Fool*, which was only part-talking. *Lights of New York* was a simple tale of a small-town boy and girl lured by the bright lights of the city. As a silent film it might have earned a modest profit. As the first all-talking picture it was a sensation, and netted a fortune. As for *The Singing Fool*, this made so much money that many cinema owners paid for the installation of their new sound equipment with the profits from this one picture, all in a week. Millions were queueing outside the cinemas of the world, and in Hollywood new sound stages were being erected, and the vast silent stages being hastily converted.

At first patrons wanted only to hear people talk and sing. To both hear and see George Bernard Shaw on Movietone, to hear the crowds at the Cup Final match, to listen to the new popular songs on the screen—the public would willingly queue. Noises and not stories, an ability to sing and talk, and not acting experience—these were the new Hollywood standards. Movement on the screen and action in the telling of a story were now less important than the words of the dialogue, the lyrics of a song. For hours the public queued beneath the posters announcing the advent of 100 PER CENT ALL TALKING PICTURES . . . ALL SINGING . . . ALL TALKING . . . ALL DANCING films. The film industry rushed to meet the demand, and let loose a fantastic selection of pictures both long and short. Endless songs of every description were sung, and sometimes murdered. Actors and actresses who might have been better silent began to talk, and went on talking, for reel after reel, all for dollars.

'If I had a Talking Picture of You-u-u!' blared the wireless sets, emphasizing that in 1928 and 1929 cinemas gathered in more money than ever before. Fox Films, with the Fox-Case

Movietone sound system, started to expand, bringing their number of theatres in America up to 325. In Hollywood anyone with the slightest experience of sound film technique was in demand. Many cinema musicians found themselves in the breadline. The pictures themselves were heavy with noise, dialogue, crackle and song. But the public returned eagerly for more.

Wallace Beery agreed with Chaplin about the talkies. 'Not so hot,' he said. 'Too many people go into motion picture theatres to sleep, and they don't want to be annoyed by a lot of conversation.' Many of the established comedians were hit hard. Ben Turpin, a favourite for years, found that his voice was not suitable for recording. The whole technique of film comedy, developed in the Sennett and Christie schools and carefully nursed by Chaplin, Hal Roach, Keaton, Larry Semon, Harry Langdon, and Harold Lloyd—to name only a few—looked like becoming almost overnight completely out of date. It was no longer enough to be visually amusing. The comedians were expected to say funny things. The whole meaning of the word 'gag' had altered.

The two-reel comedy was now suffering from a severe depression. The double feature programme, on the 'two pictures for the price of one' basis, had towards the end of the twenties hit the short comedy hard. There was no longer room for 'the comic'. Instead, a 'B' supporting picture, often of indifferent quality, but claiming to be a 'big' picture, was to be found in every three-hour programme. The short comedy, after being given away free as an inducement to buy the feature film, was now out in the cold. It was no longer profitable to spend money on them, or to plan them carefully. Those which survived were hastily written, and filmed in a few days. Only the Laurel and Hardy short comedies, now talkies, could hold their own. And in time these favourite comedians were forced to abandon the two-reeler in favour of feature films.

One of the most important of the comedy schools was now closed. Nearly every famous screen clown had graduated in one- or two-reelers, a valuable training ground which had established many reputations. Where were the new comedians to come from?

The answer came from the stage and the radio. As purely

visual comedians, many thought that Chaplin, Harold Lloyd, and Keaton were on the way out. In America the Marx Brothers, Jimmy Durante, and a whole host of other brilliantly verbal actors looked like taking their place. In Britain there was to be a host of newcomers, admirable players for the new technique, but none of them *clowns* in the strict meaning of the word.

If Gloria Swanson, Mary Pickford, George Arliss, and finally the great Garbo could talk with success on the screen—so can we, said the silent comedians. Many of them had little choice; it was talk, or go under. Totally ignoring the advice of Larry Semon in 1922—'a comedy is only as funny as its gags' (by which at the time he meant visual gags) the comics started to talk. Much of the humour was lost in the first crudity of speech, and for some months the top-heavy dialogue was simply not amusing. The comic line, the American wise-crack, the sharp retort—these had invaded the screen, and had replaced the comedy of movement, the visual gag, the art of knockabout and slapstick. In Europe the public at first found the American accents bewildering, and missed much of the dialogue. Chatter, chatter, chatter, went the talking machines. All that had been highest in motion picture art had suddenly been swept away. In later years, when films had quietened down, and Hollywood had realized that 100 per cent talking was not essential, the whole tone of comedy was different, for the true art of screen pantomime had been lost. Only when a silent Chaplin film, or part of an early Sennett picture, was revived, could a new generation realize what comedy films had lost with the coming of sound. Only the drawing-room comedy, the comedy of conversation and wit, had benefited.

Music now flooded the cinemas, accompanying every mood, and misinterpreting many a situation. Warner Brothers and other studios bought up whole music publishing companies, to secure exclusive libraries of music. Warners signed up a team of popular composers which included Sigmund Romberg, Oscar Hammerstein II, Jerome Kern, Henry Warren, and Oscar Strauss. Soon audiences all knew the words and music of 'Mine Alone', 'Singing in the Rain', 'The Song of the Dawn', and 'Tiptoe Through the Tulips'.

But the pantomime was over. Buster Keaton, with Anita

165

Page and Trixie Friganza in his first talkie, *Free and Easy*, related the adventures of a publicity novice in a film studio, who by sheer incompetence and stupidity attains the position of a star. The *Bioscope* trade paper thought the picture very amusing, but did not readily accept Keaton as a talkie star:

It will be generally admitted that Mr Keaton's funniest scenes are those in which he does not speak, a striking example, in a double sense, being that in which he is selected as a sort of punchbag in a test for various ladies who are being chosen for the part of a husband-beating shrew . . . with the use of his voice Mr Keaton definitely leaves the ranks of those supreme fun makers, including, besides himself, Mr Punch and Charlie Chaplin, whose misfortunes rouse laughter unhampered by human sympathy. He becomes a human being, and therefore has to abandon a form of entertainment in which he was supreme, and enter into competition with many already well established in the same line.

*

Meanwhile Al Jolson's *The Singing Fool* and newsreels like British Movietone News for August 14, 1929, which included the speech of the Prince of Wales and Lord Baden-Powell at the Scouts' World Jamboree, were making cinemas in Britain hastily install sound equipment. In Wolverhampton the first hall to change from silent films was the Agricultural Hall, the largest in the town, which re-opened with *The Singing Fool*. In the following September the Queen's, Wolverhampton, installed sound equipment. Elsewhere all over Britain and America other cinemas were doing the same. At the Havelock Picture House, Sunderland, the first Wearside cinema to feature talkies, some 121,000 people went to see *The Singing Fool*. The Queen's Hall, Newcastle-on-Tyne, started off with *Show Boat*, playing to capacity audiences at each of the four daily performances. At the nearby Stoll theatre *The Singing Fool* ran for more than eight weeks. In Sheffield enormous crowds besieged the Central Picture House to see *Broadway Melody*, and the Regent to see *Movietone Follies*, following a record six-week run of *The Singing Fool* which had been seen by 150,000 Sheffield people.

At this time the Roxy cinema, New York, was taking 700,000 dollars in four weeks with *The Cockeyed World*, in which Victor McLaglen and Edmund Lowe, with very little story but plenty of wise-cracks, played Flagg and Quirt. The film world was making a fortune out of the talkies, and everyone wanted to be in on it. Even Mack Sennett, the great master of silent film comedy, was making a full-length feature picture—*Midnight Daddies*.

*

For British producers the talkies, aided by the rising quota law which forced British cinemas to book English pictures, proved a wonderful opportunity. Between 1929 and 1939 a whole army of new British screen comedians appeared, recruited mainly from the music halls, musical comedy, and the radio. Gracie Fields, Will Hay, Max Miller, Will Fyffe, Tommy Trinder, Arthur Askey, Tommy Handley, Ernie Lotinga, Leslie Fuller, the 'Crazy Gang', Sandy Powell, Arthur Lucan and Kitty McShane, Frank Randle, Elsie and Doris Waters—these were a few of the stage stars who entered the film comedy field in the thirties and forties. There were many more. The Aldwych team —Tom Walls, Ralph Lynn, Robertson Hare, and Mary Brough— were transferred almost bodily from the Aldwych theatre farces to the film studios. Jack Hulbert and Cicely Courtneidge came from the revue and musical comedy stage to contribute dancing, singing, and clowning on musical comedy lines. Bobby Howes and Stanley Lupino did the same. Leslie Henson (who had first filmed with Hepworth) now found himself much in demand for screen farce. Nelson Keys, Peter Haddon, Herbert Mundin, Alfred Drayton, A. W. Bascomb, Fred Emney, and Hugh Wakefield became familiar figures to millions of British cinema patrons. Henry Kendall, an engaging light comedian who was a considerable success on the stage, was by 1935 more in demand in British studios than any other actor. Sir Seymour Hicks became for a time the master of the slightly risqué screen comedy and farcical situation. Arthur Riscoe proved himself to be more amusing than most British producers had the wit to appreciate, and Claude Hulbert, Claude Dampier, and Kenneth Kove became masters in the art of being screen 'silly ass' types.

Jack Buchanan sang and danced his way into the hearts of immense audiences in a series of light comedies with music; and, as we shall see, even this did not exhaust the list.

However good these individualists were the standard of film production in Britain seldom matched their ability. Most of their pictures were prolonged music hall acts, musical comedies, and stage farces—photographed from a limited number of angles. Of all the British comedy films made between 1929 and 1939, only ten stand out as being above average in treatment, direction, and general appeal, although there were many more which were amusing:

1. Will Hay, Moore Marriott, and Graham Moffatt in 'Oh, Mr Porter', directed by Marcel Varnel. Although this team were to make many more comedies, this was probably the best.
2. Jack Hulbert with Cicely Courtneidge in 'Jack's the Boy', directed by Walter Forde.
3. Gracie Fields in 'Sally in Our Alley', directed by Basil Dean.
4. George Formby in 'Keep Your Seats Please'.
5. Tom Walls, Ralph Lynn, Robertson Hare, and Mary Brough in 'Thark'. Mary Brough was memorable as 'Mrs Frush of Fark', and Walls and Lynn shared a hilarious sequence in a bedroom in the haunted house. Every time Tom Walls pressed the lever of the soda water syphon, Ralph Lynn nearly jumped out of bed with fright.
6. Sydney Howard in 'Up for the Cup', directed by Jack Raymond.
7. Charles Laughton in Alexander Korda's 'The Private Life of Henry the Eighth', rich in satire, and a milestone in British production, being international in appeal.
8. Leslie Howard in 'Pygmalion', directed by Leslie Howard and Anthony Asquith. In connection with the making of a later film George Bernard Shaw is said to have exclaimed to film producer Gabriel Pascal, 'The trouble is that you are interested only in art, and I am interested only in money'. This one was an artistic success which made a lot of money.

9. 'Say it With Flowers', directed by John Baxter, with Mary Clare, Ben Field, and George Carney. A modest film about Londoners, rich in comedy and human sentiment.

10. Gordon Harker and Binnie Hale in 'This is the Life'. Not an outstanding comedy, but memorable for a hilarious burlesque operatic ending. Harker himself gave many other distinguished performances.

There were of course many others, but these ten were typical of the better British comedies of the thirties.

*

But to return to 1928—the year in which audiences in Britain were crowding into the cinemas which had been wired for sound, to see and hear Al Jolson in *The Jazz Singer*. It was a year still rich in silent comedy. Chaplin was to be seen in *The Circus*, Harold Lloyd was in *Speedy*, Chester Conklin was in *Tell It to Sweeney*, Monty Banks was in *Week End Wives*, Syd Chaplin and Betty Balfour were in the English film *A Little Bit of Fluff*, and Walter Forde was in *Wait and See*. These were only a few of the last of the big silent comedy pictures. There were ninety British pictures produced during the year, thanks to the quota law, and to the enterprise of a Scots solicitor named John Maxwell who had taken over the British International Studios at Elstree, and was determined to make more British films.

During 1929 the industry on both sides of the Atlantic was forced to adjust itself to the new medium. But there were many cinema owners who still remained unconvinced that talkies had come to stay. It was not until December 1930 that almost all the picture theatres in America and Europe had become wired for sound. Meanwhile the equipment manufacturers were reaping a rich harvest.

Two of Britain's best offerings in 1929 were talkies—Alfred Hitchcock's *Blackmail*, which had started as a silent film, and A. E. Dupont's tri-lingual *Atlantic*, based on the story of the Titanic disaster. Other early English talkies included *Juno and the Paycock*, *Arms and the Man*, *Dark Red Roses*, *Kitty*, and *The Manxman*. The comedies were headed by Walter Forde's *Would You Believe It?* Sydney Howard in *Splinters*, the first

English talkie revue, *Elstree Calling*, and Harry Tate in a new version of his music hall sketch *Motoring*.

The Americans offered more. There was George Arliss in *Disraeli*, Metro-Goldwyn-Mayer's spectacular *Broadway Melody*, Ruth Chatterton in *Madame X*, Ronald Colman as *Bulldog Drummond*, Norma Shearer in *The Last of Mrs Cheyney*, and Warner's overwhelming *Gold Diggers of Broadway*. *Rio Rita*, starring John Boles and Bebe Daniels, introduced two new comedians from the stage, Bert Wheeler and Robert Woolsey. Ex-jockey Woolsey and his partner had appeared in the stage version, and were filmed in their original roles. Later they appeared together in *The Cuckoos, Dixiana, Half Shot at Sunrise, Hook, Line and Sinker, Diplomaniacs, So This is Africa, Hips Hips Hooray, Cockeyed Cavaliers*, and *Kentucky Kernels*. Their natural successors in later years were Abbott and Costello.

Hollywood romance was provided by Charles Farrell and Janet Gaynor, who sang and talked in *Sunny Side Up*, and from France came Maurice Chevalier, to star with Jeannette Mac-Donald in Ernst Lubitsch's gay *The Love Parade*. Chevalier, one of the first really great international stars of the sound film, had been born of humble parents in one of the poorest suburbs of Paris. When his father died he was eleven, and he went to work, winning an amateur contest two years later at a local theatre by appearing as a red-nosed comedian and imitator of popular stars of the day. When eighteen he became dancing partner to Mistinguette, the legendary idol of the Paris stage. Invited to America by Jesse Lasky to star in *The Innocents of Paris* (1929), Chevalier made an immediate hit, and after starring in *The Love Parade, The Big Pond, The Playboy of Paris, The Merry Widow*, and other pictures, went to Britain to make *The Beloved Vagabond* before returning to France to star in further French films.

One of Britain's early talkie stars was Sir Harry Lauder, who had long before the 1914 war acted and mimed for synchronized pictures. He had also appeared with Chaplin in a 500 foot film made in America for the War Loan. That was in 1918, when the name of Lauder was as well known as that of Chaplin. In 1923 he adapted his famous song *I Love a Lassie* as a film, and four years later it was announced that he was to receive ten thousand pounds for starring in Welsh-Pearson's version of John Buchan's *Huntingtower*. Later the grand old man of the music halls appeared in *Auld Lang Syne*, and in a dismal Fox-British quota picture called *The End of the Road*. However, his success as a film personality did not equal that of his fellow-countryman Will Fyffe, who made his film début in the thirties, and was soon recognized by Hollywood as a fine character actor and master of pathos. Will Fyffe made several pictures in Britain and America, and on the outbreak of war in 1939 was invited to return to Hollywood, which he refused to do because he felt that the place for a Scot during the war was in Britain.

*

One of the first English musical revues was *Elstree Calling*, directed by Adrian Brunel in 1930 for British International Pictures in twelve days at a cost of about £13,000. In Britain alone the film was booked for five or six times its cost, and it was later given eleven new sound tracks, all in different languages. In Australia and New Zealand, where the public was anxious to hear the English voice on the screen (as opposed to the American) the picture was a tremendous success. In Cape Town a cinema was called *The Elstree Bioscope*.

Elstree Calling relied on the music hall and musical comedy stars of the day for its performers, and for good measure added one or two screen players who were under contract at Elstree. The cast list was as follows:

Anna May Wong	John Longden
Jack Hulbert	Bobby Comber
Cicely Courtneidge	Hannah Jones
Gordon Harker	Helen Burnell
Will Fyffe	Lawrence Green
Teddy Brown	Ivor McLaren
Lily Morris	Beksoff
Donald Calthrop	The Three Eddies
Jameson Thomas	Charlot and the Adelphi Girls
Tommy Handley	

The London *Daily Mail* called *Elstree Calling* 'by far the best talking film revue'. It was in fact little more than a collection of music hall and musical comedy acts, connected by a slender story. But there was humour, singing, dancing, and a little bit of everything in it, which was what the public wanted. Furthermore, it was directed resourcefully, and it delighted those members of the audience in Britain who had grown rather tired of the American nasal accent.

It might be interesting to compare extracts from two trade press revews, showing how this typically English picture stood up against the might of Hollywood, as revealed by a similar musical revue film :

The Bioscope, February 12, 1930

'Elstree Calling'

(British International Pictures)

It was an ambitious idea to present a film revue including such a cast of popular favourites in every branch of musical and dramatic entertainment, but Adrian Brunel, with the co-operation of Alfred Hitchcock, Andre Charlot, Paul Murray, and Jack Hulbert, has completed a very difficult task with gratifying success. . . . Mr Brunel has had the happy idea of connecting the different items by the services of a broadcaster, with glimpses of Gordon Harker trying to participate in the revue by getting it on a television set of his own construction, and the constant interruptions of Donald Calthrop, . . . and it is to be regretted that Harker only succeeds in seeing and hearing Tommy Handley say 'Good Night, everybody,' for every item is well worth seeing and hearing . . . the whole revue is a very successful attempt to present together so varied and brilliant a collection of popular artists.

The Bioscope, February 19, 1930

'Happy Days'

(Fox Films)

Minstrel show revue introducing Fox stars in a show arranged as a benefit for an old show-boat owner now down on his luck. Slight love interest. Lavish settings, many giving effect to novel ideas. A few good song numbers; some excellent chorus singing and dancing. Such story as there is merely introduces the Fox players in one special show, which makes up quite 75 per cent of the picture. Among those who contribute numbers are Janet Gaynor, Charles Farrell, Victor McLaglen, Edmund Lowe, El Brendel, Frank Richardson, J. Harold Murray, Whispering Jack Smith, Marjorie White and Richard, Dixie Lee, Shaun Lynn and Ann Pennington and George MacFarlane.

Three months later a colour version of *Elstree Calling* was available, and *The Bioscope* was reminding its readers that 'the continuous humour makes dull moments impossible, while the director deserves thanks for getting together such an extraordinary collection of talented artists.'

But the competition from Hollywood was very strong. At Universal City Carl Laemmle, whose earlier fortunes we have considered, had already completed the production of the spectacular new musical revue *The King of Jazz*. To produce and direct this mammoth film the English stage producer John Murray Anderson had been invited to leave his favourite Broadway. He was lodged in luxury on the outskirts of Universal City for several weeks before Carl Laemmle sent for him. Anxious to get to work, and to know what plans had been made for the film, the Englishman was impatient with the delay, almost aghast at the lavish expenditure which he felt would never be permitted in his theatre world. At last he was ushered into the presence of the great Carl Laemmle. He was bursting to get on with the job; but Laemmle merely looked at him. 'Turn around,' he said. 'That certainly is a beautiful suit. That must be an English suit . . . yes, it is. Where did you get it?' After this, they talked about English suspenders—or braces, as John Murray Anderson called them.

The King of Jazz, put out at a time when half of the world's films were still silent, but re-issued many times in later years, was an immense financial success. Anderson's flair for elaborate and tasteful production was enhanced by the careful use of colour. In London *The Bioscope* reported 'the settings, which are on a colossal scale, are in most instances of extreme beauty and in every case of dazzling brilliance. The colouring is rich and tasteful, and the photography of consistent excellence.'

Supporting Paul Whiteman and his band were Jeannette Loff, Laura La Plante, William Kent, John Boles, George Chiles, and a large cast. Bing Crosby appeared as one of a vocal trio in a speciality number with the band. Richard Cromwell was a crowd artist. A cartoon in colour showed how Paul Whiteman introduced jazz into the desert. The four theme songs, 'I'd Like to Do things for You', 'Song of the Dawn', 'Happy Feet', and 'A Bench in the Park' were soon being whistled and sung all over

173

America and Europe. In 1931 and 1932 the picture returned, to make more money. It directly influenced the appearance in 1932 of the British dance band leader Jack Payne in *Say It With Music*, which in a more modest way was also a tremendous success. What is more, it confounded the many critics who said that the talking picture was dying, or could not last, by setting a new standard in musical films.

But Universal did not have it all their own way. *Paramount on Parade* boasted a star list which included everyone on the studio pay roll. Supervised by Elsie Janis, it presented magnificent dance spectacles, a dozen theme songs, and featured Maurice Chevalier, George Bancroft, Evelyn Brent, Clive Brook, Nancy Carroll, Ruth Chatterton, Gary Cooper, William Powell, Harry Green, Jack Oakie, Clara Bow, Dennis King, Richard Arlen, Charles Rogers, and Helen Kane.

William Haines, starring in *The Girl Said No* (Metro-Goldwyn-Mayer) appeared as a young man fresh from college starting out on a business career under the impression that he knows everything. The Haines charm was supported by Leila Hyams, Polly Moran, and Marie Dressler.

Meanwhile Al Christie, hopeful that sound would give a new lease of life to the two-reel comedy, was offering *The Fatal Forceps* with Ford Sterling, Bert Roach, and Will King, *The Duke of Dublin* with Charles Murray, Marie Dressler and Polly Moran in *Dangerous Females*, and Louise Fazenda in *Faro Nell, or In Old Californy*. The novelty of the talkies meant that all kinds of films could gain a showing. While Benita Hume and Ivor Novello were filming Novello's play *A Symphony in Two Flats* (with the theme tune played by Jack Payne and his BBC Band) someone else had persuaded Davy Burnaby, Betty Chester, Gilbert Childs, Laddie Cliff, and Stanley Holloway to appear in a modest picture version of their highly successful stage show *The Co-Optimists*. And Charles Laughton and Elsa Lanchester were making a modest series of two-reel comedies written by H. G. Wells and directed by Ivor Montagu, called *Bluebottles*, *The Tonic*, and *Daydreams*. Even Walter Forde was singing (only one song) in *You'd Be Surprised*. He compared favourably with the American gag-comedians, but he was soon to leave the screen in order to become a director.

On October 6, 1930, Paramount Pictures released in Britain *The Love Parade*, a musical comedy on spectacular lines, with witty and amusing dialogue, tuneful music, and clever direction by Lubitsch. It assured the popularity of Maurice Chevalier for many years. From Warner Brothers—the pioneers of talkies— came Al Jolson in *Mammy* and *Say It With Songs*, Edward Everett Horton and Patsy Ruth Miller in *The Hottentot*, the first 100 PER CENT TECHNICOLOR ALL TALKING, ALL SINGING AND DANCING REVUE—*On With the Show*, with Betty Compson, the all-colour *Gold Diggers of Broadway*, Ted Lewis and his Band in *Is Everybody Happy?*, and a dozen dramas, featuring George Arliss, John Barrymore, Pauline Frederick, Grant Withers, Dolores Del Rio, Monte Blue, and Thomas Meighan. Warners were wisely ploughing back their profits, to make sure that in the thirties and forties they could stand up to their rivals, and would never again have to rely on Rin-Tin-Tin or chance— in the form of the talkies—to save the day.

That Hollywood could sometimes laugh at itself was made apparent in *Show People*, directed by King Vidor, with Marion Davies and William Haines. This was described by *The Bioscope* as 'a screamingly funny satire on Hollywood life, full of funny situations with interesting and highly amusing shots of life in the Hollywood studios, with casual appearances by Charles Chaplin, Norma Shearer, George K. Arthur, Douglas Fairbanks, and a score of other celebrities. Whenever we in this country produce a film like this, we shall have acquired the grace to enjoy a real laugh at our foolish selves.'

CHAPTER TWELVE

The Thirties

THE TALKIES WERE now growing up. The constant break-downs in the apparatus, the first juvenile faults in the recording, these had at last given way to a more mature use of sound. Talk for the sake of talking was no longer the rule. Universal's memorable *All Quiet on the Western Front* (1930) proved that the restricted use of sound was more effective than a barrage of conversation. Griffith's first talking picture *Abraham Lincoln*, *Journey's End*, *Hell's Angels*, George Arliss in *Old English*, M.G.M.'s *The Big House*, and Garbo in *Anna Christie* were all rich in conversation, even bursting with dialogue, but it was *All Quiet* which set the standard for the future.

Meanwhile Chaplin was putting the finishing touches to his silent *City Lights*. He had met Virginia Cherrill at a football match, and persuaded her to play opposite him. At a nearby studio Harold Lloyd was making *Feet First*, and for MGM Marie Dressler and Polly Moran were filming *Caught Short*, to be followed by *Reducing* and *Politics*. At the Fox studios Will Rogers was making *So This is London*, following the success of *They Had to See Paris*, which had earned a profit of about 700,000 dollars for the company.

Will Rogers had started his long association with the stage back in 1905, performing as a cowboy spinning ropes. At the Union Square Theatre in New York a chance remark changed his act, and transformed him into an outstanding comedian-philosopher. Rogers, grinning broadly at the audience, remarked casually 'Spinning a rope is lots of fun—if your neck ain't in it.' The audience roared with laughter. And from that moment Will Rogers became a comedian. It was Sam Goldwyn who persuaded him to start filming in 1918. 'When Goldwyn decided to make fewer and worse pictures, he sent for me,' joked Rogers. He made his début in *Laughing Bill Hyde*, made at the Goldwyn studio at Fort Lee, New Jersey, where he later appeared in

30.
*Fred Astaire and
Ginger Rogers in*
FOLLOW THE FLEET

31.
*The Magic of Holly-
wood. A sixty acre
studio provides the
setting for a sequence
in the musical film*
ROSALIE

32.
*Will Hay,
Graham
Moffat and
Moore Marriott
in* OH, MR
PORTER

33.
*Abbott and
Costello in the
second version
of* RIO RITA
(1942)

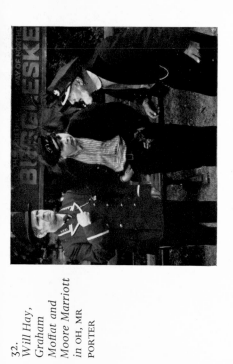

34.
*Laurel and
Hardy in*
BLOCKHEADS

35.
*Fred Mac-
Murray, Bing
Crosby and
Donald
O'Connor in*
SING YOU
SINNERS

Almost a Husband (1919), *Honest Hutch* (1920), *Boys Will Be Boys* (1921) and other films.

Rogers did not return to the screen until 1929, when he became one of Fox's biggest money makers. According to Frank Borzage, the director of *They Had to See Paris* and *Young As You Feel*, he was an outstanding screen comedian because he had the gift of making audiences forget the wise-cracking character, seeing only a simple human being torn with emotion. Altogether he made some fifteen pictures for Fox, which made him one of the best-loved comedians on the screen. After *Happy Days* (1930) came *Lightnin'*, *Ambassador Bill*, *Business and Pleasure*, and *Too Busy to Work*, in which he appeared as a carefree tramp. In 1933 came *State Fair*, with Rogers as a lovable pig farmer, and *Doctor Bull* in which he played a country doctor. In *Mr Skitch* he was a shop proprietor, and in *David Harum* a banker and horse dealer.

'It's a terribly hard job,' said Will Rogers. 'The guys that tell you they can be funny at any minute, without any effort, are guys that ain't funny to anybody but themselves. I depend on the newspapers for most of my inspirations. Some days there is material for several good lines. Then there may be a week when there isn't a little thing worth mentioning. About once a month I turn out a gag that I get a big kick out of myself.'

For many years 'America's Unofficial Ambassador,' as he was widely known, had been famous as a wit and a philosopher. He was in fact very like the characters he played on the screen. After playing polo with the Prince of Wales he said, 'The Prince was well mounted. He knows good horse-flesh when he sees it. I was ridin' a coupla dogs. One I could have got off and outrun myself.'

When Rogers was killed in an aeroplane crash all America mourned his passing. He had completed only three of the ten pictures which he was required to make under a new contract with Fox, for which he was receiving 200,000 dollars a picture. There was nobody to replace him, and nobody has done so. Perhaps Eddie Cantor summed him up best when he said 'Will Rogers was probably the most beloved man of our time. He was one man in the entertainment world who more than balanced by his exemplary life any of the scandals involving people of the theatre. He was the most charitable, most tolerant man I have ever known. There wasn't an atom of envy in his system.'

*

In Britain the newcomers were consolidating their positions. Although their pictures did not claim attention in America, home audiences and a large public in Australasia, South Africa, and other parts of the world found the new British talkies entertaining. The new comedy centre seemed to be Elstree, where Stanley Lupino was making *Love Lies*, Nelson Keys and Sydney Howard were starring in *Almost a Divorce*, and Ralph Lynn and Winifred Shotter were appearing in *Chance of a Night Time*. Scripts were being prepared for two further Sydney Howard films, *Up for the Cup*, and *Tilly of Bloomsbury*, and Seymour Hicks, Edmund Breon, and Margot Grahame were making *The Love Habit*.

All these players were from the theatre, and for stage actress Margot Grahame *The Love Habit* was to prove a turning point. She had made her film début in *Rookery Nook*, after appearing in the play at the Aldwych theatre. Although her part had been only small she was offered the leading role with Seymour Hicks in the farce *The Love Habit*, her performance arousing great interest and gaining her a contract at Elstree. Everyone, headed by Hannen Swaffer, predicted a great future for Margot Grahame, who was now much in demand in British studios, playing roles which required the glamour and beauty which most English screen actresses did not seem to possess. The average British leading lady was cold and distant, often talking with an incredible so-called Mayfair accent. A young star who had charm, beauty, and vitality could walk off with the picture, if she had acting ability.

Inevitably, Margot Grahame went to Hollywood, where in 1935 she won a coveted role in John Ford's production of Liam O'Flaherty's *The Informer*, a memorable film which gained an Academy award, and a long-term contract for Margot. Now followed leading roles in R.K.O.-Radio Productions, opposite Herbert Marshall, Frederic March, Chester Morris, Akim Tamiroff, Richard Dix, Anton Walbrook, and other leading stars. The *Picturegoer* magazine found her performance as Milady in *The Three Musketeers* 'exceedingly good'. She added beauty and a polished performance to an exciting production of *Michael Strogoff*, shone brightly in *The Arizonian* with Richard Dix, and in Cecil B. de Mille's *The Buccaneer*, and partnered Herbert Marshall attractively in *Fight For Your Lady*. When she returned to England to star with Phyllis Calvert in *Broken Journey* (1948) she started a new career in British films, went to Italy to appear with Orson Welles in *Black Magic*, and later played in *I'll Get You For This*, *The Romantic Age*, *The Crimson Pirate*, and *The Venetian Bird*, adding glamour and genuine acting ability to all her pictures. Yet her whole film career had started in the British and Dominions studio at Elstree, with two or three lines in a minor role in *Rookery Nook*.

While Margot Grahame was making *The Love Habit* for Harry Lachman, another newcomer to the screen was making her début with Gene Gerrard only a few hundred yards away, at the British International studio next door. The picture was called *Out of the Blue*, and the newcomer was named Jessie Matthews. She had started her career dancing in the side-streets of Soho, and had risen to stardom on the stage in Cochran revue. Although she did not attract particular attention in *Out of the Blue*, Jessie Matthews was soon to be Britain's leading musical screen star, following *There Goes the Bride* with *The Man from Toronto*, *The Midshipmaid*, *The Good Companions*, and a number of highly successful musical comedy pictures, of which *Gangway* and *First a Girl* were the best.

At Ealing, where imposing new studios had risen next door to the old Barker studio, Basil Dean was introducing another newcomer to the screen—Gracie Fields, who was 'having a go' at the pictures, with Ian Hunter in *Sally in our Alley*, which had been adapted by Miles Malleson from the play *The Likes of 'Er*. This relatively modest picture proved to be a tremendous money maker. It introduced Gracie Fields to an immense new public which was soon demanding not only more film appearances from her, but more gramophone records, more broadcasts, and more music hall appearances. Within six years Gracie Fields was the most popular actress on the stage, screen, or radio, in Britain. Her several films, although not up to the high technical standard of Hollywood, could often make more money in Britain than the most star-studded and expensive of America's mammoth productions. 'Our Gracie' became a national figure, a symbol of the working girl, singing through the years of the depression.

She had started her career twenty years earlier, singing in a local cinema. After playing in a revue called *Yes I Think So* at Manchester, she went to London to appear in 1915 at the Old Middlesex music hall, and in 1918 appeared in the revue *Mr Tower of London*, which had a phenomenal run until 1925. Sir Gerald du Maurier engaged her to play in *S.O.S.* at the St James's theatre in 1928, and in the same year she appeared at her first Royal Command Variety Performance before the King and Queen at the London Coliseum.

After *Sally in Our Alley* Gracie Fields made several other films, including *Looking on the Bright Side*, *This Week of Grace*, *Sing as We Go*, *Queen of Hearts*, and *Shipyard Sally*. Her American film career was not an outstanding success, but she herself could not give a poor performance, or fail to captivate audiences with her tremendous personality, the quality and range of her voice, her unique sense of comedy, and her identification with the working girl.

In 1935 came *Look Up and Laugh*, made at Ealing by Basil Dean. In this Gracie Fields was supported by Alfred Drayton, Douglas Wakefield, Billy Nelson, Harry Tate, Robb Wilton, Tommy Fields, Jack Melford, and Kenneth Kove. The fifteenth name in the cast was that of a recently discovered film actress, Vivien Leigh, who had previously appeared in two films, *The Village Squire* and *Gentleman's Agreement*. 'It seems almost inconceivable,' reported *Film Weekly* magazine, 'that J. B. Priestley could have written the story.' The comedy was broad slapstick, with a galaxy of music hall comics wallowing in soapsuds, running amok in a china shop, getting mixed up with hoses, and indulging in a dizzy flight in an aeroplane out of control. The picture was a tremendous success, and, in a broadly unsophisticated way, was funny. Why should not J. B. Priestley write a good hearty slapstick knockabout farce if he wanted to? It seems a pity that other leading authors have not followed his example, deluging the screen with soapsuds and hose-water, until it runs down among the audiences, causing havoc among the critics who like their farces French and their comedy conservative. Soapsuds instead of sex!

To direct Gracie Fields in *Queen of Hearts* at Ealing, Basil Dean called in Monty Banks. He had never before met her, but he had for long wanted to direct her in a film. With subtlety he applied a little glamour, which made Gracie more acceptable in the United States. By April 1937, British picturegoers were asking 'What will they do to our Gracie in Hollywood?' But they need not have worried, for she won all hearts—including that of Monty Banks—although she had ceased to be a symbol of the British working class.

1931 was rich in British discoveries. A rising scene stealer named Gordon Harker was playing with Bobby Howes in *Third Time Lucky*, with Leslie Henson in *The Sport of Kings*, and with Richard Bird in *The Professional Guest*. Harker, the son of a famous stage scenic painter, was already well known on the English stage, and had made his screen début in a small part with Carl Brisson in *The Ring*. Now he was stealing the honours from the stars. A protruding lower lip, a fruity cockney accent, and a muttering and abusive contempt for both the rich and haughty and the police—these were his first characteristics. Often he was the burglar who stole not only the silver, but also the film. Soon he was to be one of the most popular of British screen stars.

Britain's lower standard of comedy was typified by *The Temperance Fête* (M.G.M. British, 1932) with George Robey as Bindle, Sydney Fairbrother as his wife, Connie Ediss as Mrs Hearty, Gibb McLaughlin as Mr Hearty, and Seth Egbert as Ginger. The *Bioscope* reported: 'George Robey's impersonations may please some of his ardent admirers, but many will think the maudlin geniality, hiccupping, and lip licking excessive. Production is mediocre.'

In contrast, the same year saw the release of the sophisticated *Service for Ladies*, directed by Alexander Korda for Paramount-British. Leslie Howard was Max, a head waiter who falls in love with a society girl while on holiday in Switzerland. The supporting cast included George Grossmith, Benita Hume, Elizabeth Allan, Morton Selten, and Cyril Ritchard. The film was highly praised in America, and helped to assure the future of London Films and the building by Korda of the vast studios at Denham.

1932 also was a vintage year for the big American companies. *The Champ* (Wallace Beery and Jackie Cooper)—a sentimental family picture—was one of the financial successes of the year, proving that people like a good cry as much as they like to laugh. Buster Keaton struggled not too happily with *The Passionate Plumber*, partnered by Jimmy Durante. Chaplin was resting on the success of *City Lights*, and was not to make another film for several years. The Keystone standard of two-reel comedies was now put on the shelf; Andy Clyde, who was starring in comedies for Sennett, made *Shopping with Wifie*, and there were several Edgar Kennedy mother-in-law mix-ups, but the old order was already dead. In Britain Wallace Lupino and Hal Walters appeared in an unamusing burlesque of J. B. Priestley's *The Good Companions* called *Bad Companions*. And bad they were.

The comedy support was left mainly to the cartoon characters of Walt Disney, and to their several rivals, who were entering the field in increasing numbers. Just as Mack Sennett had met rivalry by maintaining a high production standard, by devising new ideas and fresh gags, so now did Disney. The *Terry Toon comedies*, *Aesop's Fables*, the *Merrie Melodies* and the *Tom and Jerry series* were, with the many other cat and mouse epics, seldom as well drawn as Disney's popular *Micky Mouse* and *Silly Symphony cartoons*. Because of his technical superiority, Disney towered above his rivals, but he always needed to be a step ahead, and in 1932 he decided to make colour cartoons.

Dr Herbert Thomas Kalmus, who had been making colour films since 1917, had with his associates just perfected the new three-colour Technicolor process. The success of their original two-colour process, particularly in the Douglas Fairbanks picture *The Black Pirate*, had led them to the eventual perfection of the three-colour Technicolor.

Directly Disney saw this he knew that it was what his cartoons needed, and he filmed his next picture, *Flowers and Trees*, in the new process. From this moment neither he nor Dr Kalmus needed to look back. The public started to queue for

Disney, and the film studios lined up for Technicolor cameras and equipment.

*

In Britain the industry was back to full employment, with every studio making pictures, for which there was plenty of talent available. In *Yes Mr Brown* Jack Buchanan was teamed with Margot Grahame and Elsie Randolph, and in *Glamour* Margot Grahame partnered Sir Seymour Hicks, and Merle Oberon was given her first brief part, saying a few lines of dialogue.

Glasgow-born Jack Buchanan had started work in an auctioneer's office, and after an initial failure on the stage of Pickard's Panoptican, Glasgow, had moved to London, where he obtained a chorus engagement at thirty shillings a week at the old Empire, Leicester Square. It was while understudying Vernon Watson (Nosmo King) that he was able to play the leading role, and soon rose to become one of London's most important musical comedy stars. Always immaculately dressed, he danced his way to Hollywood with Jeanette MacDonald in *Monte Carlo* (1930). In Britain his early films included *Squire the Audacious* (1923), *The Happy Ending*, *Settled Out of Court*, *Bulldog Drummond's Third Round*, *Toni*, and *Confetti*. His later talkie successes included *Paris*, *Man of Mayfair*, *Goodnight Vienna*, *Brewster's Millions*, and *When Knights were Bold*. Of the British light comedians Jack Buchanan was rated high at the box-office, although his films could not compare technically with American musical productions.

A comedian with broader appeal was Sydney Howard, who had started his acting career by joining an amateur concert party while still working in a paper merchant's business. Everybody told Sydney that he should go on the stage, so he gave up business to spend a summer with a small concert party at Cosy Corner, St Anne's-on-Sea. After touring in revues he went into the army, and on being demobilized in 1919 he resumed his touring. In 1927 Albert de Courville invited him to London to play in the revue *Box of Tricks*, which led to an important part in another revue, *Hit the Deck*. He made his film début with Nelson Keys in one of the first British talkies—*Splinters*, and was soon making *Tilly of Bloomsbury*, *Splinters in the Navy*, and *Up for the Cup*, in which he appeared as a gormless young man from the North of England who visits London for the Cup Final. These pictures firmly established him as a film comedian, after which Herbert Wilcox, who was then in charge of production at the British and Dominions studio at Elstree, set his directors and script writers on to thinking up new plots and gags for Sydney Howard. The results included *Up for the Derby*, *The Mayor's Nest*, *It's a King*, *It's a Cop*, *Girls Please*, and many more. The standard of comedy was not always high, but it appealed to most Britons. Some years later Sydney Howard co-starred with Gracie Fields in *Shipyard Sally*, and helped Gordon Harker to make *Once a Crook* into an amusing success. In his last film part, as the photographer in J. B. Priestley's *When We are Married*, he stole the acting honours, bringing the film vividly to life directly he appeared.

Over at the Gainsborough studios at Islington, Jack Hulbert was filming. A Cambridge education had led him and his brother Claude first to the amateur stage and then to the London theatre. In *Elstree Calling*, Jack Hulbert had done little more than a stage act, but in *Sunshine Susie* (1931) the English version of a German film, he danced and sang to such effect that he suddenly found himself the British film comedian of the year. Hulbert is the tall fellow with the dancing feet and the big wide grin, who dances his way through offices and along pavements . . . as everyone would secretly like to do. His gaiety, his fresh sense of burlesque, and the very twinkle in his eye, spell disaster to officialdom and dull routine. Everything is suddenly Spring when Hulbert appears. Anything might happen, but—by George—what fun it all is!

The Ghost Train, in which he shared honours with his talented wife Cicely Courtneidge, *Jack's the Boy*, in which Walter Forde directed them, and *Love on Wheels*, with Gordon Harker, followed rapidly. For *Happy Ever After* the Hulberts went with Sonnie Hale to join beautiful Lillian Harvey in Germany. The picture was directed by Erich Pommer as a bi-lingual film, but the results were not altogether successful. One of the most amusing sequences had nothing to do with the Hulberts, but showed Lillian Harvey in a fantastic dream, arriving in Hollywood as a film star. This satirical touch was cleverly produced and photographed. But the rest of the film, in spite of attractive music and songs, was patchy.

However, a moderate success was no set-back to Jack Hulbert. His long chin, a powerful personality, and the sheer joy of hard work kept his name up in cinema lights throughout the thirties. After *The Camels are Coming* (1933) for which he went to Egypt, came *Jack Ahoy*, *Falling For You*, *Bulldog Jack*, and *Paradise for Two*. Of his later pictures the best was *Take My Tip*, in which Hulbert and Cicely Courtneidge proved that the films in which they appeared together were notably funnier than those in which they appeared separately. When Cicely Courtneidge had made *Soldiers of the King* and *Aunt Sally* the results were considerably less amusing than in *Jack's the Boy* or *Take My Tip*. Hollywood seemed unable to do justice to the Courtneidge humour, especially in *A Perfect Gentleman*, and a return was wisely made to filming in Britain.

Then there was the Aldwych team—a hilarious company of players whose names became by-words in Britain during the thirties. Before its original presentation at the Shaftesbury theatre, London, in April 1922, the play *Tons of Money* had been hawked around London for years. Then Tom Walls and Leslie Henson realized its possibilities, and put it on. When the play moved to the Aldwych theatre—then the white elephant of the London stage—everyone prophesied its failure, but it ran for 737 performances and started the fortunes of everyone associated with it.

Tom Walls, ex-policeman and actor, who was to be film director, Derby winner, football pools promoter, and towards the end of his career a film character actor, was partnered by the supreme English silly ass—Ralph Lynn. The film version of *Tons of Money* (1931) was directed by Tom Walls, with Ralph Lynn, Yvonne Arnaud, Mary Brough, Robertson Hare, and Madge Saunders. In this and in *Mischief* and *Just My Luck* Ralph Lynn appeared without Walls, but the farces in which they both appeared, together with Winifred Shotter and the Aldwych team of players, were the more successful.

Rookery Nook, *Plunder*, *Chance of a Night-Time*, *Thark*, *On Approval*, *Leap Year*, *The Blarney Stone*, and *For Valour* were a few of the Aldwych films, some adapted from stage farces, some written for the screen. When the Walls–Lynn partnership was broken, only Robertson Hare was left to appear in this type of film, making infrequent appearances with Alfred Drayton or Gordon Harker, to remind cinema patrons of the golden days of the Aldwych team. But some twenty years after its first showing, the comedy *Thark* was still showing in cinemas in Britain.

Fighting Stock (1935) written by Ben Travers and directed by Tom Walls, showed Walls in a favourite role, as a testy baronet with a roving eye for women, a passion for port, and big ideas for his career as a fighting man. His nephew (Ralph Lynn) was a silly ass with a roving eye, but no fighting instincts. Robertson Hare was the browbeaten little secretary with strong leanings towards respectability. The plot, like most of the later Walls–Lynn films, hardly lived up to the reputation created by the author and the team some years before.

Ralph Lynn had started acting at Wigan, appearing in a wild and woolly melodrama called *King of Terrors* for a princely thirty shillings a week. In *Women and Wine*, at Nottingham, he played five parts for a pound a week. 'They called me the travelling lunatic asylum,' he revealed in later years. 'I was for ever rushing to and fro changing my whiskers.' At one time he earned a precarious living as a billiards marker. Then came 1922, the stage success *Tons of Money*, and some eight years later a unique position on the British screen.

*

Transferring a subject to the screen is a difficult task. Sometimes the finished product bears very little resemblance to the original.

J. B. Morton, 'Beachcomber' of the *Daily Express*, once went to a conference at the Shepherds Bush studios, where his famous Narkover characters were being incorporated in a film called *Boys Will be Boys*. To his surprise he discovered that Will Hay was to play not the part of Dr Smart Allick, but the role of Alexander Smart.

Mr Morton protested that it did not make sense, that the 'Beachcomber' public would expect to see his character Smart Allick and nobody else, and that the name Alexander Smart meant nothing at all. It was ludicrous, and of course, Mr Hay *must* be Smart Allick.

But it was no use. Mr Morton protested further, and at greater length, all without result. They did not seem to see his point. And Will Hay appeared in the film as—Alexander Smart.

CHAPTER THIRTEEN

The British Quota Boom

WHEN IN 1933 a young film casting director picked up a script at the new studios at Littleton Park, Shepperton, Middlesex, he did not realize that he was beginning a career. The studio was a single small round stage which had been built in the grounds of the sixty acre park, close to the old manor house, which had in its time sent a pack of hounds to join the Duke of Wellington's troops in the Peninsular War. The young man's name was John Baxter.

Baxter had no knowledge of films when he first went to the tiny studio which was so ambitiously named Sound City. All his experience had been gained touring the provinces with opera, comedies, and revues. But he had kept his eyes open, and was especially familiar with the people of the industrial areas, and the world of the music hall. In his spare time he observed keenly not only how people lived, but what they said, the jokes that made them laugh, the troubles that made them grumble. In the depressed areas of the late twenties and the early thirties there was often plenty to complain about.

At Sound City Baxter was the casting director, responsible for the choosing of players, and the gathering together of the 'crowd' or 'extra' artists. It was while he was sitting in a car, driving down to the studio, that he idly picked up the film script, and looked at the typescript. What he read interested him greatly. 'I wish I could help to make a picture like this,' he said. His wish was realized only a week later, when he was asked to act as associate director on the film, a modest little picture about an ex-officer of the 1914 war, who is down but not quite out. When things look desperate, he receives an invitation to attend a regimental reunion at a large London hotel. The officer attends, and after dinner gives all the money he has in the world—a single note—to help an unfortunate comrade.

This film, directed by Ivar Campbell, was called *Reunion*. It was modestly made, and it took only a fortnight to produce.

But it received such favourable press notices, and such enthusiastic comment from the public, that the little team at Shepperton, half professional and half amateur, was greatly encouraged. It was felt that John Baxter, in particular, could add a touch of sincerity which was seldom found in British studios.

If Hepworth had been encouraged by Wardour Street, London, to continue making films into the thirties he might have found a worthy partner in Baxter, for at a time when the accent in most British studios was distinctly American, and Elstree and Shepherd's Bush were devoting their attention to glamour and bedroom farce, here was a new director who actually wished to reflect the English scene, to put real people, with their native humour, on the screen.

Not for years, and never in Britain, had anyone attempted to film a story about down-and-outs, the submerged tenth of a metropolis, the embankment and alley dwellers of the world. It was a subject which Chaplin had personally portrayed in *City Lights*, and von Sternberg had depicted in *The Salvation Hunters*. But to get too far under the skin of humanity was considered by the film industry to be uncommercial, to court financial disaster. Wardour Street therefore noted with surprise that Baxter had been asked to direct a film called *Doss House*, without a woman in the cast, with no star names. Not a blonde, no theme song, not even an attractive title. How could it be a success?

Doss House cost some £4,000 to make, and was filmed in a single modest set, representing the inside of a London 'flop house'. Here were collected all the dregs of humanity—the men of the streets and the gutter, who might seem to the casual observer to be men of yesterday with no future, but who were in fact down, but not out. Warmly and with rich sentiment, Baxter moved his camera among the characters, bringing out the Cockney humour, the problems of people, the determination of the forgotten. The players were mostly small-part actors and crowd artists, some of whom were themselves desperately in need of work. The clothes they wore were genuine, the make-up was slight, the air was thick with smoke and the smell of humanity crowding together for warmth and comfort. But above all rose the humour of the down-and-out, his only pro-

tection against a society which had little use for him. All the
flotsam and jetsam of life was crammed into sixty minutes by a
cast of players to whom in later years Baxter offered work
whenever it was possible.

Doss House was a tremendously moving experience, claiming
the immediate attention of the press. In his innocence of film
methods, Baxter had moved his camera freely up and down the
lines of faces, in and out among the players, in their rags and
newspapers, their sacks and tatters. The microphone was used
sparingly, so that without knowing it, Baxter made what is now
known as a semi-documentary picture, for it was a film with
only a slight story, but possessing great social significance.

The czars of Wardour Street paid very little attention to it,
for two reasons; it did not boast a star name, and it was cheaply
made. These two factors were enough to condemn it. But fortunately the public liked it, and the film made a handsome profit.
So Baxter was encouraged to go ahead, and think of another
bright idea.

Song of the Plough came next, a modest tribute to the farmers
of Britain, written by Reginald Pound and filmed almost entirely on the Sussex downs, around Lewes. With a little money
to spare, Sound City could afford a slightly more ambitious
picture, and Baxter now concentrated on filming all the everyday events of the English countryside—the ploughing, the sow-
ing, the harvesting, the market and the country fair, the village
inn and the sheepdog trials. Stewart Rome (who had been in
Reunion) played the part of a gentleman farmer, hard hit by
agricultural conditions in the early thirties, and Allan Jeayes,
David Hay Petrie, and some relatively unknown players completed the cast. The real hero of the film was the cameraman
who had gone with Baxter out into Sussex and had photographed superbly what Hilaire Belloc has described as

> . . . along the sky the line of the Downs,
> So noble and so bare.

The film opened with scenes of horses ploughing against a
background of high white clouds. It would be difficult not to be
moved by the beauty of these sequences. Yet on seeing them, one

important film magnate was heard to say, 'Well, when is the picture going to *start*?'

Baxter did not forget to introduce laughter into *Song of the Plough*. His postman, his crowd at the fair-ground, the demonstrator with a patent stain-remover at Lewes cattle market—all contributed humour. The picture went into the programme at the Empire, Leicester Square, was given a special press show by Metro-Goldwyn-Mayer, and was then booked on the Odeon cinema circuit. When it reached Australia, New Zealand, and South Africa, it earned considerable applause, for it gave many people overseas *their first opportunity* of seeing rural England.

Baxter now looked around for another homely story, and found it in the tale of a London flower seller (Mary Clare), set against a cheery background of Covent Garden market, and the fruity humour of cockney life. *Say It With Flowers*, with Ben Field and George Carney, was produced by Julius Hagen at Twickenham under a quota film contract with Radio Pictures. It was Hagen who had wondered when *Song of the Plough* was going to start. Now he had given Baxter a contract to direct for him, and was making at least £2,000 per picture, per fortnight.

For his part as a fish and chip specialist George Carney, one of the great names of the English music hall, spent days haunting the little eating-shops around Shoreditch and Hackney, studying not only the way people spoke and moved, but their viewpoints and opinions. While making careful mental notes of everything he saw, he heard a road-sweeper say to a companion: 'Well, you can say what yer like abaht old Alf, but 'e sweeps rahnd a lamp-post as pretty as any bloke I ever saw!'

Inevitably, Carney's characterization in the film was brilliant, but he came of a school which does not exist today. For a long time he had been with Karno's 'Mumming Birds', and it was there that he struck up a friendship with Chaplin which never waned. In those days Carney used to sing a song called 'On the Promenade,' and night after night Chaplin would stand in the wings and watch. Years afterwards, in 1921, Carney was lunching with Chaplin at the famous Brown Derby in Hollywood. During lunch, Carney casually mentioned his old act. In a flash Chaplin had jumped up, and was performing the entire act, singing the whole song from beginning to end, complete with the comedy patter. He had remembered everything.

In *Say It With Flowers* two famous music hall stars, Florrie Forde and Charles Coburn, appeared. This started Baxter off on a music hall path which was perhaps not always entirely successful, for other producers and directors were doing the same thing. Flanagan and Allen, Tommy Trinder, George Robey, Lucan and McShane, Frank Randle, and other variety stars appeared in his pictures, but his comedy touch was surer when his comedians were only incidental to the story, providing relief for a more important theme. The story and the film itself have always been more vital than the mere presence of a comedian, as Chaplin had first pointed out to Mack Sennett many years previously. Where Baxter ignored this rule the film suffered.

His next subject was *Flood Tide*, a story of London's river, in which George Carney stole the honours as the bargee. In *A Real Bloke* Carney was assisted by Mary Clare, who helped him to put something of the humour of a cockney navvy on to the screen. Baxter's later films, *Love on the Dole*, *The Common Touch*, and *Men of Yesterday*, all contained comedy cameos. In Walter Greenwood's *Love on the Dole* the young north country lad (Geoffrey Hibbert) staying in Blackpool for the first time, creeps into the bathroom to inspect the bath—something he has never before been able to use, for they haven't got a bath at home. It was Baxter's way of reminding his audience that not everyone in the world owned a bath on Cecil B. de Mille lines, although Hollywood might suggest it.

In most of his earlier films Baxter depended for his comedy and character studies on a number of highly dependable players who were hand-picked from the theatre, music hall, and screen. Faces with character in them were what he wanted, and he found them among such artists as George Carney, Mark Daly, Johnnie Schofield, Edgar Driver, Roddy Hughes, Dick Francis, Len Morris, Freddie Watts, Harry Terry, and Vi Kaley. These were some of the 'regulars,' the folk who could be depended upon to give their best performance every time, having years of experience behind them. Many felt that, like Hepworth, Baxter should form a stock company of such players, but it would have been a costly undertaking. Instead he had to be content to use the 'regulars' whenever he could, and some of these players had but to appear on the screen to steal the picture. Many could have done well in Hollywood if they had gone there.

For Baxter, George Robey starred in *Birds of a Feather*, adapted from the novel *A Rift in the Loot*. This was a farce, the Prime Minister of Mirth playing the part of a sausage king who rents a castle in order to be a country gentleman, with disastrous results. During the making of this picture at Shepperton, Robey was required to stand in a hall while Veronica Brady, as his wife, dropped a vase on to his head. Thin wax vases were produced by the property department, and Robey watched a demonstration in which the assistant director, Bob Jones, stood still while vases were thrown down on to his head. Robey rehearsed the scene, falling back with the shock, then slowly recovering and opening his eyes.

'Now look, George,' said Baxter, 'when the vase hits you, you glance up, see Veronica up above you, and register anger, like this. You're furious at getting the vase on your head. We shall take a close-up.'

George Robey thought for a second. 'A close-up?' he said. 'Now look here, wouldn't it be much funnier, I meantersay, if I recover, then I roll my eyes like this, look up, and see Veronica up above, and say nice and loudly . . . "You . . . . . !" '

Everybody in the studio gasped. It was a word which had not then been heard on the screen. But Baxter did not flinch, nor did he bother to explain to Robey that it couldn't go onto the screen. 'That's right, George,' he said. 'You go ahead.' And that is how they filmed it, so that next day, when the day's work was projected in the studio theatre, everyone crowded in to see the scene in which George Robey so magnificently exclaimed on the screen the word which no one had ever heard in a film. But, not surprisingly, this sequence did not appear in the completed picture, being left on the cutting-room floor.

The technique so successfully employed in later years by Michael Balcon at Ealing was first foreseen by John Baxter in the thirties, and was captured by him in all his more serious pictures. For about £4,000 it was possible to make *Doss House* or *Song of the Plough*, completing the picture in three or four weeks for delivery to the distributors, who paid a pound a foot for the film—about £6,000 for a sixty-minute subject. This method of making quick money appealed to many financiers, for while Baxter and a small minority were struggling with limited means to make worth-while pictures, Britain's screens were being cluttered up with many 'quota quickies' which were anything but distinguished. These films had to be shown by law, but at such cinemas as the Empire, Leicester Square, they were often shown only in the mornings, to empty seats or to the theatre cleaners. Of the supporting features, Baxter's were almost the only British quota films to be shown at every performance in this cinema.

'If you can make them laugh, you can make them think,' said Baxter. In one film he wished to show boys playing cricket in the cobbled streets of an industrial city, a sequence intended to emphasize the fact that in the big cities of Britain there are hundreds of children who have no playing-fields, but must play in the streets. Baxter knew that the best way to put this over was by means of a comedy 'gag'. He therefore opened his sequence with the game of cricket in progress in a yard—the wickets painted on a wall, the group of working lads enjoying their lunch-hour game. The bowler delivers the ball, the batsman hits out, and the ball soars away out of the picture. The players stand still and wait silently, and suddenly there comes a crash, followed by the tinkle of broken glass. At once the game is abandoned, as all the players rush off in different directions.

Baxter is a shy, retiring man, who has been known to go and see a Frank Capra film instead of attending one of his own trade shows. When he and a partner ran a film casting agency in London's Regent Street, his office was visited daily for several years by a queue of film 'extras,' the guinea-a-day crowd artists, who hoped for work. Some were young and well dressed, but many were old and struggling to keep up appearances. It was a hard life. Just before Christmas one year Baxter said to his casting assistant, Archie Woof: 'Archie, have a look at the books and see who had a bad year. We could afford to do something for about a hundred of them.'

Archie Woof, who knew nearly every actor and actress in London by their Christian names, and needed no list to say which could do with a helping hand, looked through the books. Then he and Barbara Emary, the production assistant, made up a hundred gift parcels, each containing a full Christmas dinner —a bird, pudding, a bottle of wine, and all the trimmings. These were taken out to a hundred little flats and dwelling places, where the forgotten 'extras' lived, to be left inside doors, or with the neighbours. In most cases the recipient did not know who had sent the parcel. These were the folk whom Baxter and Archie Woof always tried to squeeze into a film, if it were humanly possible.

John Baxter's pictures were rich in human sentiment and comedy, and the team which grew up around him at Shepperton in the early thirties was destined in later years to contribute largely to the making of the best type of British films. At Sound City, Norman Loudon had collected in his studio many new-comers to the industry, who were trained under the 'quota quickie' system. These included Anthony Kimmins (as film star and director); John Bryan, who later won an Academy Award as art director of *Great Expectations*, and produced *The Card*; Laurence Irving; cameraman Hone Glendinning; director Ralph Thomas (who started as a junior in the cutting rooms); pro-ducer Ralph Bettinson; producer Raymond Stross (who started as a clapper-boy); cameraman Guy Greene (who was also to win an Academy Award); Edward Woods, the stills photographer who was to become head of the stills department of the Rank organisation; assistant director Anthony Gilkinson, who was to become a producer; art director Ralph Brinton; dress designer Elizabeth Haffenden; continuity girl Martha Robinson, who became an author; private secretary Barbara Emary, who be-came a producer; and Frank Launder, who for a time read the scripts in the scenario department. There were many more. Events occurred quickly at Shepperton. John Clements made his film début in a two-reeler called *No Quarter*. An almost un-known actor named Hugh McDermott stepped forward as Stanley to say 'Dr Livingstone, I presume,' to Percy Marmont, playing in *Livingstone* for James FitzPatrick. James Mason, playing juvenile lead in *The Mill on the Floss*, sat in the studio restaurant enjoying a one-and-sixpenny lunch. George Arliss, Will Fyffe, and Paul Robeson met together at tea-time, all working in the studio on different films. Shepperton was a hive of activity.

Other centres for the making of 'quickies' were at Teddington and Twickenham. At Teddington the Warner Brothers-First National company produced a regular supply of quickly-made films, some good, some bad, and many indifferent. In recent years it has been the practice to condemn the British 'quickies,' but the technicians who made them received valuable training. At Teddington there were two art directors who became producers—Peter Proud and Michael Relph. Mario Zampi, Baynham Honri, and Ralph Ince, the veteran actor and director from the old American Vitagraph company, were among the team which Irving Asher assembled. Roy William Neill, who directed many of the pictures, had worked for several leading American studios, and had directed *Viking*, one of Hollywood's first colour pictures. He could claim to have discovered Carole Lombard, Constance Bennett, Jean Arthur, and Edmund Lowe. Alice White had started her studio career as his script girl.

In the thirties and during the first years of the 1939 war the Teddington team produced several hundred feature films, including a large number of comedies. Among the thousands of players who enjoyed the unique spirit of comradeship which existed in such studios in those days were Max Miller, Will Fyffe, Claude Hulbert, Dorothy (Chili) Bouchier, Margot Grahame, Bebe Daniels, Laura La Plante, Roland Young, Oliver Wakefield, Elizabeth Allan, Cyril Ritchard, Billy Hartnell, Richard Greene, Marie Lohr, Wally Patch, Charles Heslop, Jack Donahue, Gus McNaughton, Henry Kendell, and Errol Flynn (in the film which took him to Hollywood).

The pictures varied from the drama of *Flying Fortress* (Richard Greene, Carla Lehmann, Betty Stockfield, directed by Walter Forde) to the comedy of *George and Margaret* (Marie Lohr, Judy Kelly, and Noel Howlett). Max Miller made a series of comedies, Henry Kendall and Claude Hulbert appeared in more farces than they later cared to remember, and Teddington anticipated the Huggett family films by producing *The Briggs Family*, with Edmund Chapman, Mary Clare, Jane Baxter, Peter Croft, Glynis Johns, and Oliver Wakefield. For *A Gentleman's Gentleman*, Eric Blore returned to England to make his British film début, having established himself on the American screen as the perfect English butler. The story was written by his brother-in-law Austin Melford, and the title was suggested by the line which Blore had introduced into the American film *It's Love I'm After*—'If I were not a gentleman's gentleman—I could be such a cad's cad.'

But not all of the Teddington films were good. In 1937 Nervo and Knox, Jack Barty, Hal Gordon, and George Carney appeared in *It's in the Bag*, which a film magazine described as containing 'worn out jokes and feeble knockabout, in a plot which takes continuity into little account.' Indeed, few of the quota pictures were notable. Lupino Lane, too often given poor material by British producers, suffered in *The Deputy Drummer* (Columbia British 1936) which the *Picturegoer* described as an 'amateurish production on stage lines, which is so incredibly weak in plot that it exercises hardly any appeal at all. Lupino Lane's dances are its only asset.' In *Trust the Navy*, made in the same year, Lane was entirely at the mercy of another weak plot, hoary jokes, and material which was quite unworthy of his talents. In the same year *Don't Rush Me* treated Robb Wilton, Muriel Aked, Peter Haddon, Hal Walters, and Kenneth Kove in similar fashion, giving nobody a chance to rise above the dismal screenplay.

Over at the Fox British studios at Wembley James Mason was starring in *Who Goes Next?*, from the play by Reginald Simpson and James W. Drawbell. At Twickenham, Morton Selten, Jane Carr, Richard Cooper, Davina Craig, and Eva Moore were making *Annie, Leave the Room!*, and at Shepperton the cast of *Radio Pirates*, by Donovan Pedelty, included Leslie French, Warren Jenkins, Mary Lawson, Enid Stamp Taylor, Teddy Brown, Hughie Green, and Roy Fox and his band. At Beaconsfield Maclean Rogers was directing *Marry the Girl*, which he had adapted with Kathleen Butler from the Aldwych farce. It starred Sonnie Hale, Winifred Shotter, Hugh Wakefield, Judy Kelly, Kenneth Kove, Cecil Parker, C. Denier Warren, and the inevitable Wally Patch, who probably appeared in more British films than most actors, and continued to delight audiences every time.

Henry Edwards, who had successfully mastered the talkie

technique after a considerable success in *The Flag Lieutenant* series, was responsible as chairman of the company for the letting of the Teddington studios to Warner Brothers. At Twickenham he directed several comedies, including Edgar Wallace's *The Lad* (with Gordon Harker), *The Private Secretary* (with Edward Everett Horton), the farce *Are You a Mason?* (with Sonnie Hale and Robertson Hare), and a new version of *Squibs*, with Betty Balfour, Stanley Holloway, and Gordon Harker. Ralph Lynn starred for him in *In the Soup*, and Harker starred in *Beauty and the Barge*.

Of the major British comedies of the thirties none was more successful than Alexander Korda's triumphant *The Private Life of Henry the Eighth*. It was said that Korda had heard a London taxi-driver singing the old music hall song 'I'm 'Enery the Eighth, I am . . .' and had been struck by the idea of making a film about King Henry. The story and dialogue were by Lajos Biros and Arthur Wimperis, and their satirical treatment of a rollicking page of history brought sudden fame to Charles Laughton and to everyone connected with the picture. For Laughton, Robert Donat, Merle Oberon, Wendy Barrie, and Binnie Barnes, it brought stardom. For Korda it meant capital, new studios, fame and fortune. Judged the best picture of the year in America, it made Hollywood look to Britain, proving that the best was acceptable anywhere. And rightly or wrongly, it told the world more about King Henry in ninety-five minutes than the schoolmasters could teach.

But it must be recognized that British films of this quality were rare. According to J. B. Priestley (writing in *World Film News* for November 1936), what was really wrong with English film producers in general was that they were too timid. 'A few years ago,' wrote the author of *The Good Companions*, 'a big English company asked me to write a film for them, and I suggested an amusing little story I had in mind that was a good-humoured satire on some aspects of the film world. 'Oh NO!' they assured me, 'we can't possibly satirize the industry!' Yet within a few months of that, Hollywood came out with some crashing satires of itself. All timidity . . . it is timidity that makes the English producers bring out a series of imitations of the milder Hollywood routines.'

This was certainly true of social comedies, which were hardly attempted in Britain, except modestly by John Baxter. Meanwhile Hollywood was producing them by the score on a most ambitious scale. Frank Capra, a master of the art of spinning a modern fairy tale in pictures, was constantly making films in which honest heroes battled with big bad business men and politicians for the sympathy of the audience and the hands of sweet young girls, like Jean Arthur. A genuine belief in the sanctity of home life, in goodness, and in the triumph of right was the recipe for a Capra picture. In *Lady for a Day* an old apple-seller (May Robson) pretended to her absent daughter that she was a wealthy society woman, and was helped in her deception by a hobo friend. For a day they managed to maintain the deception, while the daughter paid them a visit. In *Mr Deeds Goes to Town* and later in *Mr Smith Goes to Washington*, the young knights in armour stood up against the all-powerful machinery of big business and power politics, and won the day. In *It Happened One Night* Capra showed a wealthy father disliking the idea of his daughter being in love with a very ordinary carefree American boy, working in a routine job. It was the small man who came out on top.

Similarly, in John Baxter's more modest *The Small Man* a group of shopkeepers threatened with extinction by a chain store get together and go to London to meet the haughty business chiefs who are threatening their private enterprise. Finding London a wonderful place, they are at first slightly awed by the huge building where the meeting is to be held. Baxter made his little group of small shopkeepers walk along imposing passages, into an immense hall. The woman with the general store, the fish shop proprietor, the baker, and the man who ran the hardware shop looked insignificant in the entrance to the magnificent offices. But once inside the boardroom their courage and sense of humour returned, and they were able to win a tough fight, finally going back in triumph to their row of shops with the assurance that there would be no chain store in their district.

For Capra, who had started his career as a gag man and writer for Harry Langdon, *It Happened One Night* won three Academy awards. Baxter's *The Small Man* is forgotten. While the human comedy treatment of the Capra picture, relying on amusing situations and light-hearted character portrayals, was widely copied in later years by other producers and directors, no other British producer bothered to make the type of film in which Baxter specialized. Perhaps, as J. B. Priestley said, they were too timid?

CHAPTER FOURTEEN

Crosby and Company

OF ALL THE many players who brought happiness into the make-believe world of the cinema, few shone more brightly at this time than Bing Crosby. He had made his film début in *The King of Jazz*, and appeared in some short musical films for Mack Sennett before gaining his first feature role in Paramount's *The Big Broadcast of 1932*.

Almost a legend by the time he made his forty-second picture in 1950, Harry Lillis Crosby had been born the fourth of seven children, and his first job had been in a pickle factory. In turn he became a janitor, a grocery van driver, a boxing match usher, a postal assistant, a farm help and a lumberjack—all before going to the University. A chance meeting with the leader of a local dance band led him to become a drummer at college dances and high school parties. When the band broke up in 1925, Crosby and the leader—Al Rinker—went to Los Angeles to form a music hall act, and as Crosby and Rinker were billed as 'Two boys and a guitar, singing songs in their own way.'

In San Francisco Paul Whiteman saw the act, and gave the boys a contract. With Harry Barris added to form a trio, they became the Paul Whiteman Rhythm Boys, and toured with the big band show for three years before appearing with Whiteman in *The King of Jazz*.

It was Crosby's appearance as a solo singer in a series of two-reelers made by Mack Sennett in 1931 which attracted the attention of the gramophone companies, and subsequently aroused interest amongst the radio sponsors.

Crosby was the first successful radio singer to become an established film star. His personality was built upon the appeal of good looks and pleasant humour, and his songs were intended to appeal to family audiences. They were gay, carefree tunes, calculated to spread a little happiness. From now on he was to bring an immense fortune to his sponsors, great wealth to himself and his family, and pleasure to all who saw or heard him.

Yet the Bing Crosby of the fifties was essentially the same personality as the relatively unknown singer of 1931. Success did not appear to have changed him.

In *College Humour* (1933) he shared acting honours with Richard Arlen, George Burns, Gracie Allen, and Jack Oakie. As a result of *Going Hollywood*, in which he supported Marion Davies, the good-looking young man with the melodious voice was rated among the first ten most popular actors on the American screen. *We're Not Dressing*, with Carole Lombard, came next. Then followed *She Loves Me Not*, with Miriam Hopkins, featuring the song success 'Love in Bloom', which threatened to rival the popularity of Crosby's 'I Surrender Dear' and 'Just One More Chance'.

All over the world people were now singing the Crosby melodies. *Rhythm on the Range*, *Sing You Sinners*, *Pennies from Heaven*, and *East Side of Heaven*, all starring Crosby, were among the most successful films of the thirties. But, as we shall see, he was to reach his greatest popularity during the war years and in the fifties, when the films in which he appeared with Bob Hope were the biggest money makers from the Paramount studios.

*

Bob Hope, who relies mainly on dialogue for his laughs, came to the films in the thirties, like Crosby. The fifth son of an English stonemason, he was christened Leslie Towne Hope at Eltham, where he was born in 1904. When the family went to America he attended high school in Cleveland, and started to learn tap dancing in his spare time. On leaving school he went to work as a clerk to a motor company, where he said afterwards that only his sense of humour kept him his job.

One day in 1920 he heard that Roscoe 'Fatty' Arbuckle was going to make a personal appearance in Cleveland. The rumour was going around that a couple of local stage acts were required to fill the bill before the appearance of the star. Hope, who had kept up his tap dancing and had learned to be an amusing master of ceremonies at motor sales gatherings, asked a friend named George Byrne if he would join him. Together they applied to the local theatre, and to their surprise they were told that they were booked. For two weeks they danced and gagged to packed audiences who had come to see Arbuckle. The great comedian liked their act, and thoughtfully introduced Hope and Byrne to the manager of a touring musical comedy show, who offered them a job at once. It is interesting that Arbuckle, soon to fade completely from the screen, should have helped a future film comedian up the ladder.

In the touring show they danced, did a black-face act, and Hope sang in a quartette and played a saxophone. When it was time for them to move on to the next town everyone helped to pack up the scenery and the props. After three weeks in vaudeville at the Detroit State Theatre they moved to Pittsburgh, and finally they reached New York, where they appeared for several weeks in a bill headed by Daisy and Violet Hilton, the Siamese twins.

One night their manager told them that he had arranged an audition for them. The show was to be a Broadway production —*Sidewalks of New York* (incidentally, later made into a film by Buster Keaton). When the great day arrived, Bob Hope and his partner nervously came out on to the stage, to face the critical gazes of Eddie Downing, Kate Smith, and Ruby Keeler. But they won the job, and appeared in their dancing act in the revue.

Hope soon realized that a dancing act, unless it was sensational, was a slender reed for a stage career. So he decided to start on his own as an entertainer—with patter. But in Chicago he discovered that a performer's life could be very lonely when he was still unknown. No one would give him an audition. 'Before long I was four thousand dollars in debt,' he says. 'I had holes in my shoes, and I was eating doughnuts and coffee. I couldn't afford anything more.'

But eventually he got a job, and was able to pay back his debts and accumulate five thousand dollars. With this backing he determined to storm Broadway, and returned to New York armed with a file of press cuttings and letters from theatres at which he had played. At first he received very little encouragement, but finally he landed a job at the Eighty-Sixth Street theatre, where he appeared just before the last act. To his surprise, he was a success. After the second show offers began to pour in, and he signed a three-year contract to appear with star billing on the R.K.O. chain of theatres. He was given a film test, and appeared in a number of two-reel comedies for Educational Pictures before joining the stage show *Ballyhoo*.

Then came a vaudeville tour, followed by a leading part in the stage show *Roberta*, during the run of which he lent Fred MacMurray his hat and cane to make a screen test for Paramount—the same company for whom he was himself soon to star.

From the stage Bob Hope took his comedy act to the radio, where he immediately began to attract the attention of film producers. Although at first he turned down offers, he was unable to resist the opportunity of appearing in Paramount's *The Big Broadcast of 1938*. In this he scored a great personal success, singing with Shirley Ross the popular song 'Thanks for the Memory'.

By 1939 Bob Hope was a leading film and radio comedian, with a big following on both sides of the Atlantic. Just as war was declared he decided to return to England, to see his grandfather, who was soon to be ninety-seven. He sailed on the *Queen Mary*, and was given a tremendous reception on his arrival in London.

Between 1938 and 1950 he made twenty-eight feature films, the most popular being *The Road to Singapore*, and its successors, in which he was teamed with Bing Crosby and Dorothy Lamour.

Asked who wrote his scripts, Hope said 'I have four or five writers. But I write most of the smart gags myself.'

At the London Palladium in 1951 he was said to be receiving a record fee for his act. Some £15,000, his earnings during his visit to Britain, was given to the Rev. James Butterworth of Camberwell Road, London, to help rebuild his blitzed youth centre, Clubland. Fifteen people accompanied Hope on his tour —four gag writers, two radio technicians, a producer, a secretary, a radio station executive, a sponsor, two agents, a honeymoon couple, and his blonde singer Marilyn Maxwell.

'I am here to work,' he said. 'I have got to get fresh material. I have not acted here before, but my stuff has been over before me . . . so when I get boned up on English personalities and the

English scene I'll get down with my gag writers and work out a complete new routine.'

Talking about golf, Bob Hope said 'My handicap is four.' When asked what the handicap of his rival Bing Crosby was, he replied immediately, 'His age.'

'I just love working,' he said. 'The government likes me to work. It lives on the money I earn. As for England, I like it. The girls whistle right back at you.'

*

Another popular comedian who made his screen début in 1929 and appeared mainly in Paramount pictures during the thirties and forties was Jack Benny. As a boy he had worked in his father's drapery store, but had bought a fiddle and started to take music lessons. Teaming up with a pianist, he played in vaudeville for four years, returning after service in the navy in the first world war to substitute patter for his violin. Soon he began to establish a reputation as a light comedian, and when playing in Los Angeles in 1928 some studio executives from Metro-Goldwyn-Mayer, looking for talent for a musical revue, saw the show and noticed how clever Benny was as a master of ceremonies. Two days later he was invited to sign his first film contract, to play in *The Hollywood Revue of 1929*. This was followed by four further M.G.M. pictures, starting with *Chasing Rainbows*, with Bessie Love and Charles King, and *The Medicine Man*. In 1935 he appeared in *Transatlantic Merry-Go-Round*, and then in *Broadway Melody of 1936*. *The Big Broadcast of 1937* and his later films were for Paramount, for whom he appeared in *College Holiday*, *Artists and Models of 1937*, *Artists and Models Abroad*, *Man about Town*, and *Buck Benny Rides Again*.

In *The Big Broadcast of 1937* Benny was seen as the manager of an American broadcasting station, with George Burns and Gracie Allen as the sponsors of a programme advertising golf balls. Shirley Ross was a crooner, and Ray Milland a newspaper columnist. Benny's comedy is of the talkie variety, depending on wisecracks and dialogue gags. A master of timing and expression, he has proved an accomplished comedian of the more sophisticated type.

In 1933 there appeared on the screen for the first time a new type of entertainer, a man who was to become the world's most popular dancer. This was Fred Astaire, whose name has become synonymous with perfection in the dance routine. He was born in Nebraska, the son of Frederick Austerlitz and Ann Gelius. He and his sister Adele took the name of Astaire early in their careers, and later made the change legal. When Fred was five and Adele just eighteen months his senior, they started taking dancing lessons, and were soon making regular appearances at school and parish concerts. When Fred was eight they went to New York as a juvenile brother and sister dancing act. Their mother, who went with them, sent the youngsters to a dancing school, where Fred learned tap dancing. Just before America entered the first world war a new stage act was born—'Fred and Adele Astaire in New Songs and Smart Dances.' For nine years they played in vaudeville, and appeared in the musical show *Over the Top*, with Ed Wynn.

After this, new shows came in swift succession. *The Passing Show of 1918* was followed by *Apple Blossoms*, *For Goodness Sakes* (which was written for them), *Lady Be Good*, *Funny Face*, *Smiles*, and *The Band Wagon*. In both America and Britain they enjoyed tremendous success, but in 1932 the partnership ended when Adele married the son of the Duke and Duchess of Devonshire, and retired from the stage. With some trepidation Fred decided to carry on alone. But any doubts which he may have had were dispelled by the thirty-two weeks' Broadway run of *Gay Divorce*, which prompted R.K.O.-Radio Pictures to star him in *Flying Down to Rio* with Ginger Rogers. Astaire was at first dubious about his appeal in pictures, having previously accepted an offer to appear in a dance number for M.G.M.'s *Dancing Lady*, with Joan Crawford. The report on his first film test had been 'Can't act, can dance a little'.

Astaire was in London with the stage production of *Gay Divorce* when cables reached him assuring him of the tremendous success of his first two films. When he returned to Hollywood, R.K.O.-Radio teamed him with Ginger Rogers in *Gay Divorce*, and followed it with *Roberta*, *Top Hat*, *Follow the Fleet*, *Swing Time*, and *Shall We Dance?*—all gay and melodious subjects to which the nimble feet of Astaire responded magnificently. The songs 'Cheek to Cheek', 'The Continental', 'Change Partners', and 'Top Hat' became international hits. Everyone wanted to dance over the roof-tops to happiness with Fred Astaire. Those who succeeded included Dolores del Rio, Eleanor Powell, Rita Hayworth, Paulette Goddard, Marjorie Reynolds, Joan Caulfield, Joan Leslie, Judy Garland, Betty Hutton, and Vera-Ellen.

In 1938 came *The Story of Irene and Vernon Castle*, and during the forties the popularity of Fred Astaire, regardless of who partnered him, never faltered. The success of his later films, *Ziegfeld Follies*, *Blue Skies*, *Easter Parade*, *The Barkleys of Broadway*, and *The Belle of New York* proved that whenever he announced his retirement from the screen—which he did frequently—the public demanded his return.

Some might prefer crazier comedy, such as Irene Dunne in *The Awful Truth*, Herbert Marshall in *Breakfast for Two*, or Jean Arthur in *Easy Living*. But family audiences flocked to see Astaire, tapping out twentieth-century rhythm.

And so to Shirley Temple, the darling of the thirties, whose songs echoed round the nurseries of the world, helping to make her one of the richest little girls in America. She was discovered by Charles Lamont of Educational Pictures when he was looking for twenty-five attractive children to play in his *Baby Burlesks* two-reelers. She made her début at the age of three, burlesquing Dolores del Rio as she had appeared in *What Price Glory?* for which she received ten dollars a day. Later, in another brief film appearance she burlesqued Marlene Dietrich, dressed in blue feathers and sequins. From this series she went to Fox Films to appear with James Dunn in *Stand Up and Cheer*.

Soon she was an enormous attraction, her fan clubs throughout the world having a membership of nearly four million. On her eighth birthday she received 135,000 presents and messages. Between her fifth and twelfth birthdays she earned over two million dollars, and by 1944 she was receiving an average of 185,685 letters a day. In Japan two million copies of a magazine bearing only her photographs were sold in six months.

According to W. H. Mooring of *Film Weekly* magazine, Shirley Temple learned her lessons for two hours each day in a luxurious private bungalow at Fox Movietone City, Hollywood. But during the making of *The Little Colonel* (1935) she spent her spare time cutting funny men out of old pieces of newspaper. And just to prove that she was a very ordinary little girl at heart, she could not be persuaded to wait for the correct moment before throwing mud at Lionel Barrymore. Mud pies hurtled through the air long before the cameras were ready, and when it was all over little Shirley Temple was discovered quietly making more mud pies on the studio floor. She wanted to go on throwing them.

While Fred Astaire, Ginger Rogers, Bing Crosby, and little Miss Temple were keeping the world's picturegoers happy, strange things were happening over in Germany, where on March 13, 1933, the Hitler government had constituted a ministry for the enlightenment of the people, under the direction of Josef Goebbels. One of the new minister's jobs was to ban the importation of certain films. A *Reichsfilmkammer* (film board) was set up, to which Jews, non-Aryans, and all political dissenters could not be admitted. In 1934, two Ufa films produced in Germany were prohibited because the instructions of the board had not been obeyed. The Paramount film *Desire* could be smuggled in only when the name of Lubitsch, its director, had been cut out. No German synchronization of *Ruggles of Red Gap* was permitted because of the Lincoln speech on democracy quoted by Charles Laughton.

But in Germany, as in every country where films were shown, there was one star whom everybody flocked to see. This was Walt Disney's cartoon character, Mickey Mouse.

CHAPTER FIFTEEN

Walt Disney

TWO FACTORS HELPED to push the two-reel comedy off the screen; the coming of the double-feature cinema programme, and the birth of Mickey Mouse.

There had been many film cartoons before. In 1909 there was Windsor McKay's *Gertie the Dinosaur*, in 1913 there had been John Bray's *The Artist's Dream*, and in the early twenties there was Pat Sullivan's *Felix the Cat series*, together with the *Tom Webster cartoons*, the *Out of the Inkwell series*, the *Lancelot Speed cartoons*, and many more. Everyone who ever says 'Don't be a Mutt' is paying tribute to *Mutt and Jeff*. But the art of Walt Disney rose far above anything that had preceded him, because of his technical superiority, the skill of his craftsmen, and the advances made by photography.

Disney was born in Chicago on December 5, 1901. His father was an Irish-Canadian, and his mother was of German-American descent. He had three brothers and one sister.

At the age of nine Walter started his first business venture, selling newspapers. He had to get up at three-thirty, and deliver papers until six. Then he went home for breakfast, and so to school. Every evening he went off on his delivery round. Business interfered with pleasure, but he managed to find time to become a member of a local 'gang', to build caves, join a couple of secret societies, and take part in amateur shows. He was interested in the stage and the cinema, and when Charlie Chaplin appeared, his happiness was complete. On amateur nights at the local theatre he gave impersonations of Chaplin, and once won a prize of two dollars. With his chum, a boy named Walter Pfeiffer, he started a juvenile vaudeville act called 'The Two Walts', and together they won prizes in several local theatres.

But young Disney liked drawing best. He did not know why, for nobody else in the family was artistic, nor did he get any particular encouragement from his parents, until he had proved his ability. But his favourite aunt supplied him with pencils and drawing-paper, and a retired doctor who lived nearby bought some of his first drawings, to encourage the young artist.

At the McKinley High School, Chicago, Walt divided his time between drawing and photography, sketching illustrations for the school paper, and taking his first motion pictures with a camera which he bought with his savings. Filming was to interest him increasingly. Not content with school all day, he went at night to study at the Chicago Academy of Fine Arts, where he learned about cartooning from Leroy Gossitt, a member of the *Chicago Herald* staff.

When he was fifteen he was supplying the passengers on the Kansas City-Chicago Railway with peanuts, candy, magazines, and apples. He loved travelling, and liked to hang on the step of the train as it pulled into a station. Sometimes he travelled on the coal car with the driver and fireman. It was a job likely to thrill an imaginative boy.

But the job ended when Walt ate some of the profits. Not that he cared, because in the summer of 1917 there was a shortage of man-power, and he was soon able to get another position working in the post office. It was inevitable, however, that he should want to enlist, as many of the young men of America were doing, in the armed forces. But after the army, the navy, and the Canadian enlistment offices had all told him he was too young, he joined the American Red Cross as a driver, and after a short period of training went to France. His ambulance was distinctive, because it was covered all over with original Disney sketches, which he had painted on to the bonnet and sides.

Disney's first job after the war was with an advertising company in Kansas City. He had to draw farming advertisements, but when the Christmas rush was over he was fired, and went back to the post office. He then decided to set up his own commercial art business, and persuaded a newspaper publisher to give him free desk space in return for advertisement drawings. Here he met a man with the extraordinary name of Ubbe Iwerks—another young apprentice artist without a steady job. They decided to go into partnership, Disney being the contact man and artist, and Iwerks doing the lettering and the office work. During their first month they made 125 dollars—good money, if only they had been able to collect it all.

Both partners were still watching the 'wanted' advertisements, and when they read that a slide company in Kansas City needed a cartoonist, Walt applied for the job and got it, at a salary of thirty-five dollars a week. He turned the commercial art business over to Iwerks, and started to draw advertisement slides for cinemas. Two months later Iwerks joined him, and together they fixed up a small studio in Disney's home, and began to make some short animated advertisement films.

'The slide company used the old cut-out method of animation,' said Disney. 'We joined arms and legs together with pins, and moved them under the camera. I had read of a new method of animation in a book which I had borrowed from the local library, so we tried it out, and convinced the boss that it was a better system. He installed it.'

The system was not really new. As far back as 1909 Windsor McKay had worked on the same lines at the old Vitagraph studio at Brooklyn. In 1914 Earl Hurd was using this principle, tracing moving characters on to transparent sheets of celluloid, and superimposing these over water-colour backgrounds. Each background was used for an entire scene, thus eliminating the earlier technique of sketching a new background for each drawing.

Disney made a short reel of local interest, which he sold to the owner of three large picture theatres. Asked to produce more, he arranged to deliver one film a week—a cartoon of local events. These he was able to make, for sale at thirty cents a foot.

It was while the artist was fumbling around in the realms of animated cartoons that Walt Disney met Mickey Mouse, then completely unknown and unnamed. He had always liked mice; their bright eyes and quick movements fascinated him, and he used to catch them and keep them as pets. One mouse, bolder than the rest, used to crawl over his drawing-board in search of the crumbs with which he was fed. Disney, noting that he seemed to have a distinct personality of his own, called him Mortimer Mouse.

The young artist was impatient. He wanted to carry his experiments further, but he could not afford to give up his job.

However, he was able to enlarge his studio—which now occupied the garage—and could invite other young cartoonists to spend their evenings with him, helping to evolve a new idea, the animation of fairy tales.

For six months they spent their evenings and week-ends on a short subject called *Little Red Riding Hood*. When it was completed, Disney took a chance and left his job with the slide company, to form his own firm, a 15,000 dollar organization created to produce modern fairy tales in cartoon form. Seven short films were completed, and sold to distributors in New York. But unfortunately the distributors went bankrupt, and Disney experienced a lean time, making a song film for a cinema organist, which gave him enough money to buy an ancient film camera, with which he walked around Kansas City taking moving pictures of babies. These he sold to the proud parents, and in August 1923 he had collected together enough money to plan to go to California. To make sure, he sold the camera.

Walt Disney arrived in Hollywood with two suitcases containing an old suit of clothes, some drawing materials, a sweater, and forty dollars. Behind him in Kansas City he left debts which it took him several years to settle. But right down at the bottom of one of the suitcases was a reel of film—the last fairy tale which he had made. The stockholders of the now defunct company had granted him this favour. With this can of film under his arm he tramped around Hollywood for three months, trying to get a job. Every film company gave him the same answer; they could not use the idea, but their New York office might be interested. Since he did not have the fare to New York, Disney sent the film instead, and prepared to wait several weeks for a decision.

The outlook was not hopeful. Walter's only comfort was his brother Roy, who offered sympathy and encouragement, together with 250 dollars. They decided to form a business partnership, but it was a tough proposition, for nobody in Hollywood had ever heard of the Disney boys, nor did anyone care about them. There were thousands of other young people trying to break into pictures. But with the help of an uncle, who lent them 300 dollars, they continued to look around for someone who might be interested in their cartoons.

Unexpectedly there came a reply from New York. An independent distributor not only liked the sample film, but demanded a series of pictures. Walt Disney threw his hat high in the air, and ran out to buy another old camera. Then they rented part of an estate office as a studio, and fixed up stands and tables out of old boxes and crates. Walter taught Roy how to work the camera, and he himself sat up night and day drawing cartoons. With the help of two girls whom they hired for fifteen dollars a week they made their first picture, *Alice in Cartoonland*. One of the girls, Lillian Bounds, later became Mrs Walt Disney.

But the first picture was not a success, and was abandoned. In it Disney tried to combine human figures with cartoon drawings, as Bud Fisher had done in 1916 in his *Mutt and Jeff cartoons*. In later years the same technique was again to be adopted for some of the Disney feature pictures.

To eke out their dwindling capital, Walter and Roy rented a cheap room and ate their meals in a cafeteria. One would order meat, the other vegetables; and they shared them at the same table. Sometimes they ate at home, after which Walter would sit for hours at his drawing board. 'We cooked, ate, and slept in that one room, and had to walk about a mile to reach the bathroom,' he recalled.

When the distributors asked for further films, the boys sent for Ubbe Iwerks, but soon they needed more assistance, and had to bring in another boy who had helped them in Kansas City. The new subjects featured *Oswald the Lucky Rabbit*, and they were distributed by Universal Pictures. They were reasonably successful, but Walt felt that they could be better, so he went with his wife to New York to see the disributors.

Universal were not very pleased with the suggestion that Disney should expand his production methods. The films were selling quite well, but this would hardly justify higher production costs. Disney insisted, and ended up by losing his contract. He sent a telegram to Roy in Hollywood saying that everything was all right, but he was full of misgivings, for he was returning to Hollywood without even a market for his pictures. Things looked desperate.

In the train he talked it over with his wife. They still had their home, a little studio, some money saved, and a few loyal friends. As far as the Disneys were concerned, *Oswald the Lucky Rabbit* was dead. What they needed now was a new character— something unusual, to star in their cartoons. As the train sped across the prairie lands Walter thought of all the characters he might use. A cat? No, that had been done by Pat Sullivan. A dog? Well, perhaps. But there were other dogs in the cartoon world, including Bonzo. Suddenly he thought of Mortimer Mouse. 'I've got it!' he shouted, jumping up. 'A Mouse . . . that's it . . . why didn't we think of it before? A Mouse—that's what we need!'

A little mouse to save the show. All the way across the continent they planned the first mouse cartoon. Mrs Disney helped with suggestions, and gave Walter the encouragement he so badly needed. If there was to be a mouse could there not also be a girl friend? With every mile they grew more excited, making plans for the mice which—did they guess?—were to make their fortunes. If Disney had only known, there was—and is—in Egypt a mural drawing of a mouse almost exactly like Mickey Mouse, drawn several thousand years ago.

The Disneys could hardly wait to tell Roy, to finish the last of the Oswald pictures under their old contract, and start on their new enterprise. Quietly and swiftly they worked, and when the first picture was completed and ready to be run through on the projector they were enthusiastic about it. But looking at it again next day, Walter was rather disappointed. The new character was an agile little fellow, but after all, only a mouse. It would hardly set the world on fire. But they packed the film up into its tin can, and sent it off to New York, praying that someone would like it. Unfortunately nobody thought it very interesting, just another silent cartoon. For at that time everyone in the film industry was excited about Al Jolson's film *The Jazz Singer*, which had just been released.

Although he could not sell his picture, Walt Disney still believed in his discovery, and he decided to make a further film. It was then that he realized that it would be possible to synchronize sound and music—even voices—with his pictures. In the middle of his second film he completed his plans, and decided at once to stop the production and make a third picture—a cartoon with sound. As far as he knew, nobody had ever made one. But it might happen at any minute. Time was therefore the important factor. In record time they made a silent film, which Walter himself took to New York, where he hoped that he would be able to add sound effects and music—an impossibility in Hollywood.

As he tramped the streets again, his money running low, Disney almost despaired that his little film would ever be shown. For some time he could not find a company which would add sound to his picture. With the boys back in Hollywood he had worked out his own method of synchronization, and his cartoon had been made with this in mind. He knew he was right, but in New York he had great difficulty in persuading anyone that his plan would work. First they wanted to try their way, which failed. Then at last they were persuaded to take Disney's advice, and agreed to record the music and sound effects as he wanted The result was *Steamboat Willie*, featuring Mickey Mouse.

The New York distributors were enthusiastic, and immediately offered to buy up the idea, tempting Walter with high prices. But Disney insisted that it was his pictures he wanted to sell, not his company. After staying in New York for several weeks, he decided to release his Mickey Mouse film independently. It was a big undertaking, but he knew that with the help of his wife and Roy he would do it.

Steamboat Willie received an enormous welcome from the public when it was shown. There was nothing sensational in it, but Mickey Mouse won everybody's heart directly he appeared, steering a river boat downstream. There was, by modern standards, a noisy musical accompaniment. But audiences loved it, for they had never before seen a musical cartoon. Soon they were to see many more. Within a month came *Gallopin' Gaucho*, and by the end of 1929, when a new contract was signed with Columbia Pictures, fifteen Mickey Mouse pictures and five *Silly Symphony cartoons* had been made. The first of this new series was a ghoulish fantasy based on the Danse Macabre. As soon as it was completed, in February 1929, Disney took it to be recorded in New York. But everyone was disappointed with the film. New York theatres were reluctant to show it because they said that skeletons dancing were not entertaining. It was finally shown in Los Angeles, but it was some time before the film was released. With the aid of newspaper cuttings, Disney was at last able to persuade the Roxy theatre in New York to show it.

In 1932 came the first Technicolor Silly Symphony, *Flowers and Trees*, and in time all the Disney pictures were made in Technicolor. Over 120 Mickey Mouse subjects, nearly 100 Silly Symphonies, nearly 90 Donald Duck cartoons, some 40 Pluto subjects, and nearly 25 Goofy pictures were made between 1928 and 1949, apart from several full-length features and a number of short cartoon films produced for the United States Government and the armed services during the war. During these years the name of Walt Disney had become internationally famous, while Mickey Mouse was a world favourite. In Germany he was Michael Maus, in France Michel Souris, in Japan Miki Kuchi, in Italy Topolino, in Greece Mikel Maus, in Sweden Musse Pigg, and in Brazil Camondongo Mickey.

Just how successfully Disney had stolen the comedy honours from the actors and actresses of the screen was revealed by Jack Hulbert. 'A few years ago,' he said, 'if a comedian fell flat on his back, or was seen to run the wrong way down a moving staircase, the average audience went into fits of laughter. Disney has put an end to all that. Cinemagoers have seen Mickey Mouse fall a thousand feet down from a precipice and get up unhurt. They have seen Donald Duck dissolve into thin air, and they have watched a whole orchestra carried up into the clouds by a cyclone. The gags of flesh-and-blood comedians fall pretty flat after that.'

Snow White and the Seven Dwarfs (1937) was Disney's first feature film, based on the famous fairy tale. The seven dwarfs stole the picture, it being generally agreed that Snow White and the prince were intruders in a magic fairyland of delightful dwarfs and attractive animals. Then came *Pinocchio* (1940), based on Collodi's famous story of a wooden puppet brought to life by a blue fairy. He goes into the world accompanied by a conscience appointed by Disney and named Jiminy Cricket, and is led astray by a wicked fox and a cat, but finally redeems himself by saving his father, Geppetto, from the belly of a whale, thus earning the right to become a real boy. The public loved the songs—'When You Wish Upon a Star', 'No Strings', and the verse sung by the wicked actor-fox:

> Hi diddle dee dum
> An actor's life is fun;
> You wear your hair in a pompadour,
> You ride around in a coach and four,
> You stop and buy out a candy store—
> An actor's life for me!

Parts of *Pinocchio* were considered by some critics as likely to frighten young children. But the same criticisms had been levelled at *Snow White*. Disney pointed out that his stories were fairy tales, in the tradition of the brothers Grimm, and Hans Andersen. In the magic world of fairyland and folk-lore it was necessary to draw both good and evil slightly larger than life. And in a Disney film right was always triumphant.

In 1940 came *Fantasia*, in which eight animated sequences were fitted to the music of Bach, Tchaikovsky, Stravinsky, Beethoven, Schubert, and other famous composers, in the form of a concert played by the Philadelphia Symphony Orchestra under the direction of Leopold Stokowski. Mickey Mouse and a magic broom appeared in 'The Sorcerer's Apprentice' to music by Dukas, and in other sequences ostriches, elephants, hippos, and alligators performed a ballet. The whole was a delightful experiment in music and vision. Paul Rotha, who had in 1930 claimed in his book *The Film Till Now* that American movies, with their British and German prototypes, were the *lowest* form of public entertainment, could now think again.

A year later came *The Reluctant Dragon*, combining humans with cartoon characters. Robert Benchley was seen walking into Disney's studios, trying to sell the idea of making Kenneth Grahame's story 'The Reluctant Dragon' into a film. He was seen being shown round, and during the visit saw a number of short films being made, before finally reaching the projection theatre, where he was shown the completed film *The Reluctant Dragon*, which he had wished to suggest for filming. At the end Benchley was seen sneaking out of the studio, afraid that Disney might ask him about his idea for a story.

In 1941 Disney completed *Dumbo*, the story of a baby elephant in a circus, who is born with huge ears. Everyone, including the other elephants, laughs at the little freak. 'Why, just look at those ears!' jeer the lady elephants, in rich society voices. When his mother is locked up for causing a disturbance while trying to protect him, Dumbo is left alone with his grief. But he strikes up a friendship with Timothy, the circus mouse, who advises him that the only way to free Mrs Dumbo is for Dumbo himself to earn success. The little elephant discovers that he can use his large ears as wings, and can actually fly. Nobody has ever seen a flying elephant—so young Dumbo becomes the sensation of the show world.

A year later came *Bambi*, with a deer as the hero, and in 1943 came *Saludos Amigos* (Greetings, friends), a combination of four musical shorts with South American backgrounds. *The Three Caballeros* (1945) was another composite musical, linked by sequences showing the visit of Donald Duck to South America.

Donald Duck, who had at first shared honours with Mickey and Minnie Mouse, was now a star in his own right. His first starring film was *Donald's Ostrich* (1937) in which he was seen as a railway stationmaster who discovers an ostrich named Hortense in a crate. When she greedily swallows Donald's radio she dances to the rhythm of a band, and when the programme changes to a motor-race commentary she dashes wildly around the station. In *Donald's Better Self* there were two Donalds—a good duck who knew he should go to school, and a bad duck who persuaded him instead to go fishing and to smoke. The good Donald wore a halo, and the wicked Donald had horns.

Some of the other creatures of Disney's fertile imagination became as popular as Mickey Mouse himself. Pluto the dog, Horace Horsecollar, Goofy, Jiminy Cricket, Thumper, and Figaro—all appeared in scores of pictures. Donald's nephews—three dreadful young ducks who were always tying uncle into knots—shared the honours. In *Donald's Snow Man*, Uncle Donald smashes up their snow man, so they vanquish him in a fierce snow battle, using mousetraps in snowballs, and melting his snow fort with hot coals. *The Eyes Have It* (1945) was a more unusual film, in which Donald was seen hypnotizing himself, and trying it on Pluto, who changes in turn into a mouse, a turtle, a chicken, and finally a lion. Eventually Pluto regains his senses, but Donald still thinks that the dog is a lion.

While making his Mickey Mouse, Pluto, and Donald Duck subjects, Disney continued to produce Silly Symphonies. *Ferdinand the Bull* (1938) was his seventh Academy Award winner. The Disney characters were now so well known that not only Disney, but also animals like Ferdinand, were receiving thousands of letters every week, written in hundreds of languages. Each animal was given a distinct personality. The draughtsmen, chosen from among the finest artists in the cartoon industry, had taken pride in making the characters go through emotions which before the coming of Walt Disney would have seemed impossible to secure. Facial expressions and actions were worked out with the greatest care, to ensure that the effects were not exaggerated.

When the United States entered the second world war the Disney studios joined the war effort. More than ninety-four per cent of the cartoon films were now devoted to training and instructional subjects. Mickey Mouse and Donald Duck put on uniforms, to teach the vast legions of air force navigators, pilots, nurses, and technicians of every kind how to do their jobs. In almost every theatre of war the Disney characters could be seen painted on tanks, areoplanes, guns, landing craft, jeeps, and ambulances. The code word for the invasion of Europe on D-Day was 'Mickey Mouse'.

Make Mine Music was Disney's 1948 feature film, with seven sequences combining animation and living characters. *So Dear to My Heart*, which came a year later, was a story film with charming animated sequences, about a little boy and a black lamb. *The Adventures of Ichabod and Mr Toad* combined in cartoon form the stories of 'The Wind in the Willows' by Kenneth Grahame and the legend of Ichabod Crane, of Sleepy Hollow.

Cinderella retold the familiar fairy story with enough licence to allow the introduction of mice to help Cinderella. It was the animals who won the day, as they had done in the Silly Symphonies, *The Tortoise and the Hare, The Wise Little Hen, The*

Old Mill, The Robber Kitten, Funny Little Bunnies, and *The Grasshopper and the Ants.*

The imitators of the Disney technique had, by 1950, invaded the market with some success. But many of their characters, while technically well drawn, were too often noisy and quarrelsome. Cats fought endlessly with mice, fantastic woodpeckers behaved as though they were back in the Mack Sennett studio, and there was no limit to the crazy knockabout. What was so often missing was the warmth and charm of Disney, which he alone seemed to possess. What Sennett would never have dared to do in his most hilarious slapstick comedies could now be done with impunity by some of Disney's rivals. Cruelty to animals—the squashing of a mouse or the decapitation of a cat—could be portrayed regularly. Of course, it was only on the screen, and only in a cartoon, and should not be taken seriously. Yet there it was, and is, for all the world to see. Can films influence behaviour?

Few of the rivals of Walt Disney could reach his artistic perfection. But sometimes cartoons of the quality of *Gerald McBoing-Boing* and the *Mr Magoo series* might come along, to challenge Disney's supremacy.

In 1951 Walt Disney presented his Technicolor adaptation of Lewis Carroll's classic *Alice in Wonderland*, adding for good measure a dash of 'Through the Looking Glass', with some fourteen Hollywood songs, some of them based on Carroll's verses. Although the result was hardly a faithful adaptation, to the millions who had not read the story of the little girl who fell down a rabbit hole, the picture seemed enchanting entertainment. And if Sir John Tenniel might have wondered a little at Hollywood's transformation of his Mad Hatter, his March Hare, the Dormouse, and the Dodo, and might perhaps fail to recognize his originals, he would surely be the first to grant Disney the artistic licence of his profession, realizing that in this modern medium Disney was expressing his own particular genius, to delight millions of people of all races, all over the world.

CHAPTER SIXTEEN

The Eccentrics

OF ALL THE strange characters of the screen, W. C. Fields stood head, shoulders, and stomach above the rest. He had already appeared in a small comedy role with Marion Davies in *Janice Meredith* (1924)—called *The Glorious Rebel* in Britain —when D. W. Griffith invited him in 1925 to star in *Sally of the Sawdust*, adapted from the Broadway musical 'Poppy', in which he had also starred. In his first big film he was a great success, so that Griffith starred him again in *That Royle Girl*, after which Fields went to Paramount, for whom he starred until the talkie era.

Few of the stars of Hollywood have earned such notoriety as this son of a cockney hawker, who ran away from home when he was eleven in order to become an actor. If he were a hawker, he reflected, he would have to get up early in the morning.

'All the men in my family were bearded. So were most of the women,' Fields revealed later. After four years of what might be described as juvenile delinquency, sleeping in doorways, on a billiards table, and in prison, he gained his first engagement as an entertainer, giving a juggling show in an Atlantic City beer garden. For this he earned ten dollars a week, with 'cakes', or board.

Later he appeared in cheap vaudeville shows, giving as many as twelve turns a day, until he achieved the distinction of playing at the bigger theatres. In his act he spoke hardly a word, but his pantomime proved so successful that it took him all over the world.

After a few years he began mixing acrobatics and novelty acts with the juggling. One of his most popular specialities was a burlesque golf game, which he subsequently introduced into a film. When Florenz Ziegfeld saw the act he booked Fields for the famous Follies, and for nine years the comedian played in musical shows with Will Rogers, Eddie Cantor, and other great names.

When Fields started his film career he announced that he had nothing new to add to the screen. 'My ambition is to bring back the old burlesque,' he said. 'It is eternal as laughter. I think the danger of the screen right now is that it will get too nice, too refined. Everyone in Hollywood is getting too ambitious. I want to restore the old hokum, the old army game. They have forgotten their simplicity. When a thing becomes too refined it loses its vitality and dies out. Highbrow too often is simply another way of spelling Finis. Every calculated moment in any creative work is hokum until it is done perfectly. Then it is art. My ambition is to bring back slapstick, two dollared up.'

That Royle Girl (1925) was followed by *It's the Old Army Game*, *The Potters* (1927), *So's Your Old Man*, *Running Wild*, *Two Flaming Youths*, a new version of *Tillie's Punctured Romance* (1928), and *Fools for Luck*. In 1928 Fields decided that he had no future in films, and left Paramount to return to the stage. It was not until 1931 that he went back to Hollywood, a greater rebel than ever, and on his own terms.

Paramount's *If I Had a Million* (1932) was probably the turning point. The picture was a mixture of comedy and drama, showing in a number of separate episodes what happens to ten different people when they hear that each has inherited a million dollars. The bequests have been made by an eccentric millionaire (Richard Bennett) who has given his money away with the aid of a telephone directory, in order to spite his relatives, who are waiting for his death. Fields and Alison Skipworth, who had in one of the several stories bought a new car, only to see it smashed up by a road hog, become rich enough to buy a score of old automobiles, in which they tour the city streets. Directly they spot a road hog they ram and batter his car, then move into another car in their fleet, and continue their search.

Soon the W. C. Fields expressions, 'My Little Chickadee', 'My Dove', 'My Glow-Worm', and 'Stand Clear! Keep your eyes on the ball!' were familiar to picturegoers on both sides of the Atlantic. The comedian had returned to Paramount in capital form, and there was no doubt that the sound medium suited his peculiar talents even more than the silent film.

During the filming of *My Little Chickadee*, in which he was co-starred with Mae West, he was given the part of a bartender. 'What's wrong, Bill?' asked the director when Fields hesitated about saying a line. Fields replied, 'Sorry, I was just thinking that it took me thirty years to find out that I was on the wrong side of the bar.'

The film *Never Give a Sucker an Even Break* was written by Fields himself, under the pen-name of Otis Criblecoblis. As Mahatma Kane Jeeves he wrote *The Bank Dick*, in which he appeared as a no-good character named Egbert Sousé, who wins the respect of the community in the last reel. In *You Can't Cheat an Honest Man* he played the part of Larson E. Whipsnade, and appeared with the dummy Charlie McCarthy, Edgar Bergen, a circus menagerie, and a society family into which Mr Whipsnade's daughter is expected to marry. The highlight of the picture was the social ball given by the family—the Bel-Goodies —which Mr Whipsnade crashes, and from which he escapes in a Roman chariot, cloak and all, across the state line.

Like Groucho Marx, Fields loved unusual names. A wealthy man, he had ever since his early days been afraid of poverty, and had therefore opened several hundred bank accounts under false names. These accounts were distributed all over the United States. Large sums of money were kept hidden away in various safe deposits, and on his person he frequently concealed a number of bulky rolls of bank notes.

As for his taste for liquor, this was the talk of Hollywood and the acting profession. He liked to 'drink martinis' by first taking a swig out of a gin bottle, and then another out of a vermouth bottle. He boasted proudly that he never drank anything stronger than gin before breakfast, and in his last years he was said to be consuming two quarts of it every day. When completing his income tax returns one year he deducted his drink bill, claiming that alcohol was essential to his trade as an actor.

'Milk!' he said. 'That whitish fluid they force down babies!' And another time—'I have spent forty-six of my sixty-seven years on a diet of olives floating in alcohol—the alcohol to be consumed, the olives to be saved to use over again in alcohol.'

His most famous screen characterization—apart from the role of Humpty Dumpty in *Alice in Wonderland*, which suited him perfectly—was the only one for which he was not able

223

to alter the plot, although he re-wrote as much of the dialogue as he could. This was the part of Mr Micawber in *David Copperfield*, for which he was paid £10,000, Charles Laughton having thrown up the role. Whether he made a good Micawber or not was a matter of opinion. James Agate thought not. 'Fields was a glorious buffoon,' he said, 'but being possessed of no more gentility than a pork pie, he could do no other with Micawber than turn him into an obese Ally Sloper, with very much the same nose and hat. And that, I submit, is not Dickens's character.'

Among the extraordinary people whom Fields collected around him was a man with a very small head—not much bigger than a big tankard, Fields said it was. 'With that small head,' he remarked, 'he'll own Hollywood.'

There is no doubt that W. C. Fields was amusing, but he was a constant trial to his friends, and his life was completely anti-social. His aim seemed to be to repay humanity for the poverty of his early days. Although many of his films contained brilliantly funny moments, there was often a vicious twist in the humour. His wit was cruel, his language sometimes obscene, and having built up a reputation for being a rebel, he took care to be an outsize one. When he developed a fear of kidnappers he used to lie in bed in his sumptuous home, carrying on loud conversations with imaginary bodyguards, in order to scare any possible intruders away. In the studios he believed that everyone was out to steal his scene, or to cut him out of the picture.

In spite of all his many defects, he was a brilliant comedian and one of the few clowns. His face alone could set people laughing. His strawberry nose, he extravagantly claimed, had been cut on a cocktail glass. Indeed, he did not seem to belong to the human race at all. According to J. B. Priestley all the truly great clowns—and Fields was in his opinion undoubtedly one of them—have the transient look, as though they are not men of this world being funny, but people from another planet, mystified by the commonplace problems of the earth. Certainly there was nothing commonplace about W. C. Fields. Even his real name—Claude William Duckinfield—was unusual, and might have come out of his own collection of strange surnames.

Some Comedy Stars of the Forties. Top left to right.—Groucho Marx, Toto, Danny Kaye, Sid Field

39. *Richard Hearne in* SOMETHING IN THE CITY

37.
Margaret
Rutherford,
Joyce Grenfell,
and Alistair
Sim in THE
HAPPIEST DAYS
OF YOUR LIFE

38.
Alec Guinness
on location for
THE LAVENDER
HILL MOB
(Ealing Studios)

When W. C. Fields died on Christmas Eve, 1946, he left behind him a fantastic legend. To his closest friend he bequeathed twenty-five dollars a week, while in dozens of towns his secret bank accounts, all deposited under false names, had to be traced. Some time before he died he was reported to have said 'I've drunk the health of so many people that now I've lost my own.'

If not the most lovable of comedians, W. C. Fields was certainly one of the most colourful clowns of the silent and talkie screen.

*

If Fields was an eccentric, so were the Marx Brothers, but with this difference; that whereas Fields behaved ludicrously both off and on the stage and screen, the Marx Brothers confined their absurdities to their work, except for an occasional lapse to keep up appearances.

There were five of them—Chico, Harpo, Groucho, Gummo, and Zeppo. Chico, the eldest, started learning the piano at an early age, and began his career playing in cinemas. Harpo also learned the piano, but could master only two melodies, both taught him by Chico, and this was his entire repertoire. Chico therefore sought jobs for Harpo as well as for himself, and because they looked alike, he was able to share the engagements.

When Chico left home to join a touring vaudeville company, fifteen-year-old Harpo lost all the jobs, and decided to give up music. Hearing that a page boy was wanted in a big hotel he applied for the job, and got it. Meanwhile, brother Groucho was developing a good singing voice and was learning tap dancing. As a boy soprano he sang in church, and also at concerts.

Their mother, Mrs Minnie Marx, was determined to encourage the five boys in their stage careers, and she toured the theatres and the agents with photographs of her young hopefuls. Eventually she succeeded in arranging a season's work for Groucho with Gus Edward's musical school. From here he joined the LeRoy Trio, in which he impersonated a girl singer. In Denver, however, his voice suddenly broke, and he became a baritone, and of no further use to the act. To earn enough money to return to New York he drove a grocery van.

Gummo had now developed a good tenor voice, which encouraged Mrs Marx to form an act which she called The Three Nightingales. This consisted of Groucho, Gummo, and a girl to sing soprano. She herself wrote and produced the act, and went out with it on tour, dressing the boys in white suits, celluloid collars, made-up bow ties, white shoes, and Panama hats. Three-year-old Zeppo was taken along with them. When Chico was persuaded to join the act they became The Four Nightingales, but since Harpo was given almost nothing to say he mimed, as he did later on the screen—like a ghost from the silent film comedy days.

In 1918 the Marx Brothers wrote a show of their own called 'Mrs Green's Reception', but it was a failure, so Harpo and Gummo joined the army while Groucho and Chico went to the camps to entertain. It was not until the armistice that they were re-united. Gummo then decided to retire from the stage in favour of the raincoat business, but young Zeppo replaced him in the act. The family, which had come of a long line of comics, now began to develop their comedy on the lines familiar to picture-goers in the thirties and the forties. There was nothing inherently crazy about the Marx Brothers; on the contrary, they were a very normal family, bound by strong ties of affection. But if craziness pays dividends, they preferred to be crazy, at least on the screen.

When the four Marx Brothers visited England they flopped badly at the London Coliseum. The audience, who were not familiar with this brand of humour, whistled, shouted, and threw pennies on to the stage. Groucho stepped forward and held up his hand. 'Friends,' he said, 'we have come a long way. The trip has been expensive. Would you mind throwing silver?'

After a poor week in Manchester they began to understand their audiences better, and returned after a brief provincial tour to the Coliseum, where a favourable press, influenced partly by Groucho's gag about the coins, had helped the advance bookings to mount up. Their reception was now entirely different. They knew at last what Englishmen expected of them, and they found that their success out of London had been reported in the newspapers. At the end of the last show the vast audience stood to sing 'For They Are Jolly Good Fellows'. It was a considerable triumph.

Chico, who was said to have been so named because as a boy he ran around after girls, was later able to sum up the craziness of the quartette. 'The reason why people like to see us doing any tomfool thing that comes into our heads is quite simple,' he said. 'It's because that's how every normal person would like to act, once in a while. Take Groucho. His line is to say exactly what he likes, and so you will see him interrupt a scene when he's making up to two rich old women, and suddenly burst out with "Well, you couple of big baboons! What makes you think I want to marry *either* of you?" And when Harpo makes a run at one of his blondes he goes at it like a three-quarter back. You see, we can't afford to have inhibitions. We just give it all we've got. If Harpo had any hesitation about jumping at every woman he sees, he would offend people and probably never get past the censor. But he goes at it so hard that it's just plumb crazy, and can't be in bad taste.'

Chico's first attempt to get married had been foiled by the minister, who had walked out when he discovered that Groucho and Harpo were eating the leaves of his pet rubber plant. Finally, the wedding took place, but as Chico told his bride, 'a comedian's wife must learn to take the bad with the worse.'

Comedians are expected to be the life and soul of the party, and this sometimes proves exasperating. Groucho, an extremely knowledgeable person, could usually be relied upon to produce a witty line at the right moment. But the brothers did not hang from the chandeliers to amuse the guests. Neither was Harpo as silent at home as on the screen. The dumb member of the team, he was justly famous for his miming and for his playing of the harp. His first harp cost him about eight pounds, and he taught himself to play it, but still could not read music.

Gummo, said to have earned his nickname as a boy because he liked wearing 'gum boots', was replaced in the act by Zeppo, and when Zeppo left to become an agent with Gummo, the act became known as The Three Marx Brothers.

'I can remember when Groucho was a choirboy,' recalled Gummo. 'He trilled a terrifying soprano until he stuck a hatpin into the bellows of the church organ, and had to resign under pressure. Then there was Chico, who was fined five dollars for smoking backstage. We raised a terrific row, the mayor was called in, and decided against a fine. To get even with us, the manager paid out our wages in nickels and dimes, so we had to sit up half the night counting out our money. Eventually we worked up a complete show of our own, but we forgot, among other things, to have photographs taken for the theatre lobbies. However, Harpo solved the problem by getting a big picture of Theda Bara, which he hung up outside the entrance. He didn't say that Theda Bara was actually in the show, but we had a packed house.'

Comedy took a hand in Groucho's private life directly he started to be a comedian. Everyone who has met him has gazed at him with the look which clowns know so well—the gaze which seems to say 'Come on, I bet you can't make *me* laugh.' Even his wedding, like Chico's, could not take place without some incident. As the minister began the service Groucho gave a signal, whereupon Harpo dived under the rug, Zeppo went into a dance, and Chico ran off with the bride. After all, it was what everybody expected them to do.

The brothers made their film début in *Humorisk*, which was completed in two weeks at Fort Lee, New Jersey, and in a New York studio. They immediately tried to suppress it, for they felt it would do them no good. Fortunately, the picture was never publicly shown. However, this poor start did not put them off. When the brothers scored a hit in the stage show *The Cocoanuts* they were signed by Paramount in 1929 to appear in a film version, *The Cocoanuts*, which was followed a year later by *Animal Crackers* and subsequently by *Monkey Business* (1931), *Horse Feathers* (1932), and *Duck Soup* (1933). Their later pictures, which included *Room Service*, *A Day at the Races*, *A Night at the Opera*, and *The Big Store*, were slightly less amusing than their earlier films. The humour seemed to be restricted by the stories, and undue prominence was given to singers and minor characters—even love interest—at the expense of what the patrons had paid to see . . . those crazy Marx Brothers. Prime Minister Winston Churchill was laughing at *The Big Store* on the day that the Nazi leader Rudolf Hess landed in Scotland. But he did not stop the showing of the film when he was told the news.

As for *A Day at the Races*, every gag had been tried out first on the public before going into the script. If it did not raise a laugh it was not included in the picture.

'It takes fully nine months to get good original comedy for a feature film,' said Harpo. 'Comedy cannot be ground out, and good comedy is rare, so that the public will not stand even for adaptations of what has been done before. No longer can a comedian expect jokes which have been told in one place to be new in another. We start with an idea, situations, and jokes which have never been tried out. We are in the dark about everything, because in the film studio you cannot tell what the audience will think.'

Some of the most famous lines which the brothers included in their earlier films are today constantly quoted by the many devotees of Marx humour. They include, to mention only a few:

'Gee, I wish I was back in the jungle, where men are monkeys.'
'How do you keep your youth?'—'I don't, he keeps me.'
'Either this man's dead, or my watch has stopped.'
'What is your pleasure, sir?'—'Women. What's yours?'

During the forties the brothers appeared less frequently on the screen. Perhaps good comedy material is harder to find than it used to be. But in America, France, Italy, and Britain, where their brand of humour has become almost a cult, even the oldest of their films can still be revived, if only on television.

Stories about the Marx Brothers are often misquoted, and sometimes become unrecognizable. One anecdote, better than most, is told of Harpo's visit to the South of France, where he stayed with Alexander Woollcott. Hearing that George Bernard Shaw was staying nearby, Harpo persuaded his host to invite the great man to lunch, and on the appointed day was sunbathing in the nude when he suddenly realized that a tall bearded figure was standing over him. He jumped up at once, quickly drawing a towel round him.

'I'm Harpo Marx,' he said, holding out his hand.

'I'm Bernard Shaw,' replied the visitor, neatly whipping away the towel from Harpo and leaving him naked. 'And this is Mrs Shaw!'

Another of the many stories concerns Groucho, who is alleged to have applied for membership of an exclusive New York club. When he was told that his application was accepted he is said to have pointed out that no club with a good reputation could possibly accept Groucho Marx as a member—therefore he would rather stay away. And he did.

Another tale relates how Groucho was once asked to review a book for a newspaper. But when he submitted the review he added the note: 'I was so busy writing the review that I never got around to reading the book. Is it good?'

Like W. C. Fields, Groucho collects strange names, and has appeared on the screen playing the parts of Phineas X. Flitterwaggle and Bogel D. Plugghfelder.

'You take a name like Bernard B. Brindlebug or Otto Blotto,' he says, 'and before you know it, somebody bobs up with a name exactly like it. We get what we think is a funny name, and look it up in the nearest telephone book, and there they are —dozens of them.'

In *A Day at the Races* Groucho was to be called Dr Hugo Quakenbush, but this looked familiar, and it was quickly changed to Dr Hackenbush. Dozens of people then wrote to Metro-Goldwyn-Mayer to say that their name had been chosen. Quite the safest bet was Ulysses Ungudunger, although Otis B. Driftwood remained a firm favourite in the Marx family for some years.

Were the Marx Brothers really quiet, ordinary folk off the stage and screen? Margaret Dumont, who stood their jibes and jokes gallantly for several years, should know. Claiming that the brothers chased her some ten thousand miles during the time that she worked with them, she reported: 'I was told that they needed an actress with dignity and poise, to lend legitimate dramatic balance to their comedy. After three weeks as Groucho's leading lady, I nearly had a nervous breakdown. He pushed me about, pulled chairs from under me, broiled steaks in the fireplace of my apartment, put frogs in my bath, and made my life miserable on the stage and off. But I don't regret a minute of it. I just love those boys.'

In Britain the nearest approach to this kind of humour was contributed by the Crazy Gang, who made several comedy films together, and were well known for their practical jokes. Making a film with Flanagan and Allen was a lively experience. During a particularly difficult scene, in which large crowds of players were employed, it was not unusual for a mysterious voice to break the silence with a loud 'CUT!', thus completely ruining the shot.

On another occasion Chesney Allen was all ready to dash on to the set dressed in an immaculate suit, when he found that the back of the coat had been ripped up, the sleeves were falling off, and the pockets had been carefully sewn together.

When a rather pompous actor turned up at the studio early in the morning, he waited all day to appear in the film, and was puzzled why he had never been asked to step forward. He decided to make further enquiries, and discovered to his surprise that his name was not on the call sheet. In fact it was obvious that he was not even in the film. Then he realized that Flanagan and Allen were starring in the picture and he began to remember the telephone call which had summoned him to report at the studio at seven that morning. But he was never able to discover exactly who had sent the message.

In the twenty-one years that the Crazy Gang were together, they performed thousands of practical jokes, mostly on each other. When Sir Laurence and Lady Olivier went to see their stage show, Jimmy Nervo arranged that in the interval they were presented with an enormous fried bloater, a thick chunk of bread, and an outsize mug of tea. But this is nothing to the birthday presents which the gang sent one another.

A team which moved easily from silent to sound pictures was the partnership formed by Stan Laurel and Oliver Hardy, who reached their peak of popularity in the thirties. Just as Chaplin had been Mack Sennett's greatest find, so Laurel and Hardy were the most notable players discovered by Hal Roach, at their best in short, often cheaply-made absurdities.

'Laurel came to Roach at the time when I was associated with him,' says Harold Lloyd. 'Later he teamed up with Hardy, and they formed a perfect complement. A product of the English music halls, from which Chaplin had come, Laurel was close to

Charlie in his field of pantomime. He was a great comedian. Their appeal was that of a couple of struggling characters, kind of in-between tramps and working men. They were always buddies, but always had differences that would get them into trouble. One reacted differently from the other in the same situation.'

Oliver Hardy began his career as a 'heavy' with Sennett, whereas Laurel's portrayal was always that of the innocent, simple, stupid, trusting individual, constantly getting his partner into trouble. Hardy, in contrast, showed great sophistication and a sense of worldliness, finding the juvenile behaviour of his gormless partner speechlessly infuriating, and looking helplessly to the camera, and therefore to the audience, for assistance which would never arrive.

'Comics now lean too much on the line gag and not the visual gag,' said Stan Laurel, when they started making talkies. 'I think that Hollywood comics, these days, are talking too much and not doing enough . . . What is comedy? I don't know. Does anybody? Can you define it? I learned how to get laughs, and that's all I know about it. You have to learn what people will laugh at, and then proceed accordingly. First of all, you should start out with a fairly believable plot, no matter how broad it is, and then work from there. But you've got to *learn* how to get on from there. Nobody's going to teach you.'

CHAPTER SEVENTEEN

The Forties

And thick and fast they came at last
And more, and more, and more.

LEWIS CARROLL : *Through the Looking Glass*

1940 FOUND EUROPE at war, with Hollywood still entertaining most of the world. To Europeans, Chaplin's *The Great
Dictator*, which was long overdue, had unfortunately lost some
of its humorous appeal, for Hitler was no longer a laughing
matter. The film had a first run at two Broadway theatres, the
Capitol and the Astor. In Britain it was received with enthusiasm. Hitler and Mussolini were reported to have seen the
picture privately somewhere in Germany, and to have found it
infuriating.

The rival of every comedian—Walt Disney—offered two
cartoon features, the delightful and at times fearful *Pinocchio*,
and *Fantasia*. The dramas were dwarfed by M.G.M.'s spectacular
Gone with the Wind, which was now released in Britain, having
grossed over two million dollars during its first run in the United
States. It was to remain the perfect example of Hollywood's
magnificence, technical skill, and superiority in the providing
of entertainment.

Nostalgia for the old days of the Keystone cops was revived
with *Hollywood Cavalcade*. When Alice Faye and Don Ameche
were not embracing, this amusingly reconstructed the Sennett
days, and gave Buster Keaton an opportunity of showing a new
generation that he was still a master of pantomime, and a great
clown.

Fred Astaire, looking slimmer and younger than ever, starred
with Eleanor Powell in *The Broadway Melody of 1940*, one of
the many spectacular song and dance films of the period,
lavishly produced by Metro-Goldwyn-Mayer. This studio also
produced the acidly witty *The Women*, in which Norma
Shearer, Joan Crawford, and Rosalind Russell gave distinguished

233

performances. For a less sophisticated public, Laurel and Hardy appeared at *Saps at Sea*, but it was noticeable that these two clever comedians did not shine so brightly in their feature films as they had done in their two-reelers.

Although Europe had gone to war in 1939 the battleground of Europe was quiet until the spring of 1940. British film production, which had been encouraged during the thirties by the quota, continued almost undisturbed. The 1939 comedies were varied, if not distinguished. Gordon Harker in *Saloon Bar*, Claude Hulbert and Monty Banks in *Honeymoon Merry-go-Round*, and Naunton Wayne and Basil Radford, who had stolen the honours in *The Lady Vanishes*, now appeared in an adaptation of a radio serial, *Crook's Tour*. Arthur Askey could be considered only partly successful in *Charley's (Big Hearted) Aunt*, and *Band Waggon*, and Jack Buchanan could have found a better vehicle for himself than *The Middle Watch*. Phyllis Calvert partnered George Formby in *Let George Do It*, and Lucan and McShane appeared in *Old Mother Riley in Society* and *In Business*. Gracie Fields's *Sing as we Go*, which had been released six years previously, was revived. And there was also an unambitious comedy called *That's the Ticket*, whose sole claim to fame is that it introduced Sid Field to the screen—almost unnoticed.

The British comedies with war backgrounds now came thick and fast. Sergeant-majors, raw recruits far from home—the tea tastes like soup and the orderly officer thinks it *is* soup—all the old gags from *Shoulder Arms* and *Dough Boys* were here. Tommy Trinder and Jean Colin starred in *Laugh it Off*, Barry Lupino was in *Garrison Follies*, Reginald Purdell and Wylie Watson were in *Pack Up Your Troubles*, Morland Graham and John Mills made *Old Bill and Son*, and Harry Korris and Frank Randle were in *Somewhere in England*.

By 1941 there were considerably fewer British comedies on the screen. Britain was tightening her war belt. Arthur Askey and Richard Murdoch, not too happily transferred from the radio, appeared in a new version of *The Ghost Train*. Because the railways were involved in the war effort they could not co-operate with Gainsborough Pictures, who were forced to use several sequences from their eleven-year-old Jack Hulbert-Cicely Courtneidge film.

Arthur Askey was not much funnier in *I Thank You!*, while the successful radio programme 'Hi! Gang', when adapted for the screen with Bebe Daniels and Ben Lyon, showed how unwise it could be to transfer good radio comedy to a new medium. One of the most amusing British films of the year was *Once a Crook*, with Gordon Harker and Sydney Howard. George Formby's *South American George*, *Spare a Copper*, and *Turned Out Nice Again* could not compare with the entertainment provided by such American comedies as *Andy Hardy's Private Secretary*, Laurel and Hardy's *Great Guns*, William Powell's *Love Crazy*, Joe E. Brown's *So You Won't Talk*, and Abbott and Costello in *Rookies* and *Hold that Ghost*.

Metro-Goldwyn-Mayer, who had for years consistently produced some of the world's finest film entertainment, now weighed in heavily with Lubitsch's *Ninotchka*, an amiable satire on world communism, starring Garbo and Melvyn Douglas.

A year later there were only forty-one new British features offered to the public. Of these nine were comedies. Many of the studios had been taken over as war factories, and large numbers of technicians and players were in the services. Arthur Askey's *King Arthur was a Gentleman* could not compare with even a modestly produced Hollywood film of the calibre of *Andy Hardy's Double Life*. Vera Lynn, who was earning a considerable reputation with the British forces as a radio singer, made a totally undistinguished musical film début in *We'll Meet Again*. Happier British comedy was provided by *Banana Ridge* and *Women Aren't Angels*, made amusing by the individual fooling of Robertson Hare and Alfred Drayton.

A British music hall comedian named Frank Randle now rose to popularity on the screen. In two modestly made knockabout comedies, *Somewhere on Leave* and *Somewhere in Camp*, he proved that to be successful in Britain a film need not be shown to the Press, nor be screened in London's West End. By the end of 1943 Frank Randle was one of the biggest film attractions working in English studios. In many towns in Britain, particularly in the north, his pictures took more money than those of Errol Flynn, Marlene Dietrich and Robert Taylor.

The local English success of such stars as Frank Randle and Norman Evans—to name only two—was based on crude music hall humour. At no time did a leading writer step forward to give them new material, fresh gags, or even a good comedy story. Instead, these comedians had to carry the whole burden of their screen appearances, repeating their music hall material.

To further his screen career, Frank Randle found it necessary to help to finance a small film studio in Manchester. A comedian of his capabilities, with a decided knockabout technique of the silent film class, should be welcomed in any British studio. In the silent era Randle would have gone to Hollywood, and would have made an international success as a droll. His comedy, directed along slapstick lines, could have been international instead of local, if a capable writer and a good director had spared him time.

*

Of all the comedy stars of the forties few rose to fame more quickly than Danny Kaye, the lanky blue-eyed comedian from Brooklyn who had been an unsuccesful vaudeville performer, a shop assistant, an insurance investigator, and a waiter. In March 1943 he left the Broadway revue *Let's Face It* to sign a five years' film contract with Samuel Goldwyn. For *Up in Arms*, based on an old stage farce called ' Nervous Wreck,' he received £25,000. In *Wonder Man* he appeared as a nervous student and also as his gangster brother. *The Kid from Brooklyn* was based on Harold Lloyd's earlier *The Milky Way*, yet was not so amusing as its predecessor.

Six feet tall, lean, wiry, with reddish-gold hair, Danny Kaye gained his greatest popularity through the screen, but not on the screen. It is on the stage that he appears at his best. When he visited London the Palladium theatre was packed at every performance. Princess Elizabeth, Princess Margaret and the Duke of Edinburgh went backstage and sat on the floor drinking champagne. King George the Sixth, Queen Elizabeth, Winston Churchill, and tens of thousands of other admirers enjoyed his fooling. But on the screen Danny Kaye, apart from his comedy songs, shone less brightly. In *The Secret Life of Walter Mitty* he played seven character parts, sang comically, and talked in an individual style of gibberish. But in spite of an unusual technique and a rich sense of burlesque, he still remained a photographed vaudeville star, and not a true film comedian.

*

While in 1941 British production was almost at a standstill, one studio—the British National plant at Elstree, controlled by Lady Yule—kept vigorously active. The company's dramas included *One of Our Aircraft is Missing*, *Contraband*, John Baxter's *Love on the Dole*, and Leslie Howard's *Pimpernel Smith*. Most of the comedies were less memorable, but for nearly a year the studio was producing the bulk of Britain's pictures.

In Hollywood production was almost unaffected, introducing new personalities like Betty Hutton to the screen. She made her début supporting Dorothy Lamour and William Holden in *The Fleet's In*, singing 'Arthur Murray Taught Me Dancing in a Hurry'. Paramount found that the public liked her particular brand of outlandish madcap comedy, in which she contorted, leaped, made hooligan faces, howled, and knocked herself out. An attractive blonde with a neat figure, she starred in her next film, *Happy Go Lucky*, and after toning down her knockabout fooling, appeared in *Star Spangled Rhythm*, *The Miracle of Morgan's Creek*, *Let's Face It*, *Incendiary Blonde*, *Duffy's Tavern*, *The Stork Club*, *Here Come the Waves*, *Cross My Heart*, and *The Perils of Pauline*, in which she burlesqued the career of Pearl White, the heroine of the serial dramas of the twenties. In *Let's Dance* she was successfully teamed with Fred Astaire.

*

Replacing the screen popularity of such partners as Wheeler and Woolsey, two new film comedians now shared honours with the established team of Laurel and Hardy. These were Bud Abbott and Lou Costello, who had won their first success in pictures in *Buck Privates* (known in Britain as *Rookies*). Their humour was at once acclaimed by the fighting forces, and their future was assured.

Their partnership was based on a simple formula, the spoken and visual gags being regarded as of more importance than the plot. Bud Abbott was born in a Barnum and Bailey circus tent,

237

his father being a publicity man and his mother a bareback rider. On leaving school he became in turn a sailor, a box-office cashier in a burlesque theatre, and a clerk in a hat store. By hard work and determination he saved two hundred dollars, and spending half of it on the best second-hand car he could find for the money, set out for Hollywood to find film work. Eventually M.G.M. hired him as a member of a studio labour gang, and later he became a stunt man. When doubling for Dolores del Rio he was ordered to jump from the second-floor window of a burning building, but ended up in hospital. This made him decide to go into burlesque, where he met Lou Costello.

They formed a vaudeville act, and after touring the United States for seven years they were seen by Kate Smith, who signed them up for her popular radio programme. From radio they went into a Broadway musical show with a newcomer named Carmen Miranda, and were seen by a talent scout from Universal Pictures, who asked the partners to sign a contract to appear in the film *One Night in the Tropics*. They were a moderate success, but the studio chiefs saw that they had a considerable screen future, and booked them for *Buck Privates*, after which they were offered a long-term contract. From now on they were to become two of Hollywood's biggest money-makers, but they did not forget the manager of the steel pier at Atlantic City, New Jersey, who had advanced them money when they needed it. He had given them the engagement which had resulted in the Kate Smith radio offer. Now they went several times a year to the steel pier to perform to packed houses, and when each show was over they repeated the same demand for salary : 'Pay us what you think we're worth, but don't make it more than a dollar.'

By 1952 they had made twenty-nine films together. *Keep 'Em Flying, In the Navy, Hold that Ghost, Rio Rita* (in which Wheeler and Woolsey had previously played), *Lost in a Harem, Africa Screams*, and *Abbott and Costello Meet Frankenstein* were among them. In their later films for Universal there was a tendency to repeat gags and situations, as though their producers were relying only on proved comedy effects. While they lacked the pantomimic appeal of Laurel and Hardy they nevertheless used visual comedy gags more than most comedians of the forties and fifties.

Two other comedians who went to Hollywood from the stage were Olsen and Johnson. Together for over thirty-six years, they had started their partnership in a basement café in Chicago, Olsen playing the violin and singing, while Johnson accompanied him on the piano. Developing a comedy act, they started a vaudeville show, and in September 1938 they converted their production into a crazy knockabout revue called *Hellzapoppin*, which was later filmed by Universal Pictures, establishing the comedians as unusual screen comics. *Ghost Catchers*, *See My Lawyers*, and *Crazy House* were in the same tradition, with absurdities piled high. To back up their extravagant gags Universal thought it necessary to introduce guests into their pictures. These included Allan Jones, and Count Basie and his orchestra. In the same way, Abbott and Costello were considered to need the support of the Andrews Sisters. Ted Lewis and his orchestra, the Inkspots, and other radio and vaudeville attractions. It would be hard to imagine Laurel and Hardy having to share honours with vaudeville stars, however entertaining. But the material given the comedians was seldom strong enough to carry a feature film alone.

Another recruit from the theatre was the writer and director Preston Sturges, who went to Hollywood in the early thirties after the success of his play *Strictly Dishonourable*. After working on several screenplays, including *Power and the Glory* and *Thirty Day Princess*, he persuaded Paramount in 1940 to let him direct his own story, *The Great McGinty*, an amusing satire on crooked politics. *Christmas in July* and *The Lady Eve* were followed in 1941 by *Sullivan's Travels*, an amusing but bitter satire on Hollywood and the motion-picture industry. *Hail the Conquering Hero* (1944) satirized war-time life in a small American town. The Sturgess touch was reminiscent of Mack Sennett, and of Charles Chaplin, but being more satirical and not introducing knockabout to any great extent, it was less popular. With Howard Hughes and Harold Lloyd he made *The Sin of Harold Dibblebock* in 1947, a film which finally emerged as *Mad Wednesday*.

In 1946 the *Kinematograph Weekly* in London was able to report that British films had secured considerable playing time in the United States. *A Matter of Life and Death, The Captive Heart, Great Expectations, Quiet Week End*, and *Appointment with Crime* could be considered well up to the standard of any American productions. But it could hardly be termed a comedy year, although Judy Canova opened her big mouth to effect in *Hit the Hay*, Leon Errol appeared to be as misunderstood as ever in the *Joe Palooka series*, and Fernandel shone brightly in the French comedy *Fric Frac*.

In Britain, a great financial success was scored by Herbert Wilcox's light-hearted *Piccadilly Incident*, starring Anna Neagle and Michael Wilding. The recipe, as in the Henry Edwards–Chrissie White silent films of yesterday, was a simple romance, with a touch of gaiety, and a few tears. It was a profitable mixture, which the public loved. But both the British and American studios seemed increasingly interested in crime pictures. Examples of the cycle of gangster and murder films included *I Was a Criminal, Hunted, Deadline for Murder, Accent on Crime, By Whose Hand?*, and *Terror by Night*. The detective film had been a rarity in the twenties, but had invaded the screen in the thirties with the help of such stars as James Cagney. During the forties crime films were more frequent than Westerns. By 1946 there were fewer laughs in the cinemas. Nobody could replace Larry Semon, Buster Keaton, Charles Ray, Eddie Lyons, and Lee Moran. The Chaplin films were few and far between. Screen fashions had changed considerably. The old comic automobiles, the carefully devised visual gags, all had gone. Heroes no longer threw pails of water at their enemies. Instead, they punctured them with bullets. Guns had replaced the gags.

*

By 1947 the J. Arthur Rank Organisation had become the most powerful film group in Britain, having an interest in over eighty companies engaged in the making, distribution, exhibition, and exploitation of English pictures. The total assets of the group were estimated in this year to exceed fifty million pounds, the various companies employing over 33,000 workers.

The group had started in 1935, when British producers were

40. *Fernandel in* COIFFEUR POUR DAMES (1952)

42. *Mr Magoo in* HOTSEY FOOTSEY

43. *Mr Magoo in* TROUBLE INDEMNITY

41. *Walt Disney's Mickey Mouse*

far from prosperous. The boom created by the quota act had turned into a depression, and there was anxiety in financial circles. It was then that J. Arthur Rank, the son of a prosperous flour miller, became interested in the battle to control the major British film interests. On the distribution side these interests were mainly dominated by American companies, and in British studios there was no guarantee of financial success. Rank therefore gained control of the 240 cinemas in the Gaumont British chain, the Odeon group of 305 theatres, and eleven holding companies. Any pictures which his companies produced were now assured of exhibition in Britain. Soon he controlled thirteen production companies and studio properties, twenty-three companies engaged in the making of equipment, two newsreels, a large distributing organization, an interest in Universal Pictures of America, and allied theatre companies in Canada, Australia, South Africa, New Zealand, and Egypt.

Rank had entered the industry to make religious films and to raise the prestige of British films. But because he had no previous knowledge of films he was forced, in an extremely technical industry, to rely greatly on the advice of Wardour Street, and the accepted limitations and demands of the box-office, by which the public's taste was measured. While allowing his many producers a fair amount of freedom, Rank himself remained responsible for their work, and for their success or failure. It was a formidable undertaking.

Since the earliest days of the now forgotten 'Flicker Alley' the British studios had been starved of finance. Hepworth and his contemporaries had fallen through lack of support from the distributors and the cinema proprietors. The big money made from the showing of films had not returned to the little studios at Walton, Beaconsfield, or Walthamstow. Production was the Cinderella of the industry. Now Rank altered all that. With two large chains of cinemas and his own releasing organization, he had a fair chance of holding a balance between studio expenditure and cinema profits. But his studios would not be idle for lack of money, if he could help it. Ironically, some of the money made from the showing of American pictures in Britain would now help to finance English pictures.

During the period 1941–1951 the Rank studios at Denham,

Iver, Shepherds Bush, Islington, Elstree, and Highbury first enjoyed a production boom, and then suffered a severe slump. Finally, by more careful expenditure, the group became economically stable. But at first every Rank starlet, every picture, and each relatively unimportant film player was so enthusiastically over-publicized that the public was led to expect marvels from British studios. The men and women who worked on the pictures were capable, some of them the best technicians in the world, but they could hardly live up to the trumpet-blowing of their publicity departments. Every minor player was labelled a 'star'. Good programme pictures were classed as major productions, and millions of pounds were spent in an abortive attempt to capture the film markets of the world. If a film was not greeted with enthusiasm in the United States, then the Americans were accused of 'freezing out' English pictures. This had not been true of the Hepworth product, or of major triumphs like *The Private Life of Henry the Eighth*, nor was it true now. The best of the Rank pictures were warmly received in America, and indeed all over the world. *Hamlet*, *The Red Shoes*, *Henry V*, *Great Expectations*, *Oliver Twist*, *In Which We Serve*, and *The Way Ahead* were among the many notable Rank pictures which could challange any Hollywood film. But sometimes there seemed to be too many cooks spoiling the broth. The technical list for *The Blind Goddess*, a minor programme picture produced at the Islington studios, was headed by an Executive Producer, a Producer, a Studio Chief in Charge of Production, a Production Controller, and a Director.

The comedy situation within the Rank empire was sometimes lamentable. The English comedians who had established themselves on the screen during the thirties were seldom invited to film. Hardly any effort was made to provide material for Jack Hulbert, Cicely Courtneidge, Will Hay, Gordon Harker, the Crazy Gang, Max Miller, Ralph Lynn, George Formby, or Jack Buchanan. What was worse, no search was made for new comedians, although Sid Field (who had been available for years, and had altered hardly a word of his stage routine) was persuaded to star in the costly and unhappy *London Town*, followed by *Cardboard Cavalier*. This was cardboard indeed, and was hardly worthy of the attention of director Walter Forde, who struggled bravely with crepe hair and an obviously contrived story, and was clearly handicapped by poor material.

Not that there was any lack of money for the discovery and training of comedians. Over a million pounds could be spent in putting *Caesar and Cleopatra* on to the screen, to almost nobody's satisfaction. This money could have produced quite a number of two-reel comedies, from which future stars could have been selected. There would have been no question about the difficulty of selling short comedies to the cinemas, for Rank already controlled the theatres.

Generally speaking, the British comedies were poor. *Poet's Pub* was a travesty of a good novel. *Helter Skelter* started with one comedian, was expanded to take in eight, and failed through sheer weight of numbers and lack of a good script. *Vice Versa* was boring, and *Warning to Wantons*, *Stop Press Girl*, and *The Perfect Woman* are best forgotten.

On the other hand, *Easy Money* was a delightful comedy drama in four episodes about various people who won a fortune in the football pools. Edward Rigby stole the acting honours as a dispirited bass player in an orchestra. Having won a fortune he returns to the orchestra he loves, and saves it from ruin by taking it over—but only on condition that prominence is given to the bass players.

Noel Coward's *Blithe Spirit*, transferred almost intact from the stage, was amusing, and so for a wider public was the *Huggett Family series*, although they lacked the sentimental warmth of the American *Andy Hardy series*. The characters of Mr and Mrs Huggett, delightfully played by Jack Warner and Kathleen Harrison, were first introduced in *Holiday Camp*, but were never fully developed on sentimental lines. The Hardy family, however, appeared wholly believable, while the Huggett family remained slightly unreal. The Huggetts led lives which were too complicated to be true. Millions of picturegoers —at least in Britain—felt that Mickey Rooney was typical of young America, and were touched by the performances given by that brilliant character actor Lewis Stone.

Kathleen Harrison had first won recognition in the thirties with her character study of a cockney mother with Wally Patch in Carol Reed's *Bank Holiday*. Jack Warner, the brother of the music hall and radio stars Elsie and Doris Waters, soon realized that to expect British producers to develop him as a film comedian was expecting too much, and wisely branched out as a character actor, appearing with distinction in *It Always Rains on Sunday*, *The Captive Heart*, *Against the Wind*, *The Blue Lamp*, and many other pictures. He soon established a distinctive following in Britain.

The John Mills production of *The History of Mr Polly*, which Chaplin had once wanted to make, was a considerable triumph, although it lacked the touch which Chaplin alone could have given it. Mills, who in 1947 was voted the most popular male star in British films, produced a film which was strong in human interest, and was well supported by Megs Jenkins, Finlay Currie, Moore Marriott, Miles Malleson, Edward Chapman, and Diana Churchill. A later dramatic subject in which John Mills appeared with Valerie Hobson, *The Rocking Horse Winner*, was one of the most polished productions to emerge from British studios since the war.

Despite excellent performances from the veteran actor A. E. Matthews, Cecil Parker, David Tomlinson, and Marjorie Fielding, *The Chiltern Hundreds* was too conscious of its theatrical origin to be wholly amusing. But it was well directed, as was *Tony Draws a Horse*, a popular picture which enjoyed success not only in Britain, Canada, Australia, and South Africa, but also in the United States, where the critical *Hollywood Reporter* trade review described the acting as 'brilliant' and classed the direction by John Paddy Carstairs (the son of Nelson Keys) as 'top flight'. Few Rank directors could earn this sort of praise from Americans, but it was there to be won, if it was justified.

The Perfect Woman deserves attention because it was typical of the earnest desire to produce a *funny* film. Every known device was dragged in to raise a laugh, yet Stanley Holloway was largely wasted through lack of good material, and Irene Handl —a natural commedienne—was not given one amusing line to say. Nigel Patrick, a newcomer to the screen from the stage, stole the acting honours, and managed with the help of Miles Malleson to infuse life into a plot which might have justified two reels, but could hardly stretch to eight-nine minutes.

*

Of all the comedies from British studios none were more popular than those made at Ealing by Sir Michael Balcon, who had several years previously joined forces with Victor Saville, first as a film salesman, and then as a producer of advertising films. Soon he was to become Britain's leading producer, but their activities with their first company, Victory Motion Pictures, revealed little promise. It was director Graham Cutts who advised them to concentrate on feature films, and with financial aid from C. M. Woolf and Oscar Deutsch, later the founder of the Odeon theatre group, a start was made in 1923 with *Woman to Woman*, featuring Betty Compson and Clive Brook. The picture was a considerable success, and assured them of a promising future.

With the assistance of a young chartered accountant named Reginald Baker, Balcon took over the film studio in Poole Street, Islington, from Paramount. This was to be the headquarters of the new company, Gainsborough Pictures. Later Balcon became production chief at the Gaumont British studios at Lime Grove, Shepherds Bush, where during the thirties he produced the majority of Britain's major films, including *The 39 Steps, Sunshine Susie, Friday the Thirteenth, Rome Express, The Good Companions, Forever England*, the Jack Hulbert and Cicely Courtneidge musicals, and the melodious pictures with Lillian Harvey, Jan Kiepura, Marta Eggerth, Evelyn Laye, Jessie Matthews, and Sonnie Hale. These pictures were assured of a world market.

Meanwhile Reginald Baker had joined producer Basil Dean at Ealing studios, and when the Shepherds Bush studio closed, Balcon was invited to make pictures there with Walter Forde. When Basil Dean resigned from Ealing, Balcon joined the board of directors and became the executive producer of the company.

During the war years the output of films from Ealing included such excellent subjects as *Next of Kin, The Foreman Went to France* (by J. B. Priestley, with Tommy Trinder starring), *Nine Men, San Demetrio, London, The Big Blockade, They Came to a City, Champagne Charlie, Dead of Night*, and *The Captive Heart*. Ealing was the brightest spot on the British film map, its war-time semi-documentaries being realistic, powerful, and entertaining. And when Balcon's team turned to comedy they made almost none of the mistakes of their colleagues at Shepperton, Denham, Iver, and Islington. The Ealing studios, backed by Courtauld money and assured of release for their films by the Rank organization, soon became the centre for all that was brightest and best in British film comedy. Perhaps J. Arthur Rank was wise to leave most of the humour to Michael Balcon. Trade marks might come and go, but it seemed that the Ealing team had inherited something of the pioneer spirit of the older studio, built by Will Barker many years before, and still visible over the wall.

Tommy Trinder, George Formby, Will Hay, Claude Hulbert, and Alistair Sim were all given better material at Ealing than could be found elsewhere. But it was with *Kind Hearts and Coronets, Passport to Pimlico, Hue and Cry, Whiskey Galore, The Man in the White Suit, The Lavender Hill Mob,* and *The Titfield Thunderbolt* that the Ealing team reached their highest level of screen comedy. The story and the situations were given prominence, and the players, having been carefully cast in character roles, were given witty lines and amusing by-play, and were encouraged to contribute cameo performances which would assist the entertainment value of the whole. The script and its treatment were considered more important than any single player. But only the best players were asked to contribute.

T. E. B. Clarke, who had joined Ealing in 1943, was responsible for the screenplays for *Hue and Cry, Passport to Pimlico, The Magnet, The Lavender Hill Mob,* and *The Titfield Thunderbolt.* 'We try to devise amusing stories about everyday people,' he says. 'While the old style of comedy is set in cuckoo land, and is full of fantastic situations, we like to invent highly improbable but not impossible themes. The humour must not be too absurd. We keep one little toe on the ground.'

Passport to Pimlico showed how the people living in part of Pimlico, in London, discovered that under an old charter the land on which they lived was in reality part of Burgundy, France. In order to create comedy situations from this improbable—but not impossible—theme, several script conferences were held in the studios. 'If the same thing happened here, in the studio, what would we do?' asked T. E. B. Clarke. It was obvious that the technicians would not all rush off to the wardrobe department, to borrow suits of armour, or French clothes. What would probably happen is the trades union officials would want to know how they stood. And so in *Passport to Pimlico* the question was set—what would the government do? Clarke and some of his colleagues went and saw some legal advisers, and gave them the problem: if people in Pimlico discovered that they were part of Burgundy, what *would* be the legal position?

The film won praise on both sides of the Atlantic. Yet, with the possible exception of Stanley Holloway, there were no big stars. It was the story and the treatment that mattered. Even the best players are unlikely to succeed without these essentials.

Whiskey Galore, written by Compton Mackenzie and set in a remote Scottish island, told the amusing story of a wrecked cargo of precious whisky and its effect on the islanders. Again, it was not an impossible theme.

One of the great discoveries of the Ealing studios was Alec Guinness. Although he had been given his first chance in the part of Herbert Pocket in Rank's *Great Expectations*, it was Michael Balcon who built up his reputation along comedy lines. Described by Leonard Mosley of the London *Daily Express* as 'the only comedian in films today (with the exception of Chaplin) who can conjure a laugh out of the air with a curl of his finger, a twitch of his face, or a flick of his foot', Guinness was the great discovery of post-war British films. In Ealing's *Kind Hearts and Coronets* he played eight leading characters. As a general, an admiral, a duke, a banker, a parson, as the D'Ascoyne brothers, and finally as Agatha D'Ascoyne, he revealed himself to be a masterly character actor, as well as a brilliant comedian.

'I must admit,' he said, 'that I'm not looking forward to the scene in which five of the eight characters I play meet at the funeral of the sixth!'

'Directing him is an extraordinary experience,' said Robert Hamer. 'There is no one to approach Guinness. When he is playing the part of a young blood, everything is wizard and jolly good fun. But approach him in the same manner when he is playing an aristocratic old Duke, and you immediately sense a frigid reaction. He looks at you as if to say "How dare you be so impertinent, young man?" I have to call him Sir.'

Guinness had not always known success. He attributed it later

247

to 'lack of food and early disappointments.' When he was hard up he once called on John Gielgud in his dressing-room at the theatre. Gielgud had £25 in notes on the dressing-table. 'Take this,' he said, offering Guinness the money. But Guinness refused, said good-night to Gielgud, and walked out—to his first job in the theatre. His film earnings during 1950 totalled about £25,000. Not a fantastic sum by Hollywood standards, but Alec Guinness was to become one of the highest-paid international stars.

After he had played in *Great Expectations* he had lunch with director David Lean, who naturally thought of him as the actor who had played nice young Herbert Pocket in the film.

'Of course, you people don't want real actors,' said Guinness provocatively. 'You just want types. For instance, you would never think of casting me as Fagin in *Oliver Twist*, would you?'

'Not in a hundred years,' replied Lean.

'Ah—but that's where you would be wrong,' said Guinness quickly. And some weeks later he was able to prove it.

In *A Run for Your Money*, *The Lavender Hill Mob*, and *The Man in the White Suit*, Alec Guinness added new lustre to the reputation already enjoyed by Ealing studios. A master of make-up, he seemed to be able to sink his entire personality in the part he was playing. This was evident when he appeared as Disraeli in *The Mudlark* for 20th Century Fox, and it was equally obvious when he became a young man who invents a cloth that will not wear out, in *The Man in the White Suit*.

Seventeen years earlier he had been a crowd player earning a guinea a day in the Evelyn Laye musical *Evensong*, produced by Michael Balcon at Shepherds Bush. Had the producer known it, one of the most unimportant actors in the studio during the making of the picture was to be in 1951 not only the leading stars of several of his films, but also the most popular player of the year in British pictures.

In this year Guinness started work on *The Card*, adapted from the novel by Arnold Bennett and produced by John Bryan under the direction of Ronald Neame—the son of Elwin Neame and Ivy Close—for the Rank organisation. As usual, the star gave a polished and highly amusing performance. Yet here was proof that there is little new under the sun, and nothing new under

248

the arc lamps. For *The Card* had been filmed before, back in 1921, by Ideal Films at Elstree. The star then had been Laddie Cliff—in some ways similar to Alec Guinness—and the picture was a success. All his actions fitted perfectly with the character which Arnold Bennett had created. The story was carefully adapted, and faithfully transferred to the screen. But few of the millions who admired Alec Guinness in *The Card* could remember Laddie Cliff in the same role. That is the tragedy of screen fame, which is so often only a passing glory.

*

An important feature of British films has always been the excellence of the supporting character player. Such troupers as Edward Rigby, Johnnie Schofield, Mark Daly, H. F. Maltby (the perfect gouty colonel), the dour John Laurie, Marjorie Fielding, Raymond Huntley, the gentlemanly and placid Cecil Parker, Wally Patch, Roddy Hughes, and Michael Medwin—these were players who in either large or small roles could be relied upon to give outstanding performances—regardless of star values.

It is said that on one occasion Johnnie Schofield was being considered for a dramatic part. *'Not on your life!'* exclaimed the director. *'The audience will roar with laughter directly he comes on the screen!'*

This is, of course, a mistaken impression, the result of an actor playing several successive comedy roles. Directors tend too often to think of types, and not of acting ability. When Chaplin first made a success in pictures a number of comedians started to be 'like Charlie Chaplin'. Naturally, it was an impossibility. Thus, Alec Guinness could play Fagin in *Oliver Twist*, having played young Herbert Pocket in *Great Expectations*. It follows that the director who believed that the audience would automatically roar with laughter directly Johnnie Schofield appeared, thought of this actor only as a type, as a funny man—and nothing more. This is, of course, absurd. Any good comedian should be able to move an audience to tears. The late Moore Marriott, who played the idot brilliantly as Harbottle in the Will Hay comedies, was a character actor of distinction, who had appeared in the melodramatic *The Monkey's Paw*, and in dozens of other serious film roles before becoming a toothless

249

old fool in knockabout comedies. Tom Walls gave up comedy parts to prove that he was a good straight actor. And Jack Warner did the same. Type casting is all too common, but it is a mistake.

An actor of the calibre of Edward Rigby, who had made his stage début in 1900, could be relied upon to give a reliable performance every time. He was only one of the many players who could steal the show. Hermione Baddeley was another, her comedy relief in *Brighton Rock* showing a fine sense of timing and human observation. During the forties there were many other British players who could contribute outstanding character studies, sometimes humorous, but always in character. These included Francis L. Sullivan, Margaret Rutherford, Joyce Grenfell, Bernard Miles, William Hartnell, Esme Percy, Basil Radford, Naunton Wayne, Wilfred Hyde White, and, until he became a star in his own right, Peter Ustinov.

The American comedies were even richer in scene stealers. Billie Burke, Donald Meek, Hugh Herbert, Edward Everett Horton, and Eugene Pallette could win honours in any sequence. So could Una Merkel, Allan Jenkins, James Gleason, Bryant Washburn, Charles Butterworth, and Charles Grapewin. And every one of these eleven players had been popular in the days of silent films.

There were many others. With thirty years' stage experience in musical comedy, opera, and drama, Walter Catlett entered films in 1929. He had grown up with Charles Ruggles, Al Jolson, and Leo Carrillo, and had known insecurity as a struggling young actor. He remembered trying to impress a landlady by telling her that one day people would point at her house and say that the great actor Catlett had lived there.

'All right,' said the landlady, 'but if you don't pay your rent tonight, they'll be saying that tomorrow.'

Then there was Franklyn Pangborn—a male version of Zasu Pitts—very much misunderstood in *My Man Godfrey, Don't Gamble with Love, See My Lawyer, You Came Along*, and dozens of other pictures, and famous as a picture stealer. And Andy Clyde, who created a film character with the aid of a pair of spectacles and a walrus moustache, making his name in a series of short Sennett comedies in the late twenties, to become one of

Hollywood's most popular supporting comedians, especially in cowboy pictures.

Another star from the Sennett days was Edgar Kennedy—the 'slow burn' comedian—who had delighted audiences with his *Average Man series* for Radio Pictures, and during the thirties and forties was continuously making pictures, as was Leon Errol, who had been Florenz Ziegfeld's star comedian for several years before entering silent films. His many pictures included—*Paramount on Parade, Only Saps Work, One Heavenly Night, Finn and Hattie*, the *Joe Palooka series*, and *Her Majesty Love*. Once he had planned to be a doctor. But instead, he preferred to support Dorothy Gish in *Clothes Make the Pirate*, and Colleen Moore in *Sally*.

Way back in the silent days young Clifton Webb had made his screen début with Richard Barthelmess. In London he had been well known as a dancing partner to Phyllis Monkman. Now he appeared as a smart Broadway critic in *Laura*, and stole the picture. He was at once offered another comedy part, in *The Razor's Edge*, followed by the starring role in *Sitting Pretty*, in which he introduced the amazing character of Lynn Belvedere, the man who knows all the answers and has done everything. The film, which told of an American family which engaged a baby sitter, only to find that the nurse was a man instead of a woman, was delightful farce. Inevitably, other Mr Belvedere films followed. Clifton Webb was no longer a scene stealer; the picture was his.

Another scene stealer who became a star during the forties was Mickey Rooney, who had first appeared in films as a baby, with Colleen Moore. After working in short comedies for Al Christie, as Mickey McGuire, he changed his name to Rooney in 1933, for the film *My Pal the King*. By 1937, when he became a member of the famous Hardy film family, he had appeared in nearly a hundred pictures.

A Family Affair, made by 20th Century Fox, introduced Lionel Barrymore as Judge Hardy, Spring Byington as his wife, and Mickey Rooney as the son Andy. It was an immediate success, and a year later M.G.M. produced their sequel, *You're Only Young Once*, with Lewis Stone as the judge, and Fay Holden as his wife. After this nothing could stop the adventures of the

Hardy family and their precocious son. Seeing the success of the Hardy films at M.G.M., 20th Century Fox immediately teamed Spring Byington and Jed Prouty in a rival, *The Jones Family series*. These were slightly more farcical than the Hardys, but were very popular.

In twelve more Hardy films young Mickey Rooney stole the acting honours, until he was too old to play the part. The formula in each film was similar. When Andy got into trouble, which was three or four times in each story, father would give him an informal but serious talk. Family life was centred around the breakfast-table and the telephone, and there was little relaxation in the house. Andy Hardy rushed up and down stairs, and was always having girl trouble. When Judy Garland appeared in the second film it was inevitable that much of the comedy would be devoted to adolescent love. But the series maintained warm family appeal, and was deservedly popular.

Two years after their first Hardy film, M.G.M. gave Ann Sothern the leading role in *Maisie*, the first of another family series. *Congo Maisie, Gold Rush Maisie, Maisie was a Lady*, and *Cash and Carry* were some of the titles.

*

A film in the Ealing tradition came from Elstree and the versatile pen of J. B. Priestley in 1949, when the famous author turned producer to film his own screenplay *Last Holiday*. The leading part, tailored to suit the personality of Alec Guinness, was that of an ordinary young man who hears from a doctor that he has only six months to live. He determines to enjoy every minute of his short time on earth, and goes off to a seaside luxury hotel, to enjoy himself. Ironically, for he has never before attracted attention, he finds that he is now a success. The ending of the story is unconventional, but true to life. And in the leading part Alec Guinness was given some of the best dialogue heard in a British film for many years.

However, partly because of its unconventional unhappy ending, *Last Holiday* was not given a first showing in a major London theatre. This did not prevent its enthusiastic reception in New York. But it was disconcerting to discover that the happy ending was still a vital requirement for a film story. *Picturegoer* magazine devoted a page to an open letter to J. B.

Priestley, urging him to continue to write and make more films. Too often, suggested the magazine, British pictures were impossibly handicapped by a poor story, a bad script, and unreal dialogue. Better films could be made only if the best authors were prepared to devote their time and talents to a medium which needed good writers with a knowledge of the cinema, the theatre, and most important of all—real people.

But perhaps the public did not want real people? That romantic light comedy could be a very profitable medium was proved by Herbert Wilcox, whose *Spring in Park Lane* (1948) had brought £1,400,000 to the box-office, of which £540,000 was paid to the national exchequer in tax. Theatre and distribution costs having been satisfied, some £275,000 was left to Wilcox, with which to pursue his profitable policy of presenting Anna Neagle in light-hearted Cinderella pictures; a policy which was to make her the most popular star in British films.

Herbert Wilcox recalls that when he first decided to make a musical picture, *Goodnight Vienna*, he began a long and arduous search for a leading lady to star with Jack Buchanan. He searched his files, recalled recent films, and sat through picture after picture—all with no result. Then a conference took him to the London Hippodrome, where Buchanan was starring in *Stand Up and Sing*.

'Jack was on the stage,' says Wilcox, 'and to while away the time I watched the show. Thus I set eyes on Anna Neagle. It was the first occasion on which I had seen her, and quite by accident.'

Jack Buchanan was willing to back the expert judgment of Herbert Wilcox, and so Anna Neagle became a screen star. According to the American *Motion Picture Herald* magazine she was in 1948 second among the international money-makers in British cinemas:

1. Bing Crosby
2. Anna Neagle
3. Margaret Lockwood
4. John Mills
5. Michael Wilding
6. Frederic March
7. Bob Hope

253

8. Danny Kaye
9. Myrna Loy
10. Gregory Peck

Wilcox followed up his success by repeating the same formula, and during the British film depression of 1948–49 his were almost the only English pictures assured of nationwide support. Many of the other films from British studios were severely criticized. But Herbert Wilcox had learned the hard way, through long experience of the film industry, in which he had started with his brother as a distributor. He had first established his reputation in 1921 with a modest feature called *The Wonderful Story*, which he directed. Then came *Chu Chin Chow*, made in Germany with British and American players. His many other early films had included *Decameron Nights*, *Southern Love*, *London*, *Madame Pompadour*, *Dawn*, *The Blue Danube*, *Goodnight Vienna*, *The Little Damozel*, *Say it with Music*, and *Nell Gwyn*, which really put him on the film map. This, his first version, was made at Elstree, and Dorothy Gish came over from America to star in it. The film was sold to First National in the United States for a record sum.

As chief of production at the small British and Dominions studio at Elstree, Wilcox introduced to the screen not only Anna Neagle, but Sydney Howard, Tom Walls, Ralph Lynn, Robertson Hare, Winifred Shotter, and many other stars. Anna Neagle made her film début in 1929, but had to wait until 1948 before becoming a leading attraction.

In America one of the highest paid stars was Betty Grable, who was in 1946 the highest paid woman in the country, with an income of £74,825 a year. She was only one of the 900 American men and women who annually earned more than the £18,750 paid to the President of the United States. Bing Crosby's salary in this year was £81,250, David Niven earned £48,500, Loretta Young some £46,666, Ronald Colman £18,956, Ray Milland £57,291, and Danny Kaye £33,482. All these were comedy or light entertainers and they headed the lists.

In 1948 came the death of David Wark Griffith, almost forgotten, but described by critic Dilys Powell as 'the Dickens of the screen'. His immensely touching passages of great tenderness had combined with his noble composition of battle and crowd scenes to add great lustre to the history of the cinema. Apart from Mary Pickford, Griffith had brought to the screen the Gish sisters, Mae Marsh, Richard Barthelmess, Lionel Barrymore, Mack Sennett, Douglas Fairbanks, and many other great names. A lover of the classical English novelists, he had once admitted that many of the innovations which he introduced to films had their origin in the works of those authors whom he so greatly admired. With Griffith's death, those who cared seriously for films looked back, and realized how great his contribution had been to entertainment, to enlightenment, and to the many fine pictures which other directors made under his influence.

CHAPTER EIGHTEEN

The Summing Up

FEW OF THE British scene stealers were more popular than Alistair Sim, a tall, thin, slightly bald Scots actor, who had by 1949 established himself as a leading character comedian. He had made his screen début in 1934 in a minor role in *The Private Secretary*, and had later contributed to the humour of the *Inspector Hornleigh series, Green for Danger, Hue and Cry, Waterloo Road*, and *London Belongs to Me*. In the film version of Frank Dighton's play *The Happiest Days of Your Life* he played the part of the headmaster of Nutbourne College, Dr Wetherby Pond, and was partnered by Margaret Rutherford and supported by Joyce Grenfell, Guy Middleton, John Bentley, Muriel Aked, and Edward Rigby. This was one of the most successful and amusing British films of the early fifties, being improbable but not impossible—in the Ealing tradition—but highly farcical. The plot is worth examining:

The holidays are over at Nutbourne College. The masters are assembled in Dr Wetherby Pond's study when Rainbow, the porter, informs them that one hundred extra trunks have arrived. It is discovered that the Ministry of Education—Resettlement Department—has allocated another school, St Swithin's, to share accommodation at Nutbourne. Apart from the fact that there is no extra food, and no room for the new-comers, all is well. Meanwhile, up the long drive a small and rather formidable party is advancing, led by Miss Whitchurch (Margaret Rutherford). This is the headmistress of St Swithin's, which is a girls' school.

With the arrival of both boys and girls the fun starts. Most of the domestic staff leave, and because of the new arrangements, the masters sleep in the attics. Miss Whitchurch claims the headmaster's bed. Mr Pond finds peace only in his bath. Next morning they both telephone the Ministry, but get no satisfaction.

Then comes news of a visit from some of the girls' parents. While Miss Whitchurch sees them, Mr Pond sets out for London and the Ministry. But at the station he is met by three governors of his school, on a surprise duty visit. They are taken on a long round-about route to Nutbourne, where a plan is quickly made so that the visiting parents will see only the girls, and the governors only the boys.

All goes well, but it cannot last. Eventually parents, governors, boys and girls—all come face to face, while a frantic Mr Pond and a frenzied Miss Whitchurch attempt to explain matters. A representative of the Ministry now informs them that all is in order, for another school is to be sent to Nutbourne —a co-educational school. Coach loads of boys and girls suddenly invade the grounds, as we leave Mr Pond and Miss Whitchurch planning their immediate departure for distant and saner lands.

*

The late forties marked the return of the voice of the first great talkie star, Al Jolson. After making a number of undistinguished pictures, he had fallen out of favour in the thirties, and had ceased to be a film attraction. Some ten years after his screen début he was virtually forgotten, almost unknown to a new generation. Columbia Pictures decided to make a musical film based on his life story and thirty-year-old Larry Parks was engaged to play the part of Jolson, to master every extravagant gesture and grimace of the black-faced coon singer, and to act before the cameras in the song sequences while Jolson's own voice was heard on the sound track. In Technicolor, *The Jolson Story* was a triumph, grossing over thirteen million dollars at the box-office, of which Jolson himself received over three million. In 1947 the forgotten star was voted the most popular singer in America—ahead of Bing Crosby and Frank Sinatra. Two years later came a sequel, *Jolson Sings Again*, with the same formula and almost as popular. When Jolson died suddenly in 1950 he was again a wealthy man, ending his life on top of the fickle entertainment world which is so rich in reversals. In its last years the first voice of the screen had found recognition with a new generation.

In 1949 the veteran English actor Sir Seymour Hicks died at the age of seventy-eight. He belonged to an age of great wit, of rich conversation and gracious living, and he was one of the finest comedians the English stage had produced, starting his career on the boards earning a shilling a night. He was to make and lose fortunes, but never to lose his fame as a fine actor, a humorist, and a writer. Nobody called out 'Author!' on the first night of one of his early plays, so he ran to the back of the theatre and shouted out for himself at the top of his voice. The audience took up the cry. Then he ran back to the stage to take the applause.

When he was earning £8 a week he proposed to Ellaline Terriss, his beautiful leading lady. Ten days later they married, and celebrated the wedding with Irish stew. The marriage lasted for fifty-four years, and was one of the great romances of the theatre. 'I owe everything to her,' said Sir Seymour.

As he lay dying, television audiences were laughing at the television showing of his film *A Young Man's Fancy*, which he had made several years previously for Michael Balcon. He did not know this, but he would have been pleased, for in the tradition of the theatre, the show was still going on.

*

From Elstree in 1951 came two widely different comedies, hoping to compete with the more lavish standards of Hollywood's *On the Town*, *Born Yesterday*, *The Groom Wore Spurs*, *Father's Little Dividend*, and Danny Kaye's *On the Riviera*. To make the comedy *Laughter in Paradise*, from an original story by Michael Pertwee and Jack Davies, producer-director Mario Zampi enlisted the services of Alistair Sim, Fay Compton, Beatrice Campbell, Guy Middleton, A. E. Matthews, Joyce Grenfell, and Leslie Dwyer. The story was about the last will and testament of an eccentric practical joker, and showed how four relatives responded to the news that they would inherit £50,000 if they completed certain tasks. Thus, a snobbish spinster who has treated her maid badly is required to become a servant for a month, a playboy has to marry the first girl he speaks to, a timid bank clerk has to hold up his bank manager with a gun, and a retired army officer who secretly writes bloodcurdling novels has to spend twenty-eight days in gaol for a genuine crime.

Laughter in Paradise proved to be one of the most profitable comedies of the year, and one of the funniest films made at Elstree. It was more successful than its successor *Top Secret*. In comparison, *Happy Go Lovely* was an opulent musical comedy in the Hollywood tradition—the type of film seldom attempted in England. With David Niven, Vera-Ellen, Cesar Romero, and Bobby Howes, it was the best British musical for many years. An American director and Hollywood influence did not alter the fact that it was an entertaining and light-hearted picture, made in Britain. In a supporting role Bobby Howes proved that he was one of the neglected light comedians of the screen.

The comedy touch was also apparent at Walton-on-Thames, where modern studios had grown up around Hepworth's house 'The Rosary', to become in the years 1950–1953 England's busiest film centre. Here a large number of independent producers was engaged in making pictures, as many as nineteen features being made in one year. Of these, *The Pickwick Papers*, *Mr Drake's Duck* (Douglas Fairbanks, Jnr. and Yolande Donlan), *The Body Said No* (Michael Rennie and Yolande Donlan), and *Murder at the Windmill* were the best comedies. When the studios themselves made a comedy, producer Ernest Roy chose as his star Richard Hearne, whose talents as a stage and television comedian had been recognized, although his film possibilities had been largely ignored.

In *Something in the City* (Nettlefold Films) he was allowed full scope for the type of visual fooling seldom seen in sound films. He played the part of Mr Ningle, apparently a city man, always punctual, by whom the neighbours set their clocks. Every morning he goes off to work, and every evening he returns to his suburban home. But in reality Mr Ningle is a pavement artist, and the double life which he has been leading for years is now suddenly revealed.

Richard Hearne is a true clown, and comes of a family of famous performing clowns. Like Buster Keaton, he is an accomplished acrobat. His pantomime is therefore silent, and fits the true film technique perfectly. In *Something in the City* and less successfully in a second film, *Madame Louise*, director Maclean Rogers recognized the value of visual fooling and allowed it to intrude on the story, so that the best parts of the picture were in fact the silent passages, sometimes with musical backgrounds. In these Hearne tumbled, fell, slipped through drain gratings, became caught up on walls, and rode in and out of a crowded store on a miniature motor cycle. It was quite evident that Richard Hearne could extract more humour *silently* from a given situation than most British film comedians. He is in every way a throw-back to Larry Semon days, an era in which talking was unnecessary. His actions speak for themselves, for he conveys an impression, a touch of sentiment, or a desire, with only the movement of a hand, a walk, a look, or an inclination of his head.

Hearne exploits the traditions of clowning. All the world seems against him; he is a stumbler, a man with too many parcels to carry, who must inevitably drop first one, and then another, and in stooping to pick them up, will drop them all. If he climbs a ladder it is only to sway, first backwards and then forwards, and then to fall off. When he is escaping through a window, in a desperate hurry, the top half of the sash will descend on his head. But if he is foolish, at the mercy of kitchen utensils, gas stoves, washing-up machines, and alarm clocks, then we are all fools; for, surely, we are in the same boat? We have all fumbled for our latch keys, and dropped our gloves in the process. Keaton, Hearne and Wisdom would take it a stage further, and end up with their gloves in their mouths, and the key lost in a gold-fish pond. But, basically, this comedy of human errors is common to all the best comedians, and it is *silent*.

※

It is important to remember that not all the best film comedies of the sixty years under review came from America. In sheer weight of tins of film, the Americans led the comedy race for some forty years. But many of the most amusing later comedies came from France, Italy, and the Scandinavian countries.

We have seen how, in the earliest days of silent pictures,

France and Italy led the world in the making of comic and trick films. We have considered the genius of Max Linder, discovered by Charles Pathé, who influenced Chaplin and possibly the whole school of American star comedians. We have paid brief tribute to Dranem, Polycarpe, Zigoteau, and Boncot of France, and to the early Italian clowns, André Deed (Foolshead), Tweedledum, Polidor, Bloomer, and Tontolini. There were of course dozens of others, from Charles Prince (Rigadin, Tarfutini, or Wiffles) to Bout-de-Zan, the child wonder who was really an old man.

After the early French comedies of Méliès (*Le Voyage à Travers L'Impossible* (1906) is a typical example) and Jean Durand's many comedies, there was in the early twenties a scarcity of good French comedies which was relieved only by *Parisette* (1921), *Le Voyage Imaginaire* (1925), and René Clair's notable *Un Chapeau de Paille d'Italie* (1927).

The lull continued during the thirties, with such brilliant exceptions as *A Nous la Liberté*, *La Kermesse Héroique*, and the early pictures of Fernandel. Indeed, until the forties there were comparatively few outstanding French or Italian comedies to compete with the tremendous output from Hollywood. Britain, as we have seen, was fourth or fifth as far as quality was concerned. But French pictures of the calibre of *Un Carnet de Bal* (a drama as good as that of any other country in the world) and *Sous les Toits de Paris* were outstanding achievements.

Since the second world war, however, there has been a tremendous revival in European films, especially in France and Italy, where producers have seemed determined to prove that Hollywood's supremacy has been largely unrealistic, not always artistic, and too often based on mere lavish spectacle.

In 1949 some 860 Italian films were exported to fifty-three countries. In 1951 nearly 1,300 were shown in sixty-eight countries. For the first time since the early silent days, Italian producers, directors, and stars had become internationally known. The names, to mention only a few of Italy's leading film personalities, the names of Aldo Fabrizi, Vittorio de Sica, Rossellini, Gina Lollobrigida, Gabrielle Ferzetti, Silvana Mangano, Franco Interlenghi, Lea Padovani, and Raf Vallone were now to be seen on posters all over the world. Their films were competing favourably with Hollywood's best.

The most popular of the Italian comedians was probably Toto, who looked like a cross between Keaton, Somerset Maugham, and Claude Rains, and claimed descent—rather seriously—from the Emperor Constantine of Byzantium. Becoming a comedian in spite of his family's wishes, this droll first appeared in Italian stage revues and made a not wholly successful film début during the thirties. From 1946, however, he was Italy's leading film comedian, his popularity being enough to guarantee commercial success for any of his pictures.

Thus, there was *Toto Cerca Mogue*, *47 Morto Che Parla*, *Toto Terzo Uomo*, *Toto A Colori*, *Toto 17 Re di Roma*, and many other pictures bearing Toto's name. De Filippo's *Napoli Millionaria*, Monicelli's *Guardie E Ladri* (*Cops and Robbers*), and Rossellini's *Dov'e la Liberta?* (*Where is Liberty?*) presented the clown in more mature roles than his earlier pictures. In the Monicelli film Toto was seen as Ferdinando Esposito, who lives by cheating foreign visitors to Rome. In the latter picture he was seen being discharged from prison after twenty-five years' imprisonment. But he finds life in the outside world so strange that he breaks into prison again, and is happy only when he is sentenced to a further term. This plot could be said to be almost tailor-made for Buster Keaton.

In France the leading comedians included Fernandel, Bourvil, and Jacques Tati. Fernandel, all jaw and teeth, described by the London *Daily Express* as owning 'The World's Most Expressive Face', earned his first success in a Paris music hall, having won an amateur talent contest. A part in a revue at the Concert Mayol led to his film début in Sacha Guitry's *Le Blanc at le Noir*, produced by Marc Allegret in 1930. Since then he has made over a hundred films, and in most of them his producers have exploited the comic possibilities of his features. The part of Isidore in *Le Rosier de Madame Husson* (*The Virtuous Isidore*) in 1932, was typical of the exploitation of the face value rather than of any dramatic ability.

During the thirties Fernandel starred in several dozen burlesque military comedies, such as *Le Coq du Régiment*, *Lidoire*, *La Garnison Amoureuse*, *Le Train de 8.4.47*, *Le Cavalier*,

Ignace, Les Blues de La Marine and *Les Dégourdis de la 11ᵉ*. He also appeared in the slightly vulgar knockabout comedies *Nuits de Folles, L'Hotel du Libre-Echange,* and *Ferdinand le Noceur*.

It was not until 1933 that his outstanding dramatic talent was revealed. His interpretation of the part of the clown Saturnin in Pagnol's *Angèle* revealed unsuspected ability as a character actor, which prompted Pagnol to provide Fernandel with further character comedy roles. With the making of *Regain* (1937), *Le Schpountz* (1937), *La Fille du Puisatier* (1940), *Uniformes et Grandes Manoeuvres* (1950), *Topaze* (1950), and *Coiffeur Pour Dames* and *Le Fruit Défendu* (1952) Fernandel was able to claim that he was the most popular figure in French films.

The comedian *Bourvil* (André Raimbourg) was a rival. Named after the village of Bourville where he was born in 1917, he came to the screen from the radio and cabaret, and could be considered more of a farcical comedian than Fernandel, neither so subtle nor so disarmingly gauche, but extremely popular.

Jacques Tati, however, was a visual comic in the best traditions of the silent screen. He at once claims our interest, if only for his film *Jour de Fête*, perhaps the most delightful comedy from French studios since René Clair's 1927 classic *Un Chapeau de Paille d'Italie*. Described by the *New Yorker* magazine as 'A film that looks like a new-day version of the sort of comedy Mack Sennett used to indulge in', *Jour de Fête* is a charming story about a village postman who sees a film about American quick-fire postal methods, and decides to introduce them into his village, with disastrous results.

Tati, with a little of the Keystone touch, is an absurdly tall and angular fellow who can raise more laughter in two minutes with a bicycle than many chattering comedians can gain in twenty minutes with a microphone.

In Sweden the leading comedian was Nils Poppe, whose film *Pengar (Money)* won the Grand Prix for its writer-director-star at the 1948 Venice Film Festival. This human comedy, reminiscent of René Clair and Capra, shows how a penniless tramp, who has decided to commit suicide, meets another hobo, who persuades him that life is worth living and that money is unimportant to happiness.

The three outstanding comedians of the Danish screen were

Carl Schenstrom (1881–1942), Harald Madsen (1890–1949) and Frederik Jensen (1863–1934). Schenstrom and Madsen were world famous as 'Long and Short', and appeared in many pictures together, including one made in Britain. Schenstrom's most famous films included *Han, Hun Og Hamlet* (*He, She and Hamlet*) made first in 1922 and again in 1932 by Lau Lauritzen, who also directed him in *Professor Petersen's Plejeborn* (*Professor Petersen's Foster-Children*) (1923), *Don Quixote* (1926) and *Vester Vov Vov* (1927).

Frederik Jensen's most successful films were *David Copperfield* (1922), *Little Dorrit* (1924), *Skal Vi Vadde En Million?* (*Shall We Bet a Million?*) (1932), and Sandberg's *Fem Raske Piger* (*Five Brave Girls*) (1933).

*

In 1950 Walt Disney, the world's acknowledged cartoon king, realized that he had a serious rival, a 38-year-old former employee of the Disney studios with the unlikely name of Steve Bosustow.

This artist, who incidentally bore a remarkable facial resemblance to Disney, left the home of Mickey Mouse in 1941 to start his own studio and to make cartoons as sophisticated in their new art form as Disney's pictures are charming in their fairytale simplicity.

The principal character in the cartoons made by United Productions of America is *Mr Magoo*, a near-sighted old gentleman whose half-closed eyes lead him from each mistake to a dozen fresh narrow escapes from disaster. In *Ragtime Bear* this doughty old character goes in search of peace and quiet to play golf, but mistakes a bear for his nephew. In *Trouble Indemnity* he takes out an insurance policy with a bogus company, and enjoys a series of hair-raising adventures on the scaffolding of a half-finished skyscraper, before arriving at the insurance office to claim for injuries sustained from a bite from a tiger rug. *Barefaced Flatfoot*, *Bungled Bungalow*, *Hotsey-Footsey*, and *Fuddy Duddy Buddy* are others in the *Mr Magoo series*. In the latter he is seen on holiday in Florida with his walrus-moustached English friend, Bottomly. Mr Magoo arranges to play tennis with his friend, and in his usual short-sighted manner he lands up, not on the tennis court, but in an enclosure where a walrus is kept for the entertainment of the guests. He mistakes the walrus for Bottomly, with hilarious results.

One of the first of the U.P.A. cartoons was *Gerald McBoing-Boing*, a seven-minute picture about a little boy who speaks no words, but can utter only strange hoots and sound effects. Shunned by his parents and playmates, little Gerald McCloy is nicknamed McBoing-Boing because of the noise he makes. But Gerald finally finds fame in a radio station, providing all the noises for the programmes, from the beat of galloping hooves to the chimes of the time signal. A sequel is entitled *Gerald McBoing-Boing's Symphony*.

U.P.A. cartoons contain less detail than those of Disney, but they are capable of containing almost as much charm. *Madeline*, the story by Ludwig Bemelmans about the youngest of twelve little girls in a Paris school, tells how they marched all over Paris in two straight lines, and 'in two straight lines they broke their bread, and brushed their teeth, and went to bed'. One night, little Madeline is rushed to hospital for an emergency operation. When her schoolmates visit her, she shows them the wonderful gifts she has received, but 'the biggest surprise by far—on her stomach was a scar'. That night the eleven girls wake up their teacher, and tell her, 'we want to have our appendix out, too.'

Here then is charm added to sophisticated treatment, to compare with the greater successes of Disney. What is perhaps more important is that Bosustow, like Disney, refuses to employ the dog versus cat or cat versus mouse themes in his cartoons. Humour which depends on the humiliation of others, or of animals, is not encouraged. Violence is not considered essential. For this reason alone, even if they were not also imaginatively conceived, the U.P.A. cartoons are well worth attention. They challenge Disney in technical perfection, but while Disney gives us tortoises, deer, badgers, and Mr Mouse, Bosustow produces modern cities drawn with simplicity of line, fast automobiles and tapering skyscrapers, and, strangest of all, the Edwardian Mr Magoo.

'He's the darlingest man I've seen on the screen for years,' wrote Elspeth Grant in the *Daily Sketch*.

*

The ranks of the true film clowns are thinning. Hugh Herbert, who died in March 1952, was one of the last of the genuine clowns. In England, Walter Forde, who had tumbled his way to film fame in the twenties, was happier as a director, off the screen.

'No, I've never wanted to go back,' he said. 'Mickey Balcon has begged me to act in a film again. But not me! Not much! I wouldn't even walk across. I'm still a shy man. . . . I don't think anything in the world would persuade me to put on grease-paint again.'

The new type of film comedian was a talking comic, like Bob Hope, Danny Kaye, and in England, Ronald Shiner, whose *Worm's Eye View*, made to a simple unsophisticated pattern in under six weeks for less than £50,000 by the former Hepworth actor, the late Jack Raymond, netted a profit of over £100,000, thus creating a demand for more Shiner in *Reluctant Heroes*, *Little Big Shot*, and *Top of the Form*.

In London, the trade paper *The Daily Film Renter* foresaw the success of *Reluctant Heroes* three months before the film was released, when it reported that whoever was reluctant, it would not be the cinema patrons. By 1953 Ronald Shiner was the most popular male star acting in British pictures. In 1954 came a promising rival from television, Norman Wisdom. In *Trouble in Store* the Rank Organisation produced a film which was, according to critic Dilys Powell, 'Full of gags, fallabout and little-man pathos'. In fact, many of the amusing gags were lifted from other, older films. The opening, with a rich car rolling by, revealing that Mr Wisdom was using it as a bicyclist's rest, was the opening to Harold Lloyd's *Movie Crazy*. Miss Powell considered that on the strength of this first film, Mr Wisdom lacked elegance, which was a feature of all the great filming comedians.

The most promising comic to enter British Films since the arrival of Guinness—if that versatile actor does not object to being called a comic—Norman Wisdom deserved better scripts than he got. The Hulberts, Sid Field, George Formby, Will Hay, Max Miller—these are a few of the British comedians with talent who did not get the scripts, who were never properly developed. Wisdom had even more talent, but would the Rank

Organisation learn the lessons of the past? Would they star Mr Wisdom in twelve two-reelers, so that he (and they) could learn the secrets which Lloyd, Keaton, Laurel and Hardy and the others had learned years ago? No; they were content to star him in picture after picture, and were satisfied that he soon became their biggest money-maker. In many foreign countries, Wisdom was a great favourite. But Americans did not like the Wisdom films, and he was not an international screen comic in the way that Lloyd and Keaton had been. It seemed that players (like Alec Guinness and Peter Sellers) reached international fame in *spite* of the British film industry, not because during the years under review there was any adventurous spirit in English production. Indeed, there was not. The best British films were still to come.

CHAPTER NINETEEN

Flashback

THE SILENT CLOWNS of yesterday were still popular, even in 1952, when James Anderson was preparing for cinema audiences a film devoted entirely to memories of the past. He was able to assemble in *Made for Laughs* scenes showing Mabel Normand, Ford Sterling, Mack Swain, and Fred Mace, the first Keystone comedian. Then there was Louise Fazenda, Charlie Murray, Max Asher, and Edgar Kennedy, with of course Charlie Chaplin, and his brother Syd. To complete the picture there was John Bunny, Flora Finch, Mr and Mrs Sidney Drew, Slim Summerville, Raymond Griffith, Oliver Hardy, and the two comics of Fred Karno fame, Billy Reeves and Billie Ritchie. All in one picture, with a youthful Lupino Lane, and Mack Sennett and his infamous Keystone cops.

Those who are fortunate enough to see a complete old comedy, perhaps at a local film society show or at a British Film Institute showing, know just how amusing the great clowns of the *silent* screen can still be. Twenty-eight years after it was made, Miss Joyce B. Clegg, of Rochdale, Lancs, saw one of these pictures, and wrote to the editor of *The Picturegoer* about it:

At a cinema repertory club recently I saw the 1923 silent picture 'Safety Last', starring Harold Lloyd. I have never seen anything so funny! The audience was in hysterics throughout. Film producers today could learn much about cinematic technique from some of the silent comedies, which depended upon action and the creation of amusing situations for their appeal, rather than upon slick dialogue and lavish settings.

In the same month another reader, Mr Gerald F. Emanuel, of London, wrote to the same editor:

Recently I saw Buster Keaton's silent picture 'The General'. It is certainly the funniest film I have seen for a long time. I hope someone will realize that Keaton, no less than Chaplin, can stand the test of time.

The test of time. That is it. How many of today's comedians will be worth seeing on the screen twenty years hence? Yet the pictures of Chaplin, Keaton, Mabel Normand, John Bunny, Harold Lloyd, Larry Semon, and Ford Sterling are constantly being revived by the major companies—such as Warner Brothers in their supporting 'Flashbacks', or on television. In the same month that Warners announced the completion of the twenty-ninth Abbott and Costello picture, *Jack and the Beanstalk*, they revealed that the older comedies die hard, for one of their supporting pictures would be a revival of Mack Sennett's *Here We Go Again*, with Charlie Murray.

*

What conclusion can we now reach after we have surveyed at length, year after year, the story of motion picture comedy and the comedians during the period 1894–1954?

We have seen how the pioneers created the traditions of visual comedy, how producers like Sennett and players like Chaplin, Keaton, Langdon, Charles Ray, and Harold Lloyd developed the technique, until by the late twenties the cinema offered almost perfect visual comedy entertainment, without a sound.

Then came the talkies, and with them a whole string of new names to exploit the comedy of speech, the wisecracks of the vaudeville stage and the radio. Once the silence was over, much of the magic of the cinema was lost. That, perhaps, is the conclusion we must reach. Today the humour is weighed down with talk. And although very few of the stage comedies of twenty years ago can be revived today and still raise laughter, yesterday's vintage silent comedies are often more amusing than modern humorous films.

It's New! It's Three Dimensional! It's the Funniest Picture ever made! scream the posters and the film trailers. But the truth is that there is very little that is new on the screen. It has all been done before, often much better. As for Three Dimensions, let us conquer one at a time. And the claim of any new film to be the *funniest* is a bold one. There have been quite a few comedies since Fred Ott's *Sneeze*, which started our story. Does any modern comedy compete with *The General?*

And so to Charles Chaplin, whose revival of *City Lights* some twenty years after it was made was hailed by *Life* magazine in America as 'the best picture of 1950'. He had made it in defiance of the early talking films, and it had outlived the best of them.

In 1951 he started work on *Limelight*, his story of the English music hall, in which he appears as Calvero, a renowned comedian of the past, who befriends a girl and saves her from suicide. When she becomes a successful ballerina his own career is fading, for he is no longer young, and has taken to hunting the bars. He wants to make a come-back, and dreams that he is sharing applause with the girl. But he fears that he has lost the ability to make audiences laugh. Then, for one wonderful evening, he again becomes the great music hall clown.

In Chaplin's own words, the film was about 'some of those Biblical people of the theatre, the simple, trusting children of God in a wild world'. It was a melodrama of tears, with only a little of the old Chaplin humour.

Ludovic Kennedy, who visited the Chaplin studio during production, sensed a return to the technique of earlier days. For two hours he watched Chaplin as an acrobatic violinist, accompanied by Buster Keaton, as a near-sighted pianist, burlesquing a riotous music hall act for the camera. During his sequence Chaplin's face reflected many of those subtle variations of expression which have become so familiar. In one sequence, reported Mr Kennedy, Chaplin got his foot stuck under the piano. There was the slow raising of the eyebrows to indicate Surprise; the freezing of the face and staring eyes to show Panic and Bewilderment; the sudden sideways twist of nose and mouth for Embarrassment; and—when his foot was at last free —the relaxing of the shoulders and pursing of the lips to show Relief and Dignity Regained.

'You know, this is real nostalgia for me. Sheer nostalgia,' said Chaplin, who had spent two years perfecting the story, and now modestly suggested that he thought it had emotional appeal. In *Limelight* he was author, producer, director, dialogue writer, composer, choreographer, film editor, costume designer, star, and the film's most exacting critic.

On Friday, December 28, 1951, the *Daily Mail* published an

account of a visit to the set made by one of its star writers, Collie Knox:

'Christmas in Hollywood did not feel like Christmas,' he reported. 'Maybe the occasion is too real for such an outpost of unreality. But I had my seasonable stocking in that within three hours I talked with Charlie Chaplin at his own studios for twenty minutes, watched him direct the first scene ever shot between him and his good-looking, six-foot-two, twenty-four year old son Syd, and was offered a part in this selfsame film, *Limelight*.

'He regarded me quizzically out of his brilliant blue eyes. "Ever been offered a part in pictures?" he asked. "You might not photograph too badly. I'll give you two lines in a scene in the old Empire Theatre in Leicester Square. Have to join the union, of course. What about it?"'

As the scene was not scheduled for two weeks, Collie Knox—tremulous though proud—had to reject what he called his 'first, and last, chance of screen immortality'.

Chaplin had stopped a rehearsal to talk to him. 'Though he's white-haired, those remarkable blue eyes, lithe figure, and air of nervous intensity give the lie to his sixty-two years. He was dressed for his role of a broken-down music hall actor. He spoke in a soft, very English voice as he told me he had taken two years to write this film, and that, apart from acting in it and directing it, he had composed all the music, scored it, and written the lyrics.'

To Knox Chaplin revealed that merely to stand on the set of the old Criterion bar made him homesick for England. He would like nothing better, he said, than to have the premiere in London, and to be there. This he was later able to do. Then he asked about London. 'Tell me about it,' he said.

Collie Knox watched him rehearse the scene seven times, and noted his incredible passion for detail.

'As the old busker,' he reported, 'he goes round the bar holding out his hat for money. He reaches a bench on which are sitting an elderly music hall manager, played by Nigel Bruce, and a young soldier in khaki, played by his son. The soldier has to look up, recognizing the busker, and go into his dialogue. Chaplin took his son again and again through the scene with

271

infinite patience but tireless insistence. At last he was satisfied and said: "That's fine. Now we'll do it all again, and then shoot it." '

Collie Knox thought that it was 'magical, how Chaplin stepped into the skin of the busker and drew it over him.' And he reported part of one of Chaplin's speeches, which ended with the words 'Time is the great author. It always writes the perfect ending.'

When he was leaving, Chaplin said to him, 'Give London my love. Remember the last time I was there and the traffic was held up in Piccadilly? But you are too young to remember.'

Before Collie Knox could tell him that he did remember, and wasn't too young, Chaplin had vanished into his portable dressing-room.

*

Above the table in the dressing-room, lit by powerful lights, is a mirror. Chaplin sits on his chair, and leans forward under the light to look more closely at himself. It may be that he is still thinking of his London, and is making up his mind to return. Or perhaps he is deciding some point about the next scene, which has soon to be rehearsed.

Did he but know it, all the history of film comedy is reflected in his looking-glass, as he sits gazing into it. Somewhere at the back of the room are the shadowy figures, the ghosts of the people who helped to bring laughter to an unhappy, mad world, but who are no longer with us. Chaplin has known them all. What memories their names bring back:

Max Linder, Larry Semon, Ford Sterling, John Bunny, Flora Finch, Roscoe Arbuckle, Harry Langdon, Ben Turpin, Will Rogers, Seymour Hicks, Will Fyffe, Charles Ray, Harry Myers, Marie Dressler, Wallace Beery, Hugh Herbert, Monty Banks, Florence Turner, Wallace Reid, Edna May Oliver, Sidney Drew, Marie Prevost, W. C. Fields, Leslie Howard, Douglas Fairbanks, Leon Errol, Mabel Normand.

Many others there are, stretching back through the years of motion picture history, too many to remember.

*

The figures at the back of the looking-glass watch silently, approvingly, as Chaplin pats back his white hair, and rising from his chair picks up his script. He looks once more at his reflection, at his Edwardian tail-coat, his high stiff collar, his brown trousers cut away below the knees, his striped socks, and his black boots. Then he opens the door and goes out on to the set, to continue work.

ACKNOWLEDGMENTS

The author wishes to tender his grateful thanks to the late James M. Anderson for his helpful co-operation and advice.

He wishes also to acknowledge the assistance of the following:

Ambassador Film Productions.
Associated British Film Distributors.
Associated British-Pathé.
The late F. W. Baker.
The British Film Institute.
British Lion Film Corporation.
The late Adrian Brunel.
Butcher's Film Service.
Cameo-Poly Film Distributors.
The late George Carney.
Columbia Pictures.
John Paddy Carstairs.
Theo Cowan.
Danske Filmmuseum, Copenhagen.
Ealing Studios.
The late Henry Edwards.
Eros Films.
Geoffrey Faithfull.
Walter Forde.
The late Gwen Grahame.
Grand National Pictures.
Jack Griggs.
The late Robert Hamer.
Richard Hearne.
The late Cecil M. Hepworth.
Maud Hughes.
International Film Distributors.
Robert Jones.
Ludovic Kennedy.
Collie Knox.
Gavin Lambert.
London Films.
The late Lupino Lane.
Violet McKay.
Metro-Goldwyn-Mayer Pictures.
Hugh Miller.
Monarch Films.
J. B. Morton (Beachcomber).
Leonard Mosley.

Ronald Neame.
Edith Nepean.
Nettlefold Studios.
Peter Noble.
Paramount Pictures.
J. B. Priestley.
The J. Arthur Rank Organization.
Renown Pictures.
Martha Robinson.
The late Stewart Rome.
R.K.O.-Radio Pictures.
The late Johnnie Schofield.
The late Hannen Swaffer.
20th Century Fox Films.
United Productions of America.
Universal-International.
Walt Disney Mickey Mouse.
Warner Bros.

The Editors of the following journals kindly permitted the quotation of extracts, and greatly assisted the author by supplying information :

The Cinema.
Daily Film Renter.
Kinematograph Weekly.
Picturegoer Weekly.
Picture-Play Magazine.
Picture Show.
Sight and Sound.

GEORGE ALLEN & UNWIN LTD

Head Office:
London: 40 Museum Street, W.C.1

Trade orders and enquiries:
Park Lane, Hemel Hempstead, Herts.

Auckland: P.O. Box 36013, Northcote Central N.4
Barbados: P.O. Box 222, Bridgetown
Bombay: 15 Graham Road, Ballard Estate, Bombay 1
Buenos Aires: Escritorio 454–459, Florida 165
Beirut: Deeb Building, Jeanne d'Arc Street
Calcutta: 17 Chittaranjan Avenue, Calcutta 13
Cape Town: 68 Shortmarket Street
Hong Kong: 105 Wing On Mansion, 26 Hancow Road, Kowloon
Ibadan: P.O. Box 62
Karachi: Karachi Chambers, McLeod Road
Madras: Mohan Mansions, 38c Mount Road, Madras 6
Mexico: Villalongin 32, Mexico 5, D.F.
Nairobi: P.O. Box 30583
New Delhi: 13–14 Asaf Ali Road, New Delhi 1
Ontario: 81 Curlew Drive, Don Mills
Philippines: P.O. Box 4322, Manila
Rio de Janeiro: Caixa Postal 2537-Zc-00
Singapore: 36c Prinsep Street, Singapore 7
Sydney N.S.W.: Bradbury House, 55 York Street
Tokyo: P.O. Box 26, Kamata

Harold Lloyd's World of Comedy

WILLIAM CAHN

Harold Lloyd is unique; an immortal comedian who has returned to the limelight recently with the enormously successful reissue of his own film classics in 'Harold Lloyd's World of Comedy'. In this book he has talked at length to William Cahn about the 'golden age of comedy' he knows so well. Mack Sennett, Charlie Chaplin, Buster Keaton, Mabel Normand, W. C. Fields, Laurel and Hardy, the Marx Brothers – all come to life in personal reminiscences and in more than 200 photographs in this handsome volume.

Mr Lloyd's anecdotes on the comedy of yesterday are supplemented by penetrating comment on today's popular comics – Lucille Ball, Red Skelton, Jack Lemmon, Dick Van Dyke, and others, from those carrying on the great traditions of slapstick to the recent 'sick' phenomenon.

When it comes to comedy we are all experts. But even among experts few are so well qualified to talk about comedy as Harold Lloyd. He is the comedian about whom James Agee, the critic, wrote: 'If plain laughter is any criterion, few people have equalled him, and nobody has ever beaten him.' Ever since pictures in America first learned to move, he has been one of the most thoughtful students of comedy. Mr Cahn, the author of many successful books, makes a speciality of working with words and illustrations to portray an era or an individual. In Harold Lloyd he has found ideal material.

'A delightful memorial volume to a great comedian.'—*Books and Bookmen.*

LONDON: GEORGE ALLEN AND UNWIN LTD